Tales from
THE MAP
ROOM

To Our Parents

Tales from
THE MAP
ROOM

Fact and Fiction about Maps and their makers

PETER BARBER and CHRISTOPHER BOARD

BBC BOOKS

This book is published to accompany the television series entitled
Tales from the Map Room
which was first broadcast in Spring 1993.
The series was produced by Julian Stenhouse
for BBC Continuing Education and
Training Television

Published by BBC Books,
a division of BBC Enterprises Limited,
Woodlands, 80 Wood Lane
London W12 0TT

First Published 1993

© The Contributors 1993

ISBN 0 563 36784 9

Designed by
Casebourne Rose Design Associates

Set in Trump Medieval by
Ace Filmsetting Ltd, Frome

Printed and bound in Great Britain by
Clays Ltd, St Ives Plc

Colour separation by
Technic Ltd, Berkhamsted

Jacket printed by
Belmont Press Ltd, Northampton

LIST OF CONTRIBUTORS

Peter Barber is the Deputy Map Librarian of the British Library.

A. Sarah Bendall is a fellow of Emmanuel College, Cambridge, and the author of *Maps, Land and Society. A history with a carto-bibliography of Cambridgeshire estate maps c. 1600–1836.* (Cambridge University Press, 1992).

Christopher Board is Senior Lecturer at the London School of Economics, and President of the British Cartographic Society.

John Paddy Browne is author of *Map Cover Art: A Pictorial History of Ordnance Survey Cover Illustrations* (Ordnance Survey, Southampton, 1991).

Tony Campbell is the Map Librarian of the British Library.

Peter Chasseaud is the author of *Topography of Armageddon: A British Trench Atlas of the Western Front* (Map Books, Lewis, 1991).

Lindsay Constable is a geography teacher at Dulwich College.

Catherine Delano Smith was Reader in Geography at the University of Nottingham and is the co-author of *Maps in Bibles 1500–1600. An Illustrated Catalogue* (Librarie Droz, Geneva, 1991).

James Elliot has worked in the British Library Map Library and is author of *The City in Maps: urban mapping to 1900* (British Library, London, 1987)

Patrick Fagan is ex-Director General of Military Survey.

Susan Gole is Chair of the International Map Collectors' Society [IMCoS], and author of *Indian Maps and Plans* (Manohar Publications, New Delhi, 1989).

David Hall is Director General of the Foundation for Science and Technology.

Gillian Hill has worked in the British Library Map Library and is author of *Cartographic Curiosities* (British Library, London, 1978).

Yolande Hodson has worked in the British Library Map Library and is map adviser to the Royal Collection.

A. Crispin Jewitt has worked in the British Library Map Library and is author of *Maps for Empire: the first 2,000 numbered War Office maps* (British Library, London, 1992).

David K.C. Jones is Professor of Physical Geography at the London School of Economics.

Emrys Jones is Professor Emeritus in Social Geography at the London School of Economics.

Roger Kain is Montefiore Professor of Geography at the University of Exeter.

G.R.P. Lawrence was Lecturer in Geography at King's College London.

John Leonard is Director of Ordnance Survey, Southampton.

G. Malcolm Lewis was Senior Lecturer in the Department of Geography, University of Sheffield and is Principal Investigator for the Amerindian and Inuit Maps and Mapping Programme.

Douglas Muir is Curator of Philately at the National Postal Museum in London.

Richard Oliver is Research Fellow in the History of Cartography at the University of Exeter.

R.B. Parry is Senior Research Fellow in the Geography Department, University of Reading.

William Ravenhill is Emeritus Reardon Smith Professor of Geography at the University of Exeter.

Rear-Admiral Steve Ritchie was Hydrographer of the Navy, 1966–71.

Dr Kenneth Sealy is Reader Emeritus in Transport Geography at the London School of Economics.

Dr John Shepherd is Reader in Urban and Regional Planning in the Department of Geography at Birkbeck College, University of London.

Andrew Tatham, formerly Map Librarian at King's College, London, is now Keeper at the Royal Geographical Society. He is a member of the International Cartographic Society's Commission on Tactile Mapping.

Helen Wallis was Map Librarian of the British Museum and British Library, 19687–85.

Andrew Wells is a Lecturer in Social Psychology at the London School of Economics.

Margaret Wilkes is Map Librarian of the National Library of Scotland.

Contents

INTRODUCTION

'Geography is about maps,
But biography is about chaps'.

Or so wrote the English author E. C. Bentley earlier this century. In this book we have tried to remind our readers that maps are also about chaps (male and female) – and their perceptions, intentions, needs, knowledge, beliefs and visions.

No map can be a literal transcription of reality. Indeed most people would be baffled and confused if map-makers did not select, clarify and even distort reality for the sake of their intended customers. A picture may say more than a thousand words, but a map can often say it more effectively..A photograph of a town, landscape or planet may contain more information, in an undifferentiated sort of way, but a well-designed map conveys its selected message

with greater impact. The reasons for this selection have been as varied as the people and institutions that have created maps and the resulting maps can usually tell the onlooker much about the map-maker's values and the culture in which he or she operated. Indeed, in the past and to a surprisingly large degree to this day, maps have had as much to do with culture and civilization as with geography.

In ancient Greece, China and Rome and in the West since the eighteenth century, cartography and scientific measurement were inseparable. Map-makers of those areas claimed with justice that their work possessed scientific integrity. However, there have been other societies and ages when 'pure science' and measurement took second place to the artistic expression of cultural, political and religious values on maps. Some present extremely complex images. Others, serving as icons or symbols, have been extremely simple in design. Nor is that tradition dead, as maps in advertisements, holiday postcards and political cartoons still demonstrate. Indeed 'scientific integrity' is hard to quantify and some of the superficially most 'scientific' of maps can be found, on analysis, to be peddling propaganda or at least a pet theory or message.

This may come as a shock to those of us who have placed an unthinking faith in the objective reality and unconditional reliability of modern maps. Dazzled by science and technology, many of us assume unquestioningly that with the near-perfection of measuring instrumentation and techniques, aerial and space photography and digital mapping, map-

(Opposite) The map-maker selects from reality: Paul Pfinzing at work, 1598. From (Paul Pfinzing), Methodvs Geometrica. Nuremberg: Valentin Fuhrmann, 1598. British Library C.115.i.2.

(Left) The reality that tells us less than the map – NASA satellite view of the world from outer space.

making has reached the ultimate reality. Those of us who condescendingly assume that ancient maps, though pretty, are 'crude' and 'naive' with little to say to later generations or different civilizations (apart, possibly, from tracking the gradual European discovery of the world), should lift the 'decorative old map' from the sitting room wall and take a closer look.

In this book, we have taken that close look by exploring the essence of the map and its relationship with the external world. We have considered the role of maps in differing societies over time, the means by which they convey information, the nature of that information and how they were actually used. There is as much here about symbols, faith, spying, deception, vanity, driving, disasters, government, war, tourism, and art as about measurement and science.

The chapters in the book explore six general themes through a series of particular examples. Each chapter has an introductory section which brings together the specific points of the whole chapter making cross references to other parts of the book where appropriate. However, each of the individual examples can stand alone as a map story. A large number of the illustrations come from the British Library which houses one of the world's great collections of maps and topographical material.

The book is not intended to be a history of maps, a gallery of pretty old maps, a study of any single map-maker, any school of map-making or the mapping of any particular area (though London does feature prominently). And the reader will search in vain for detailed discussions of surveying methods, geographical information systems, digital mapping or for maps of the great discoveries. But, if we have succeeded in demonstrating that maps are about chaps – and about life – we shall be satisfied.   PETER BARBER and CHRISTOPHER BOARD

A TISSUE OF LIES

Maps are one of the greatest illusions known to man and yet we instinctively put our faith in them.

Disregarding the evidence of our own eyes, we assume, when using maps, that they are a substitute for reality. But there is no way in which they can be – in all respects. Not even the biggest maps can reproduce absolutely everything about the area they depict while the most precisely surveyed map, created using the latest technology, cannot capture all aspects of the globe's roundness on a flat surface. Far from being objective portrayals of the world around us, maps have often served to lend credibility to aspirations, theories, and, quite frequently, misunderstandings. Indeed some maps have been more or less pure fantasy, even if they use cartographic conventions, while others have largely or completely ignored the visible world in order to depict features – physical, social, political and religious – that cannot be seen. Sometimes, particularly for security reasons, map-makers will intentionally suppress or distort information. The cost of making maps has also exerted a negative influence, leading sometimes to outdated or even incorrect information being reproduced over the centuries or to depictions of groups of features which have never existed together at the same time, creating phoney images of what appears to the uninitiated to be 'reality'.

The fact is that map-makers have no alternative but to choose what they want us to see and how we are to see it. Mere social convention often unconsciously dictates what they insert and how we react. Some maps reflect the objectives of their makers by playing down the narrowly geographical features in favour of cultural ones. Ideology has influenced the selection and through the centuries the content of maps has been manipulated to add authority to every cause from militant Christianity to advertising. In order to add clarity to the selected message, whether it be geographical or more broadly cultural, the map-maker will mix pictures and symbols, disregard natural colour, alter the true relationship of places and the distances between them and play false with relative size.

The Scale (but small Respect not truth in all.

A Scale of Half an English Mile.

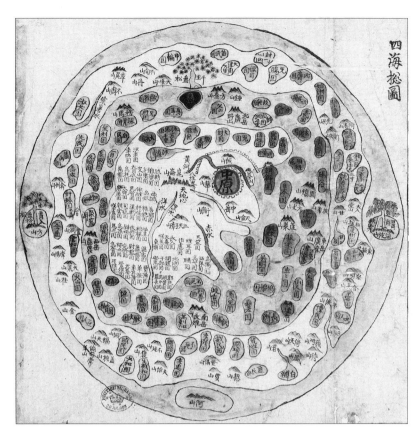

四海揔圖

(Opposite) An early hint ('The scale's but small. Expect not truth in all') at the limits of veracity. Detail, showing the scale cartouche, from the Hollar map of London and Westminster, 1685. Guildhall Library: Howgego No.35.

(Above) Sino-Korean world map of 1800, based on a prototype of c.1500 AD showing China (Middle Kingdom) within the Great Wall at the centre of the world, with the rest of the world at the edges. British Library Maps 33.c.13.
When other societies chose to place their culture at the centre of the map, similar images resulted: compare this with the Christian Psalter world map of about 1260 centred on Jerusalem (p.23).

Yet no map is a total illusion. However ill-surveyed, untrue or fanciful, it contains some elements of reality and mirrors its creator's views and cultural background in a way that frequently transcends the simple representation of the physical world. In this way, so-called 'inaccurate' or 'crude' old maps can be of immense importance to students of history because they can reveal the mentalities of past societies, civilizations and even individuals, such as Elizabeth I's great minister, Lord Burghley (see pp.88). Because of its very artificiality, a well-constructed, purpose-linked modern map will also be of far greater assistance to the contemporary user than any simple duplication of reality, whether they're in search of specific answers to important spatial questions or just trying to solve problems with a spatial element to them.   PETER BARBER

A MATTER OF SCALE

On 13 September 1631 the Dutch won a famous victory, the battle of Slaak, over their former Spanish masters. The Spaniards had sent a large fleet northwards in the hope of wresting the mouth of the River Scheldt from the Dutch and freeing the Spanish-controlled town of Antwerp from the Dutch blockade that had all but strangled it since the 1590s. The fleet lost its way in the mist, however, and ran aground. In the ensuing battle the Dutch captured 76 Spanish ships and 4140 soldiers.

(Above and top right) Getting it wrong. Two Dutch silver medals by J. Looff commemorating the naval battle of Slaak, 1631. British Museum.

To celebrate the Dutch success, the Zeeland authorities ordered the striking of several medals, some of which were decorated with maps. At least two, both oriented with south at the top, were cartographic disasters. In an effort to depict the whole story on one of them (above), Looff, the medallist, tried to copy everything on the much larger map that served as his model. The names of the towns, rivers, sand banks and islands at the

mouth of the Scheldt are all given. The ships and opposing forces are shown and identified in the key, which also names the Dutch commanders. The result is a riot of lettering that drowns the coastlines and obscures the letters of the alphabet which the key is supposed to clarify! The other medal (above) also fails miserably – but for the opposite reasons. This time the physical relief and the ships are depicted, and superbly. The inscription attributes the success of the battle to God, and a legend on the other side names the victory and lists its most important consequences, but the total absence of any other text leaves the uninformed outsider totally mystified as to what the map actually shows.

Looff had failed to realize that maps cannot be complete and objective representations of reality, no matter how large they are. At the same time, they must go beyond reality by depicting the most important physical, but also non-physical, features in words or symbols. Selectivity is essential but, as the two Dutch medals show, it is by no means easy for the map-maker to display the necessary discipline. The resulting map is inevitably only a partial and subjective view of reality, depending on the map-maker's intentions, assumptions and beliefs, and on the size of the surface, and thus the scale of the map, available to them.

The late-seventeenth-century English map-maker, William Hack, who worked in the

Getting it right. A detail of William Hack's map of Jamaica, 1682, showing the land around Port Royal. British Library Add. MS 5414.4.

Docklands area of London, has successfully grasped these points in his manuscript map of Jamaica (above) which was dedicated to the pirate, 'Captain' Bartholomew Sharp. Ignoring the detailed depiction of the terrain, Hack concentrates on the coastline, power and economic structure of the island. Towns, such as the capital Port Royal, forts, parishes and plantation owners are named and located, as are the beacons which communicated news of danger from pirates, invaders and revolting slaves. In the space provided by the sheep's skin on which the map is drawn,

Hack gives not so much an objective image of seventeenth-century Jamaica as a clear and pleasing administrative and economic guide for pirates or governors alike. Sharp may have used the map for piracy off Jamaica in 1684, but within a few years it was safely in the hands of a member of the Governor of Jamaica's household.   Peter Barber

LOOKING AT THE WORLD

The earth is spherical but most maps are flat. It is, therefore, impossible to capture all the aspects of this curved surface on a single, two-dimensional map. Projections of the round earth on to flat paper can retain accuracy in certain respects but only at the cost of distortion in others. The projection which the map-maker selects for a map depends either on their own intentions or those of their employer – though these are rarely stated explicitly. The result, over the centuries, has been a multitude of images of the earth, all of them containing some truth and some distortion, serving some ends but prejudicing others.

Projections can be of immense value in providing new ways of looking at the world, and are becoming ever more so as computers allow a hitherto unattainable flexibility in creating exciting and purposeful new ones. Above all, projections affect the very way we perceive our planet. However lofty their creators' motives, they all have emotive and political undertones.

Most people today are accustomed to the projection named after Gerard Mercator, the sixteenth-century map-maker, mathematician and instrument-maker. By mathematically calculating the spacing of the straight lines which represent the parallels, or lines of latitude, so they become further apart the further they are from the Equator, he compensated for their true length and hence managed to retain angles. At each single point, scale is in fact correct in all directions but it increases progressively so that higher latitudes cannot be represented, the Poles being at infinity. Distances can only be measured along a latitude line and a different scale ratio is required for each one. However, the familiar Mercator map of the world is the right choice for any map user who needs to know correct shapes, true angles or accurate bearings. It solves the navigator's problem of reconciling directions or bearings on the spherical globe with those that can be drawn on a flat sheet.

The Mercator projection does so at a price, however, and that is the exaggeration in the relative size of land masses the nearer one gets to the Poles. Cartographers have long been aware of this problem and have invented various so-called 'equal area' projections in order to compensate. One of the best-known is that created by Gall in the mid-nineteenth century and revised in recent years by Arno Peters. It shows the land masses in their true proportions, but in doing so it distorts coastal shapes and skews the global framework, creating an image which has been likened to

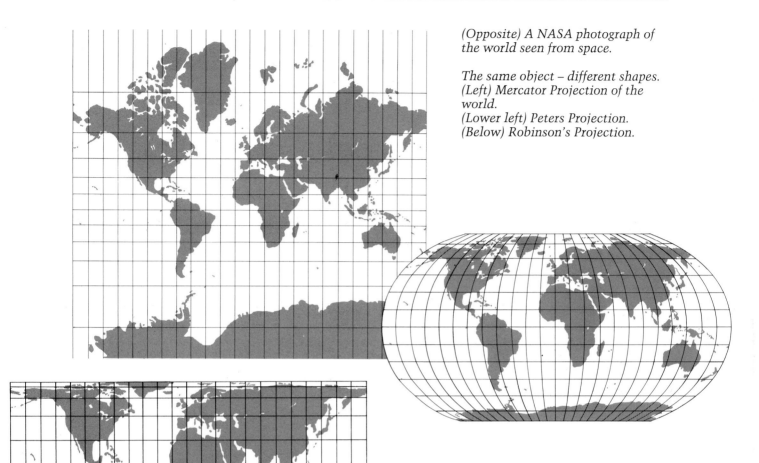

(Opposite) A NASA photograph of the world seen from space.

The same object – different shapes. (Left) Mercator Projection of the world. (Lower left) Peters Projection. (Below) Robinson's Projection.

hanging much of the world on a washing line strung along the Arctic.

The Mercator projection may have been intended by its European originator for practical navigation, but it also has the effect of enlarging the size of the developed world – often the lands of the former European colonial masters – at the expense of the Third World which generally lies closer to the Equator. Furthermore it became the standard image of the world used by the European colonialists (see the stamp on p.25). Not surprisingly, therefore, it has caused increasing irritation to Third World countries. They and the organizations in which they have a major voice, such as Unesco, have encouraged the use of equal-area projections (notably the Peters projection), which show their true size – though not shape – on the globe. To claim, however, as they often do in the literature accompanying the maps, that this projection is really 'new' or 'truer' than the Mercator projection is an oversimplification.

The political implications of map projections featured in the Cold War. Until recently, the Mercator projection served American opinion-formers well by magnifying the size of the Soviet Union, and thus the apparent size of the Soviet 'threat' to the USA. The ending of the Cold War has seen the popularization of the Robinson projection in such widely read American magazines as *National Geographic*. This projection, created by the distinguished American cartographer Arthur Robinson in 1963, reconciles elements of the equal-area and Mercator projections to produce an image of America's new 'ally' which is altogether smaller, relative to the USA, and a good deal less menacing.　G. R. P. LAWRENCE

COLOUR AND CLARITY

Features in the landscape were originally shown on maps in the form of pictures, and some still are, but by the nineteenth century there were standard ways of representing most of these features. As a result, maps were easier to read.

For example, roads differed from region to region – some were muddy, others dusty or stony or paved with flat stones, to which were added concrete and asphalt, and this information had to be shown on maps. Users also had to have some idea of the roads' relative importance. Map-makers began to indicate this by the width or boldness of the roads' edges, but once colour printing became commonplace more important roads could be shown in red, less important ones in yellow and unimportant ones left uncoloured. Conventionally, woodlands were shown by bird's-eye views of groups of trees usually in black or green (see p.89), but gradually, on smaller-scale maps, it became acceptable to use continuous green instead. By far the most universally accepted convention is to show all water features in blue – the sea and lakes in lighter blue, rivers and canals as blue lines or double blue lines when watercourses are wider.

Probably the most difficult task faced by the cartographer is how best to represent the rise and fall of the ground on flat paper. Hill ranges were once shown pictorially (when they would look like uniform little heaps of sugar – see p.30), or with lines of short pen-strokes lying in the direction of the greatest slope, but these methods gave no indication of the actual shape of the land, nor of its height. These techniques were gradually supplemented and often replaced by contours – lines joining points at the same height above mean sea-level. Many map-readers find it hard to appreciate the shape of the ground from the study of contours alone, so other methods are used in combination with contours. This 1937 Ordnance Survey map of Skye uses several ways of enhancing the contours to create the effect of relief. Increasingly dark brown shading is added to zones above 1000, 2000 and 3000 feet. Yet more shading

is applied to steep slopes: those facing north-west are in orange, those facing south-east are in purple-grey. The map is effective and attractive, but it was extremely expensive to produce.

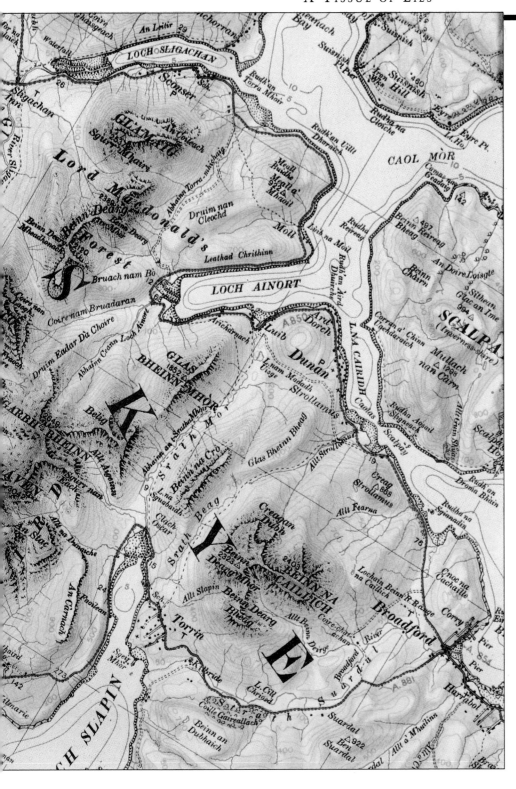

Ordnance Survey.
Special District
(Relief) Map, Skye,
1937. (1:126,720).
(Detail.)

Whenever this technique of shading is used to generate a pictorial effect of landscape illuminated from afar, the imagined light source comes from the top left-hand corner of the map, otherwise hills will look like holes, and ridges will seem to be valleys even though in the northern hemisphere there can be no sunlight from the north-west.

CHRISTOPHER BOARD

IMPORTANT IS BIG!

The map of the Valley of Kashmir in India (below) demonstrates the importance of understanding the content of a map before assuming it could have no value to a modern traveller. It dates possibly from the first half of the nineteenth century and, at first glance, appears crude, possibly unfinished, and grossly distorted in scale. Unlike many indigenous Indian maps, this one has inscriptions neatly lettered in orange in Devnagari script. Someone, perhaps unfamiliar with the area, wanted to be able to identify the places in their own language and added Urdu translations to some of the names.

The focal point is the River Jhelum, with its many bridges. It is shown flowing from its source

on the left, through the town of Srinagar, and on to the Wular Lake, with a dangerous eddy as it flows out of the valley to the plains beyond. The emphasis of the map is on the waterways. At this period goods were moved by boat, and most people found it quicker and more convenient to be paddled in the typical Kashmiri versions of the gondola, even for long journeys, rather than pick their way along uneven paths. So the river is shown as both a traffic lane and an obstacle crossed by bridges. But the 1½ miles (2.4 km) of its course through the town of Srinagar occupies almost as much space on the map as the roughly 30 miles (48 km) from there to its source, and similarly the 8 miles (12.8 km) from the town to

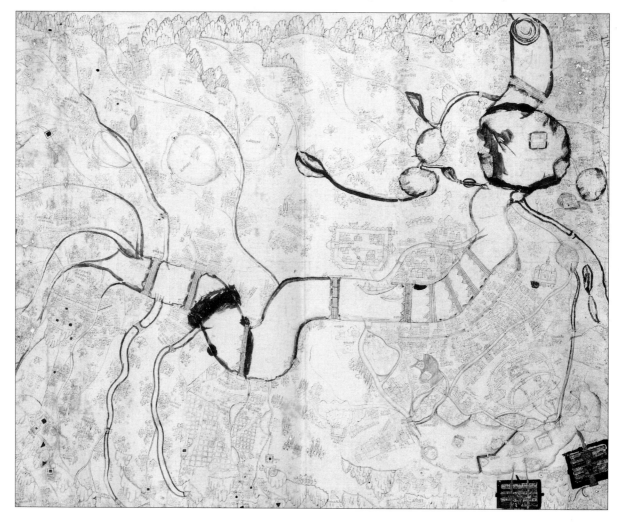

the Wular Lake is much condensed, since there was little of importance to depict on that stretch.

Only two of the numerous Mughal gardens are shown, and those are the two maintained by the rulers of the province as pleasant picnic sites and suitable venues for audiences with visiting dignitaries. The commercially profitable saffron fields, however, are clearly shown with their squared beds below a large loop of the Jhelum.

Within the town the enclosed fort, its administrative centre, is prominently shown, but an older fort on the Hari Parbat hill can hardly be seen. By the time this map was drawn the fort was in ruins, but it is still one of the dominant features of the valley, visible from afar. Other parts of the town are very sketchily shown, but all the important places that a traveller might want to visit have been marked – even the new line of poplars between the river and the Dal Lake.

Once the geographical scale is no longer the overriding feature of map-making, it is possible to include even more material that is relevant to the purpose of the map and to reduce or ignore any that is unnecessary. In this way the eye of the viewer is drawn to what the cartographer considers to be the reason for the map, instead of having to observe each detail and evaluate its importance individually. This was a point grasped as much by the medieval map-makers of Europe as by their Indian counterparts of the last century – and, only a few years ago, by the creator of the Sloane Ranger map of the world (below). Yet even the most scientifically measured modern maps indulge in some exaggeration of the true size of what are considered important features, such as the width of major roads on the smaller-scale Ordnance Survey maps (see pp.14–15) and of all roads on A-Z town atlases.   SUSAN GOLE

(Opposite)
Anonymous
manuscript map of
Kashmir Valley.
British Library
Oriental and Indian
Collections (Cat.
F.V.4). Size 80 × 60
cm. Paper.

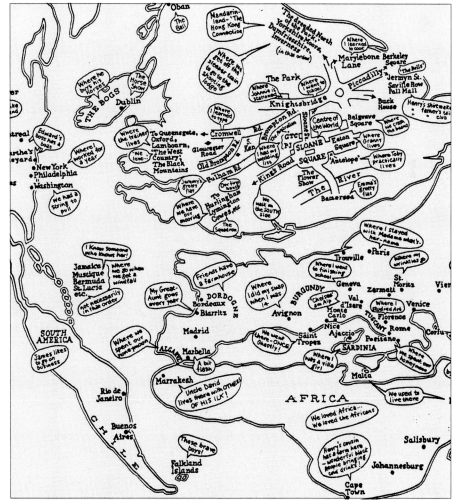

(Right) Anonymous –
'Rangerland – Sloane
is where you find it',
London, 1982.

WHAT THE EYE CAN'T SEE . . .

Most maps may be regarded as mirrors of reality, depicting the visible features of the world. At the end of the seventeenth century map-makers began to develop a new type of map, known as the thematic map. Its purpose was to depict the distributions of particular phenomena, and to illustrate theories about them. The earliest examples are the world map of ocean currents by the Jesuit Athanasius Kircher, drawn in 1665, and the maps of wind systems (1686) and of the variation of the compass (1701) made by the British geographer, Edmund Halley.

It was in the early years of the nineteenth century that thematic mapping became a major activity. Studies in the natural sciences, the industrial and social revolutions of recent times and the development of statistics had stimulated the demand for maps that represented the geographical complexities of physical and cultural phenomena. Alexander von Humboldt, the great German geographer, might comment in 1811, 'It would be ridiculous to express by contours, moral ideas, the prosperity of nations, or decay of their literature; but whatever relates to extent and quantity may be represented by geographical figures', but even he did not anticipate the range and sophistication of future thematic mapping. During his lifetime map publishers were already venturing into the speculative realms of comparative religion and culture inspired by developing ethnographical studies. The 'Chart of the World Shewing the Religion and Civilization of Each Country' by James Wyld, 1815 (right), is an example. Yet it is also an example of the pitfalls of such mapping. Although it may appear to be based on scientific research, it is actually composed of a mixture of fact, supposition and personal bias.

Wyld claimed that the map was an objective representation of the areas occupied by the differing tribes or races of the world, and by the different religions and their relative strengths within these areas (indicated by the portion of the boundary line in the relevant colour). The subjectivity is, nevertheless, immediately apparent

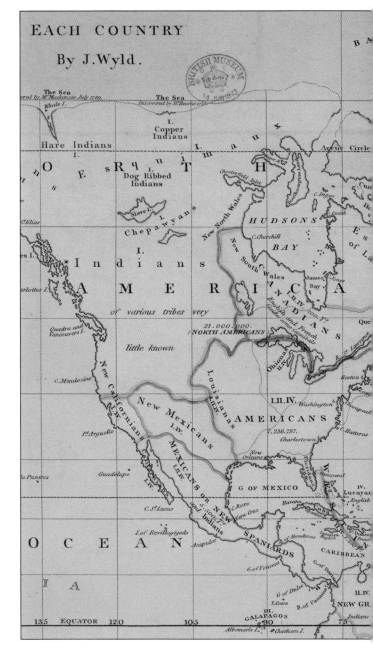

to modern eyes. In the key to the religions (embracing theism, Judaism, Catholicism, Protestantism, Greek Orthodox, Mohammedanism, sabeism, idolatry and scepticism), scepticism and atheism are equated with 'Absolute Ignorance', black is the colour of Judaism and, in the ranking of levels of civilization, the scale runs from I ('comprehending the savage') to V ('the most civilized nations as England, France &c'). The civili-

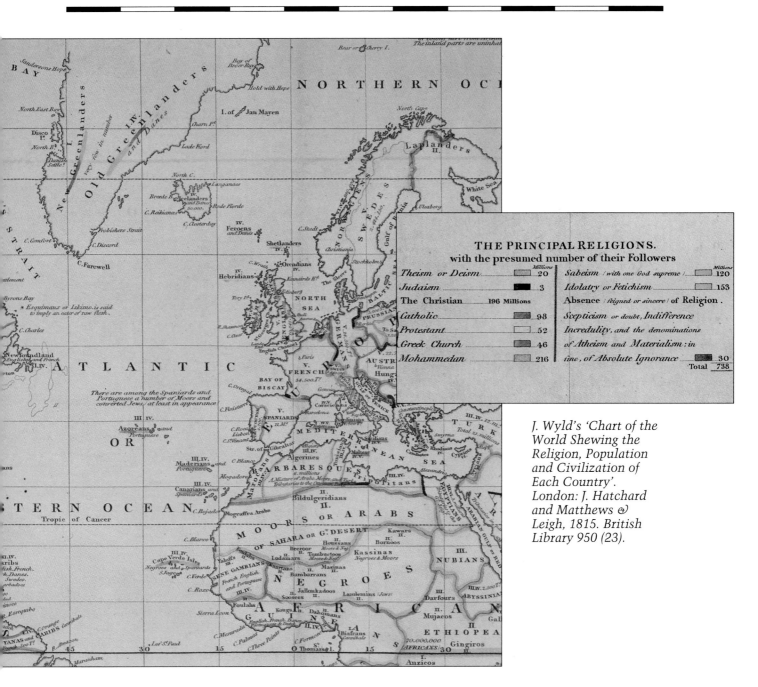

The Principal Religions table:

THE PRINCIPAL RELIGIONS. with the presumed number of their Followers			
Theism or Deism	20 Millions	*Sabeism* (*with one God supreme*)	120 Millions
Judaism	3	*Idolatry or Fetichism*	153
The Christian	196 Millions	Absence (*feigned or sincere*) of Religion.	
Catholic	98	*Scepticism or doubt, Indifference*	
Protestant	52	*Incredulity, and the denominations*	
Greek Church	46	*of Atheism and Materialism: in*	
Mohammedan	216	*fine, of Absolute Ignorance*	30
		Total	738

J. Wyld's 'Chart of the World Shewing the Religion, Population and Civilization of Each Country'. London: J. Hatchard and Matthews & Leigh, 1815. British Library 950 (23).

zation of the USA, containing Catholics, Protestants, idolators and atheists in almost equal measure, is judged to vary between II and V. Canada fares little better with its mixture of 'English and French besides some Cannibals' – a similar mixture to that in Guyana. Such judgements seem laughable today and, by the end of the century, greater experience, a more critical grasp of statistics and more sophisticated cartographic techniques led to the creation of thematic maps, such as Charles Booth's 'Poverty Maps' (see pp.146–7), which made a serious contribution to the understanding of major social problems.

For all its naivety and prejudice, however, Wyld's map and others like it do provide a glimpse into an educated Englishman's view of the world in the year of Waterloo, when his country was at the height of its power.

HELEN WALLIS

TRIVIA – OR THE ESSENCE?

'So Geographers in Afric-Maps
With savage Pictures fill their gaps
And o'er unhabitable Downs
Place Elephants for want of Towns'
Jonathan Swift (1667–1745), On Poetry: A
Rhapsody (1733)

After the cult of science took hold from about 1700, and the last corners of the globe were 'discovered', so increasingly restrictive assumptions have been made about the purpose and nature of maps. They have been regarded as having everything to do with accurate knowledge of the physical world and precise measurement of the earth's surface, and nothing to do with anything else. One of the earliest people to hold such views and to ridicule what others have since scorned as 'mere decoration' on maps was Jonathan Swift, the creator of *Gulliver's Travels* (in which Gulliver's maps were very scientific), and his views have gone echoing down the centuries.

When Swift wrote his verse he presumably had in mind a map like the one shown here. It was published in Amsterdam by Willem Blaeu, the founder of the leading Dutch map publishing firm during the golden age of Dutch cartography, when Amsterdam dominated the European map market. It was largely thanks to the work of Portuguese mariners, since 1450, that Blaeu was able to show the coastline of Guinea in some detail (see p.86 for a later map). The hinterland, though, was then virtually unexplored. While regrettable from the purely cartographical standpoint, it gave Blaeu space to elaborate on the aspects of Guinea that were of greatest importance to likely purchasers of the map: its exotic animals, its ivory – and Dutch control of its slave trade. Amidst the bays and headlands there are such slaving and trading centres as the Dutch Fort Nassau and the rival Portuguese fort of Sao Jorge de Elmina. Elephants, lions, monkeys, baboons and alligators, which were, after all, actually to be seen there, are depicted in the inland areas. The seas are shown

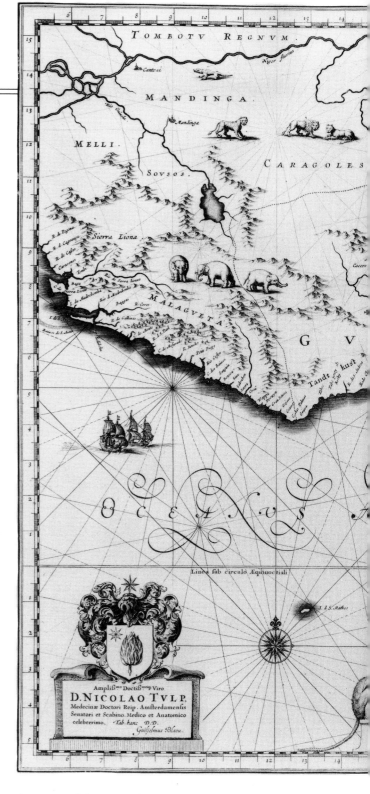

dominated by Dutch ships. Two young black cherubs carry an ivory tusk while two adults (the female holding a parrot), adorn the map's title. Accompanying them are more baboons, directly reflecting the Dutch view of the natives that underpinned the slave trade.

The map demonstrates the older view that maps could be as much about the world's differing peoples, flora, fauna, religions, legends and his-

'Afric-Maps': W. Blaeu, 'Guinea' from W. and J. Blaeu, Le Théatre du Monde ou Nouvel Atlas, Amsterdam, 1635. British Library Maps C.4.b.3 vol 2.

tory as about the accurate depiction of coastlines, rivers and towns. Of course, the limitations of scale meant that the cartographer had to be selective, but a nod had to be made in the direction of broader culture. (On medieval world maps, where there was a conflict, very often the physical information was sacrificed, such as in the Duchy of Cornwall world map on p.160.) If there was not room in the map itself, cultural features were included in the borders (see p.78) or, at the very least, would adorn the title or scale bar. Medieval world maps had the same encyclopedic objectives and to this day tourist maps continue the tradition (see p.55).

PETER BARBER

MAPPING A CIVILIZATION

At first glance few pictures can be further removed from 'the truth' than the frontispiece (right) to the manuscript known as the Fejervary Screenfold, one of the few Aztec manuscripts to have survived the destruction that followed the capture of Tenochtitlan (Mexico City) by Cortés in 1521. Yet the frontispiece, which was originally owned and probably created by priests of the Toltec faith, maps the empire and civilization of the Aztecs.

It is divided into four segments or lobes, with intervening diagonals radiating from a centre in which stands the fire god (or Lord) Xiuhtecutli. Flanking a tree in each of the segments are the remaining eight Aztec gods who, with the fire god, represent nine of the thirteen moons into which the Aztec year of 260 days was divided. The four sets of smaller symbols (or glyphs) placed one above the other in some of the intersections represent the 20 days of each moon, which collectively correspond to the span of a human pregnancy (the gods were regarded as a form of midwife). In the intersections are symbols culminating at the top in stylized maize, a reference to the Aztec belief that man was created in the image of maize. The circles on the birds flying above the maize symbolize years. The picture therefore represents the Aztecs' framework of time and belief.

At the same time the map depicts their surroundings. The four segments may represent the four sections into which Tenochtitlan was divided. They certainly represent the four provinces into which the Aztecs divided their empire, each surrounded by its own sacred river and dominated by its particular gods, with east at the top and the actual physical geography distorted to fit within the pattern. The trees refer to the origins of the Aztecs and the birds on them to the differing types of tribute which each province of the empire brought to Tenochtitlan at different seasons of the year. The four red staves represent streams of blood flowing from the fire god on top of the sacrificial altar at the centre, separating the underworld of the death god (right) from the upper regions of the rain god (left).

Most of the earliest, prehistoric, maps are

(Above) Fejervary Screenfold created before 1521 in Tochtepec area, Mexico. Merseyside Museum, Liverpool. HMAI 118.

(Right) 'Psalter' World Map, c.1260. British Library Add. MS 28681.f.9.

now believed to be spiritual representations, or 'fossilized prayers', like the Fejervary Screenfold and the more familiar thirteenth-century European world maps, such as the Hereford *Mappamundi* and the 'Psalter' map (right). In all of them physical geography is more or less distorted in order to accommodate the map's principal purpose: to provide a framework within which the creators' Christian view of human existence, faith, history and knowledge can be expressed in pictures. The world is variously shown as dominated or held by, or even as the body of, God or the gods. There are allusions, particularly in the Hereford *Mappamundi* which is surmounted by an illustration of the Last Judgement, to the passage of time and the transience of human existence. If the Aztec world is centred on Tenochtitlan, after 1100 the Christian world is increasingly shown as being centred on Jerusalem. To this day, adherents of a variety of religions and sects feel the urge to 'map' their beliefs and world views.

PETER BARBER

THE MAP TAKES ON AN IDEOLOGICAL HUE

The main map shown here was the first world map to use the Mercator projection (see pp.12–13) as perfected by the English mathematician, Edward Wright. It incorporates discoveries in northern Russia around Novaya Zemlya which had been made in 1594–5, and so must have seemed remarkably up-to-date and accurate when it first appeared in about 1597.

However, its geographical content took second place to the other messages it contained. Published in the Netherlands, which had been engaged in a war of independence against Philip II of Spain since the 1560s, the map was created by a Protestant, Jodocus Hondius, who had been a religious refugee in England. The scene at the foot of the map, showing the Christian Knight struggling against (reading from the left) Worldly Vanity, Sin, Carnal Weakness, the Devil and Death, might be dismissed today as mere conventional morality. Yet Hondius's contemporaries, who were as familiar with visual allegories and the Bible as we are with crossword puzzles and television programmes, would have known differently. They would have noticed that the face of the knight bore more than a passing resemblance to Henri IV of France (an ally of Elizabeth of England), who was then going through a critical phase in his war against Catholic Spain. The chalice borne by the figure of the World ('Mundus') is identified as having once been owned by the Whore of Babylon – a familiar Protestant term of abuse for the Papacy. The biblical texts further emphasize the message that the scene represents the fight between (Protestant) good and (Catholic) evil.

The map itself develops this ideological message. The Latin title, roughly translated as 'a map of the lands of the whole world in which the struggle of the Christian Knight on Earth . . . is graphically depicted', implies that it is an allegory of a struggle that was actually taking place throughout the world. The detail rubs salt into the

Catholic wounds. There are no Spanish or Portuguese shields over the lands outside Europe which, in Catholic international law (and on most maps), were claimed by Philip II. Worse still, the discoveries of the Protestant English in Russia and North Canada are emphasized and those of the Catholics understated, while an inscription deals in detail with the foundation of that thorn in the

(Left) Jodocus Hondius, 'Typus Totius Orbis Terrarum, in quo et Christiani militis certamen super terram (in pietatis studiosi gratiam) graphice designatur', 1596–7. British Library Maps 188.k.1 (5).

(Below) Canadian stamp from 1898 showing the British Empire. British Library Philatelic Section; Stanley Gibbons (1989), 166, 167 or 168.

(Above) Soviet stamp of 1927 commemorating tenth anniversary of the October Revolution. British Library Philatelic Section; Stanley Gibbons, Europe, iii, 505.

Spaniards' flesh, the first English colony of Virginia.

The Catholics gave as good as they got in their own maps, the adornment of which implies that the world beyond Europe should be dominated by an alliance of Iberian power and militant Catholicism. Accurate maps, although they may be highly selective and subjective, have continued to be used by people with ideological messages. If, in 1898, using the colour red and a simplified and suitably centred map of the world, the Canadians were able to proclaim on a stamp that 'We hold a vaster empire than has been', Stalin's Soviet Union was able, a few decades later, and using exactly the same techniques, to make much the same point about Communism.   PETER BARBER

IN THE REALMS OF
LOVE AND ALLEGORY

Maps frequently show lands that do not exist. Many have specific literary origins, from the *Utopia* of Sir Thomas More's political commentary through Swift's satirical Lilliput and Brobdingnag in *Gulliver's Travels* to twentieth-century fantasy and science fiction. In *Treasure Island*, the map came before the story, but usually the map serves to illustrate the text and is derived from it.

Other imaginary lands, however, exist only as maps, although they have rarely owed their existence to pure fancy and a simple desire to decorate. Some prosaically explain and illustrate the cartographic symbols used by a particular map-maker. Invented countries could be used to great effect in political broadsheets; others could be designed as lighter satires or even to provide moral or religious guidance.

One very popular theme for such maps, from the seventeenth century onwards, was love and marriage. The map below is unusually large and complex. This elaborate satire combines geographical and military imagery with cartographic convention in considerable detail and the result is a far greater sense of realism and immediacy than is common in 'love maps'. The date is about 1730; the approach reflects the cynicism fashionable at the time. Rather than the usual straightforward

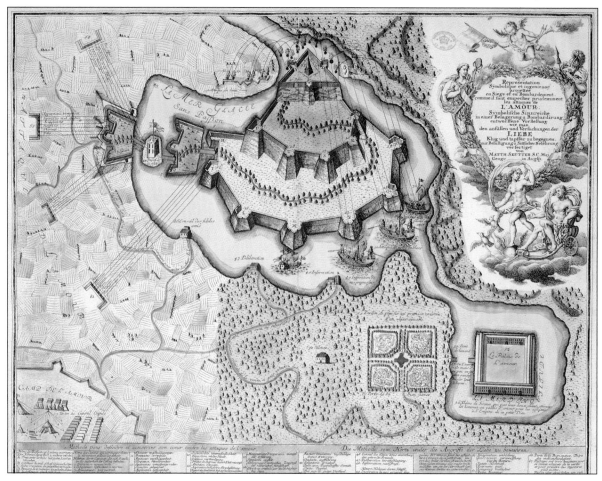

depiction of the realms of the emotions, with or without a recommended route between their hazards to the goal of true love and/or marriage, we have a carefully worked-out siege map. Here is no geographical code of behaviour for a suitor – instead, amatory pursuit is seen as a military campaign, with the woman rather than the man as the aggressor. Man is not seeking to win the love of his lady, but rather is ensconced in a secure fortress, surrounded by a frozen, passionless sea, preparing to withstand the bombardments of the fair sex whether in the form of virtues or feminine wiles. His armoury includes prudence and experience; his fortress is entered by the bridge of wisdom. It is surrounded by batteries of tenderness, charms, despair; by ships armed with beauty, birth, pleasant conversation. General Cupid is encamped nearby with his army and sirens tempt the unwary to the Palace of Love. The conventions of mapping and warfare are combined with fantasy to give strength and vitality to an abstract,

only partly humorous, lesson in morality.

In contrast, many seventeenth-century Dutch painters, notably Vermeer, introduced accurate depictions of real maps into their works for symbolic or allegorical reasons. At one level the painting by Vermeer below is an accurate portrait of a seventeenth-century Dutch interior. Its reality is underlined by a prominently displayed wall map of the provinces of Holland and Westfriesland by Balthasar Florisz van Berkenrode, which was first published by the leading Dutch map publisher Willem Blaeu (see pp.20–21) in 1620 and went through numerous later editions. At another level the map, as is commonly the case in such paintings, may emphasize the worldliness, superficiality and, by implication, the deeper moral dangers in this apparently innocent scene of dalliance between a cavalier and a smiling girl, which is really an allegory of the battle of the sexes.

GILLIAN HILL

(Opposite) The siege of love pictured on a map. Matthias Seutter, 'Representation Symbolique et Ingenieuse Projettee en Siege et en Bombardement, comme il faut empecher prudemment les attaques de l'Amour'. Augsburg, c.1730. British Library Maps C.26 f.4 (42).

(Left) The siege of love mapped on a picture. Jan Vermeer: Soldier and Smiling Girl, *1657. Frick Collection, New York.*

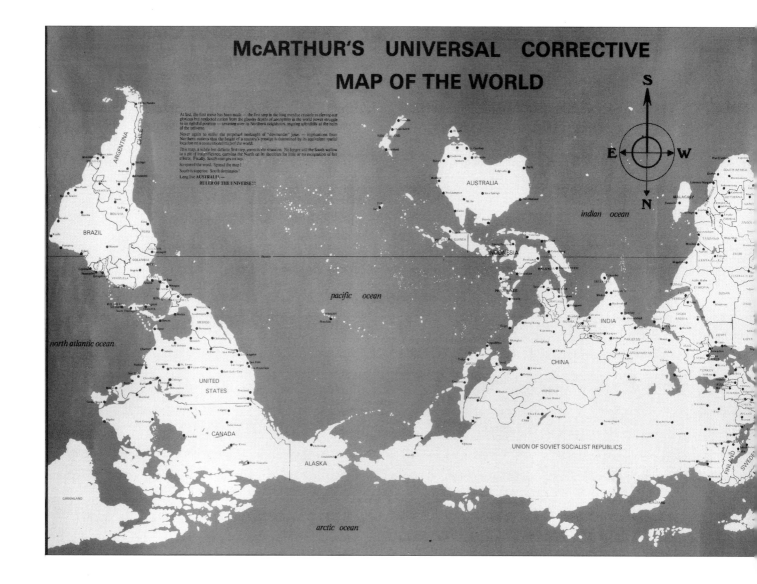

UPSIDE DOWN AND RIGHT WAY UP

'At last, the first move has been made – the first step in the long overdue crusade to elevate our glorious but neglected nation from the gloomy depths of anonymity in the world power struggle to its rightful position – towering over its Northern neighbours, reigning splendidly at the helm of the universe. Never again to suffer the perpetual onslaught of "downunder" jokes – implications from Northern nations that the height of a country's prestige is determined by its equivalent spatial location on a conventional map of the world . . . No longer will the South wallow in a pit of insignificance . . . South is superior . . . Long live Australia, Ruler of the Universe!!'

So reads the caption on the map above, otherwise a normal Mercator projection map, which not only places Australia at the top but also at the centre, a position subtly emphasized by shading out the other countries. The map-maker has a valid point, but is far from being the first to make it.

(Left) The South Triumphant. McArthur's Universal Corrective Map of the World. Created by Stuart McArthur of Carlton, Melbourne, Australia, © 1979. Distributed by Rex Publications, 413 Pacific Highway, Artarmon 2064, Australia. Ph: 428 33566.

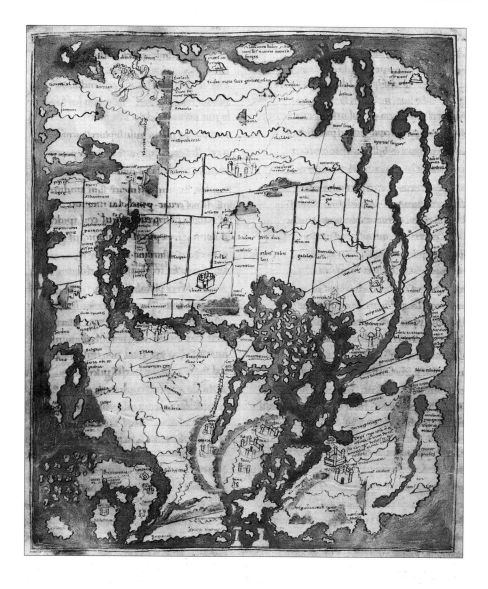

(Right) Orientation or Pointing East. The 'Anglo-Saxon' or Cottonian World Map, c.1035. British Library Cotton MS Tiberius B.V.f.56.

In fact, there is no 'right' way up for a map. The north orientation of most maps is no more than a convention which may stem from the simple fact that most European compasses produced after 1600 were made to point north. Before that a sizeable proportion of maps pointed south and a few, in the same way as place settings around a circular table, had no single orientation. Indeed, the very word 'orientation' reveals that some of the earliest maps pointed east (*oriens* in Latin), probably because Paradise, or its pagan equivalent, was for centuries believed to lie in the eastern-most part of Asia and is shown in that position on the 'Psalter' world map of about 1260 (see p.23).

Both the 'Psalter' map and the even earlier 'Anglo-Saxon' world map above, made by an English scribe in about 1035, represent this earlier convention. The location of Great Britain at the bottom left reveals that the map is oriented to the east. A clue to its origins in classical antiquity lies in the fact that it is centred not on Jerusalem, as one might expect from a map produced in a Christian land, but on an island, Delos, that was sacred to the ancient Greeks. Whether the map-maker realized its significance, however, is doubtful – habit dies hard and can become unquestioning. The fact that most people today are unsettled by anything other than a north-pointing map demonstrates the strength of custom. PETER BARBER

SEDITION IN THE COLONIES

In 1670 Charles II ordered the Council of Plantations (i.e. colonies) 'to procure Mapps, Platts or Charts of all . . . our . . . Plantations abroad, together with the Mapps . . . of their respective Ports, Forts, Bayes [and] Rivers.' Most colonial governors readily obliged but Barbados lagged behind. In 1675, the new governor, Sir Jonathan Atkins, was asked for a map. In July 1679 he was sharply reminded of 'what their Lordships have already demanded without effect, viz. description and map of the country'.

In fact, a local surveyor, Richard Forde of Bridgetown, had probably prepared this map (below) and sent it to London to be printed by

December 1674. It is quite admirable in its way. The panel at the bottom right gives an excellent summary of the population, economy and constitution; the coastlines, bays and rivers are drawn relatively accurately. The major landscape features, roads and parishes are all shown. The sugar plantations, the source of the island's considerable wealth, receive particular attention. Not only are their owners named, but Forde distinguishes between the windmills, watermills and cattle mills that were used to grind the sugar cane. This map has been acclaimed as the first economic map of an English American colony, and Forde himself was so proud of it that, in January

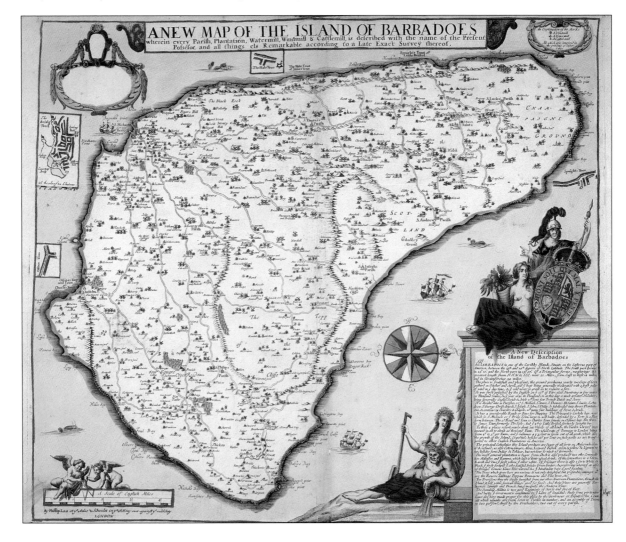

1675, he persuaded the Barbados assembly to prohibit copying of the map for seven years under pain of a fine of 2000 lb (900 kg) of sugar!

So why didn't the Governor send a copy home earlier? The answer is to be found in the letter that he sent to his masters on 21 May 1680. 'I cannot commend it much' he snarled '. . . that it is true in all particulars I cannot assume . . . [Forde] is a Quaker as your Lordships may perceive by his not mentioning the churches nor expressing the fortifications, of both of which they make great scruple.' This was the crux of the matter. The coast of Barbados had been sprinkled with forts, like Jamaica (see p.11), since it was first settled by the English in 1620, but no trace of them is to be seen on the map despite the King's express command that they be shown.

Forde was a rare exception to the general rule that map-makers reflect the values of the establishment in their work. Most of these values are so taken for granted that the 'objectivity' of the content of maps tends to be accepted unquestioningly by contemporaries. The questions only come later, when the values of society change and the map's content appears to be 'strange', or when a contemporary non-conformist, like Forde, produces a 'subversive' map, excellent though it may be in its own right. It is then that Governor Atkins's snarls find their modern echo in outraged letters to the press.

PETER BARBER

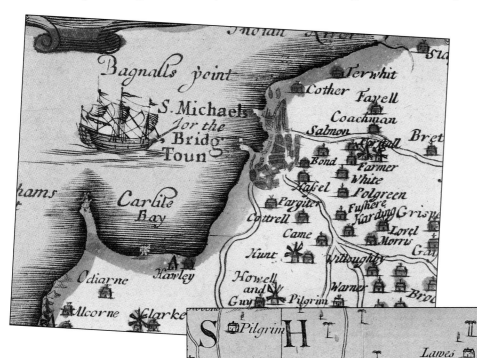

(Left) Detail from Forde's map opposite, with west at the top, showing the area around Bridgetown (without forts).
(Below) Detail from William Mayo's map 'A new and exact map of the island of Barbadoes', London 1722; reissued c.1750. Showing the area around Bridgetown (with Charles Fort, St. Anns Castle etc.) and with east at top. British Library * 82350 (7).

(Opposite) Richard Forde's 'A new map of the island of Barbadoes' c.1675. Reissued with minor additions by P. Lea c.1685. British Library Maps 185 m.1 (17).

WHAT THE BIRD DOESN'T NECESSARILY SEE

Many maps, and particularly larger-scale topographical maps such as those of Ordnance Survey (OS), give the impression of being a 'bird's-eye' view. As the map becomes larger scale, the detail becomes less generalized and stylized; the OS 1-inch and 1:50000 maps show quite fine detail, bolstering the illusion of a bird's-eye view. In fact, certain details are omitted, notably field boundaries, but long custom probably makes most map-users overlook this, and assume the map is a view from above of a moment frozen in time.

The three map extracts here include two examples of a 'moment frozen in time'. The other one looks equally convincing but in fact has only a very limited relationship to reality.

The first extract (below left) shows the city of Lincoln as it was when the Ordnance Survey first mapped it in 1819–21. At this time the population was just under 10000.

The third extract (below right) shows Lincoln in 1886, by which time it was the meeting-place of six railway lines, the population had risen to nearly 40000 and the built-up area had expanded considerably. This map was based on the first complete OS survey of the district to be carried out since 1819–21. There is no reason to suppose that either the 1819–21 or the 1886 surveys contain inconsistencies, once one accepts that field boundaries are omitted and that in the later map

(Below) What the bird saw in 1821. Part of Ordnance Survey Old Series, sheet 83, published 1824, from a copy printed c.1838. British Library Maps 148.e.27.

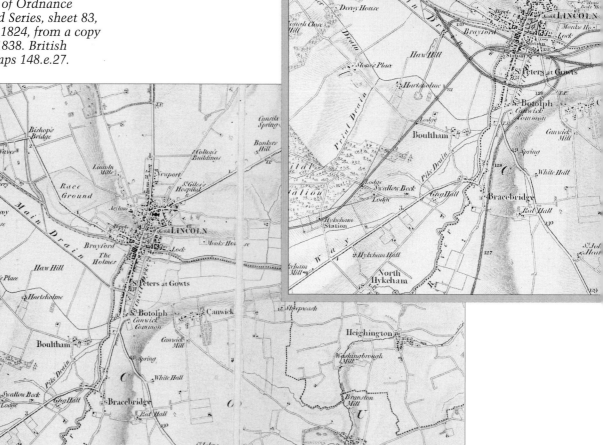

the names of some suburbs are left out because of lack of space.

In contrast, the second extract (centre), published in 1893, is a mass of subtle inconsistency. Superficially, it appears similar to the 1819–21 survey, and indeed much of the detail is unchanged, but the railways are conspicuous additions; the newest of them was only completed in 1882. There are several other additions at Lincoln, such as Union House, Cottage and St Anne Bede House, as well as a few elsewhere, such as Pyewipe Inn (near the top left corner). In fact, these additions were surveyed between about 1849–50, at the same time as the first railways were added to the map. During the nineteenth century there was great pressure on the OS to complete the primary survey of the country before updating already published maps. However, the explosive growth of the railway system could not be ignored, and at first the surveyors adding the railways were also permitted to add other changes which they noticed. Being close to a railway, the Pyewipe Inn was added, but not the new county Lunatic Asylum (near the bottom of the third extract), which was out of sight of the surveyor and therefore not recorded. By the time the later railways were added, no other revision was undertaken: this sometimes led to improbable situations, illustrated here by the road north from Boultham, which on the second extract appears to have been turned into a dead-end by the railway, but which on the third extract is shown much more plausibly, diverted to run parallel with the railway.

Although it might be thought that 'it couldn't happen today', in fact it does. It is common for new roads, in particular, to be added to maps without any other updating, the philosophy, both then and now, being that a partially updated map is better than none.

RICHARD OLIVER

(Left) What no bird, or human, ever saw (like this anyway!). Part of Ordnance Survey Old Series, sheet 83, published 1824, with railways up to December 1890 inserted, from a copy printed in October 1893. British Library Maps C.C.1.t.

(Below) What the bird saw in 1886. Part of Ordnance Survey New Series, first edition, sheet 114, published 1891. British Library Maps 1175 (243).

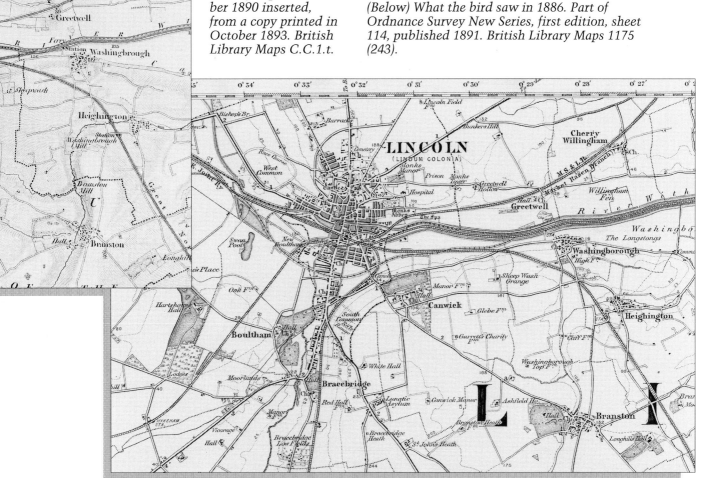

CUTTING COSTS

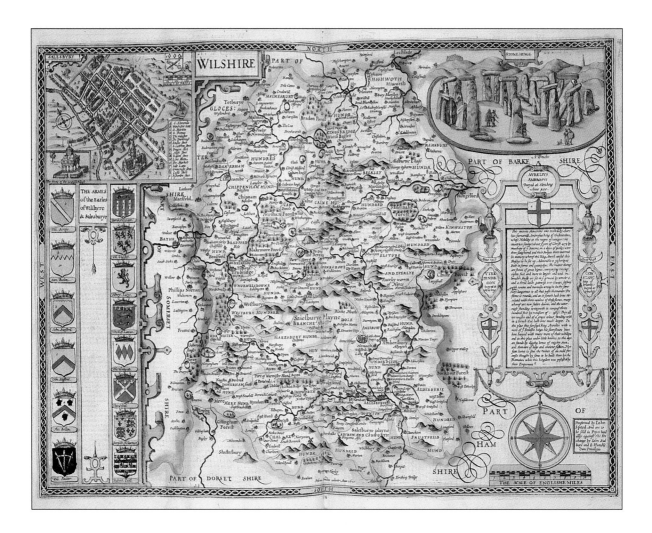

From the first atlas ever published (a 1477 edition of Ptolemy – see p.36) right up to the mid-nineteenth century, most printed maps were produced from engraved copper plates. In this process the image would be cut in reverse into the copper, the lines filled with ink and the plate pulled under great pressure through a rolling press.

The cost of the plate itself and of its subsequent engraving represented a sizeable investment for a map publisher. If carefully handled, a plate could last for well over a century. Altering the plate meant further engraver's fees, and replacing it meant a repeat of the whole initial expense. Viewed in this light, with map publishing seen as a purely economic activity, it is not surprising that the owners of map plates went to considerable lengths to avoid changing or replacing them.

Copper is a soft metal. Although its softness was a help to the engraver, it also meant that the pulling of impressions gradually wore down the engraved image. While it was usual practice to recut the engraved lines, some publishers sold maps that were so faint they were barely legible. Plates might also break at the corners, or develop cracks that had to be riveted together. In other words, map publishers were first and foremost businessmen who were more interested in exploiting an investment than in improving it.

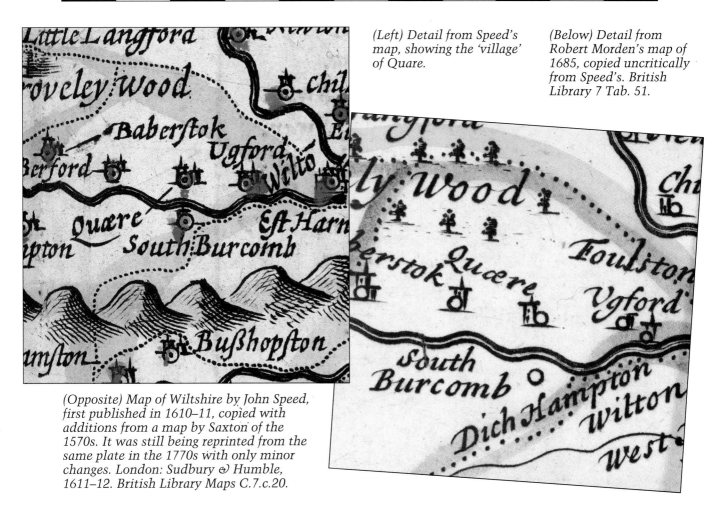

(Left) Detail from Speed's map, showing the 'village' of Quare.

(Below) Detail from Robert Morden's map of 1685, copied uncritically from Speed's. British Library 7 Tab. 51.

(Opposite) Map of Wiltshire by John Speed, first published in 1610–11, copied with additions from a map by Saxton of the 1570s. It was still being reprinted from the same plate in the 1770s with only minor changes. London: Sudbury & Humble, 1611–12. British Library Maps C.7.c.20.

British users were fobbed off with out-of-date maps for both sea and land. Throughout the eighteenth century, sailors had to make do with charts produced by a single firm, Mount & Page, in an era before monopoly commissions. Their maps were up to a century old, thus ignoring life-threatening changes to sandbanks and estuaries.

For maps of England and Wales the situation was even worse, because of the very high cost of resurveying the counties. These had been first mapped in the 1570s by Christopher Saxton, yet the results were still on sale two hundred years later (see p.88 and p.141). Despite some cosmetic improvements, they remained pictures of an Elizabethan landscape which had by then undergone fundamental changes.

In the upsurge of confidence created by the Restoration, and Charles II's optimistic promises of royal bounty, several publishers talked of new surveys of England. None succeeded and, in fact, the least ambitious of these schemes, which was the re-issue of the Dutch county maps that were copies, at two removes, from Saxton, landed its instigator Moses Pitt in a debtors' prison. So copies were relentlessly made of copies and re-worked plates were often passed off as new. Some of today's map publishers deliberately hide a particular feature on their maps so they can easily spot any unlicensed copying. A mythical Wiltshire village had, inadvertently, the same effect. Where Saxton left unnamed the village of North Burcombe, his first copyist, John Speed, wrote *Quare* (which was the equivalent of a question mark) but forgot to resolve the question. His imitators unwittingly perpetuated this query until well into the following century.

What we learn most of all from the plagiarism that was a way of life for most early map publishers is the ignorance or tolerance of the buying public. If you supposedly get what you pay for, it is no less true that you get what you will put up with.

TONY CAMPBELL

FANTASY AND MISUNDERSTANDING

People often ask to see the map inscribed with the legend 'Here be dragons', yet there is no such thing. Dorothy L. Sayers coined the phrase for her detective story 'The Dragon's Mouth', and invented the map, too. It was said to be in a Ptolemy, edited by Sebastian Münster of Basle in the sixteenth century, symbolizing the 'Marvels of the East'. These were usually depicted on medieval maps as a fringe of monstrous beings decorating the continent of Africa (see pp.160–61). For many centuries such fantasies and misconceptions haunted the world map and enthralled European armchair travellers.

Cartographic errors also played a role in plans for exploration and discovery. When the *Geography* of Claudius Ptolemy, written in about AD 150, was revived in Europe in the fifteenth century, the work was regarded as a model of scientific method and was revised in the light of contemporary knowledge. One major error, however, was not corrected but was exaggerated – Ptolemy's world map shows the continent of Eurasia extending over 180 degrees instead of 100. The Chinese discoveries of Marco Polo, the thirteenth-century Venetian traveller, now had to be added to Ptolemy's eastern Asia. As a result of this and other corrections, Christopher Columbus calculated that the distance from the Canary Islands westward to Cipango (Japan) was 2400 miles (3860 km), whereas the true distance in 28 degrees North was 10600 miles (17060 km). His figures plotted on a modern map put Japan in the Virgin Islands of the West Indies and Cathay (China) on the west coast of Mexico.

As European discoveries advanced, the New World of America became the home of some of the fantasies which had abounded in the continents of Africa and Asia. Myths were not abandoned but transplanted. In South America the Spaniards' quest for gold was fed by tales of a kingdom of El Dorado, meaning the 'gilded one'. Sir Walter Raleigh sailed in 1595 to discover for England this El Dorado, believed to lie somewhere between the Amazon and the Orinoco

rivers. He returned with a report of the 'large and beautiful empire of Guiana', and drew a map of it showing the large lake of Manoa and, at its western end, the city of Manoa, called by the Spaniards El Dorado. Raleigh also described tribes with their heads in their breasts, the *anthropophagi*, and Amazonian warrior women. These were duly depicted when Jodocus Hondius made an engraved version of Raleigh's map for publication in Amsterdam in 1599.

In *Gulliver's Travels*, which was first published in 1726, Jonathan Swift satirized the geo-

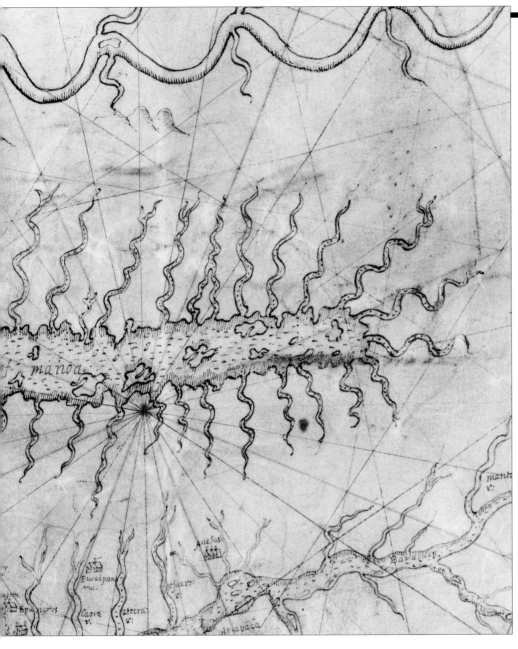

Sir Walter Raleigh's manuscript map of Guiana and El Dorado, 1595. Detail showing area around Lake Manoa. British Library Add. MS 17940 a.

graphical errors which had become established features of maps. Thus, in 1703, Gulliver discovers the bulbous peninsula of Brobdingnag on the coast of California, which for many years had been shown on maps as an island rather than the peninsula that it really is. People today tend to share Swift's scorn for the inaccuracies, misunderstandings and fantasies on old maps (though in the future similar comments may be made about some of today's more flamboyant speculations about the universe). Yet these fictions were regarded as reality in their time and provided the bases for very real historical events.

If Columbus had known the truth, he would not have set sail in 1492 to discover the western passage from Europe to Asia. If Raleigh had known the truth he would not have undertaken the last, disastrous voyage to South America in search of the gold of El Dorado that led to his execution on Tower Hill in 1618. Cartographic fantasies often have a grain of truth in them, but even when they have lacked it, they merit more than modern ridicule.

HELEN WALLIS

ON THE ROAD: NAVIGATION MAPPING

Presumably prehistoric humans found their way about by wandering in the landscape. Strangers broke new ground by securing the help of guides who knew the way to the 'other side', to the source of the river or great lakes. Some, who explored what they regarded as the unknown, made records of their journeys. These were put together to make drawings or maps of these previously 'unknown' lands. First of all travellers conquered their ignorance of the land, and then the seas, which presented a special challenge because traces of previous journeys were invisible. Eventually the air and outer space have been traversed by balloons, aircraft, rockets, space shuttles and satellites.

Gradually, travellers of all kinds demanded aids to enable them to reach their destinations more quickly, more surely, to know where they had been and whether they were on the best route. Since Roman times distinctive strip-like maps have been created for travellers, and that basic shape continues today. Eventually they wanted to know if they could expect the comfort of nightly stopovers, refreshment and interesting diversions such as monuments, fine scenery or refuelling stops for horses or cars. The great escape from the town by train, and especially bicycle, generated a demand for more specialized maps, some of which were attractively re-packaged to persuade these travellers to buy them. Some wanted to go faster, others didn't want to think about confusing choices of route, but all wanted to reach destinations at their own chosen pace. Now there are travellers who journey for the sake of it, like those who take part in orienteering, or the walkers and ramblers in the countryside and the enthusiasts looking for history on town trails. Gradually the requirements of people with disabilities are being taken into account with new approaches to map design.They have all created a demand for maps of very different kinds.

People move about so much in the modern world aided by all kinds of transport that they frequently need to know whether they have arrived at the right place and, if in the right building, how to reach the correct floor or room. Each method of transport has spawned maps to suit its mode of operation. The

Roman legion had its roads, camps and fortresses and distances between them; the merchant seaman had maps of ports, rocks and wrecks; the holidaymaker often wants to know how quickly that long gap between breakfast and bed can be comfortably filled. To encourage travellers on the Underground in London, new diagrammatic maps were evolved which were copied worldwide. For many, London is better known from these brilliant devices than it is from the streets above. Taxi drivers by contrast ply their trade above ground in precisely the opposite manner by knowing the rich detail of the roads, landmarks and traffic conditions in all parts of the inner city. Their mental map of the city would be hard to better. The speed of travel requires the navigator and the passenger to expect maps of different scales, amounts of detail and emphases if journeys are not to end in disaster. You can have maximum choice from all the routes visible on an air photograph to a selection whose names can be identified. The walker needs frequent landmarks, the pilot needs a few large and unmistakeable objects, as well as his target, to be clearly legible on the map.

Now we can command a computer to tell us the quickest, easiest, prettiest, safest, cheapest or shortest route by road. Soon within London's girdle, the M25, motorists will be able to receive, as they drive, computerized warning of accidents, roadworks and congestion. If they decide to take the advice offered by these computer navigators, they will still need maps to tell them how to escape without getting totally lost. Maps have become indispensable for almost all kinds of travel.

CHRISTOPHER BOARD

(Opposite) Travel by land: seventeenth century travellers and their map. Detail from Wenceslas Hollar's frontispiece to John Ogilby's Britannia, Volume the First *(London, 1675). British Library, maps C.6.d.8.*

(Right) Travel by sea: Romeyn De Hooghe, 'Carte Nouvelle des costes . . . depuis la Brille jusques à Dieppe avec une Partie des cartes d'Angleterre', Amsterdam, 1693. National Maritime Museum JA1 001.

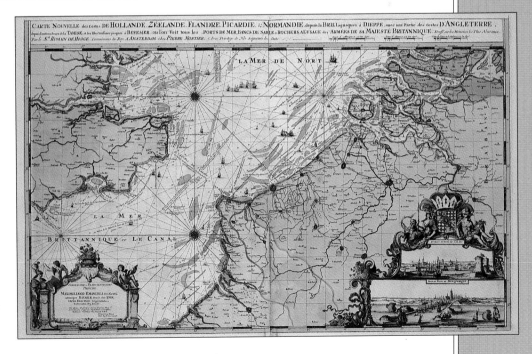

TRAVELLING IN UNCHARTED TERRITORY

In their earliest, preliterate, stages of cultural development, people throughout the world made and used drawings that had some of the characteristics of modern maps. From the Age of Discovery onwards, explorers and colonists from Europe requested and used such maps to obtain information about lands unknown to them. Assumed by Europeans to be somewhat inaccurate versions of their own maps, native maps seemed superior and preferable to spoken language as a means of receiving such information. However, they were fundamentally different from European maps, rather than just inaccurate versions of them.

The contemporary copy (opposite below) of an early eighteenth-century American Indian map is a good example. It represents more than 400 000 square miles (1 036 000 square km) of what is now the south eastern United States of America. It appears to be a representation of the mental image of this part of North America held by one Indian nation. They would have travelled in this region without needing the drawn map but the colonists new to the region wanted it drawn in order to travel and trade with friendly peoples.

As the representative of the British Crown, Governor Nicholson of Carolina had a duty to find out about French activities in the Mississippi and Ohio valleys to the west and north west and their relationships with the many tribes in the region. This map was part of the finding-out process and was made for him by a friendly Chickasaw chief. At the time it represented what, for the English, was unknown territory. It appeared to show the patterns of rivers and Indian paths and the distribution of Indian tribes and French settlements in relation to these. The latter were represented by circles (or semi-circles), the different sizes of which were evidently intended to indicate relative differences in size, population or perhaps political power. The original map on deerskin would not have had a title or names because the Indians had no equivalent of a script.

The writing, therefore, must have been inserted on the copy by an English official after asking the Indians for the information.

Though a valuable source of political intelligence, this map would not have helped the English to estimate distances, determine directions, anticipate hazards or do any of the other tasks involved in planning and undertaking journeys in unknown territories. Like all maps made by preliterate peoples it shows only relative position. Twisting paths and meandering rivers are shown by straight lines occasionally changing direction. The eastern coast of the Gulf of Mexico is almost represented as a straight line, but omits Florida. The South Atlantic coast is not shown, though the 'English' (the colony in and around Charleston) are indicated. On the left (western) edge of the map, the Red and Arkansas Rivers are each rotated clockwise through 45 degrees in relation to the Mississippi River, doubtless to squeeze them on to the deerskin. The map below, however, reveals that they are part of a fairly systematic distortion. The Chickasaw chief placed his own tribal area near the centre of the skin, about which the scale, as revealed by the reconstructed lines of latitude and longitude, is relatively large (see pp. 16–17). Away from the centre the lines become increasingly twisted and more narrowly spaced. Whatever other medium the chief had used the map would have been shaped differently. In all cases, however, the centre of the 'world' shown would have remained at the centre of the map, enlarged in relation to the margins because it was the nucleus of the Indian political system. Whether or not the cartographer is conscious of it, even a diagrammatic map is shaped to communicate a particular point of view.

At the time, and within the culture in which it was made, such a map is unlikely to be misunderstood. At a later time, or within a fundamentally different culture, it will almost always mislead.

G. MALCOLM LEWIS

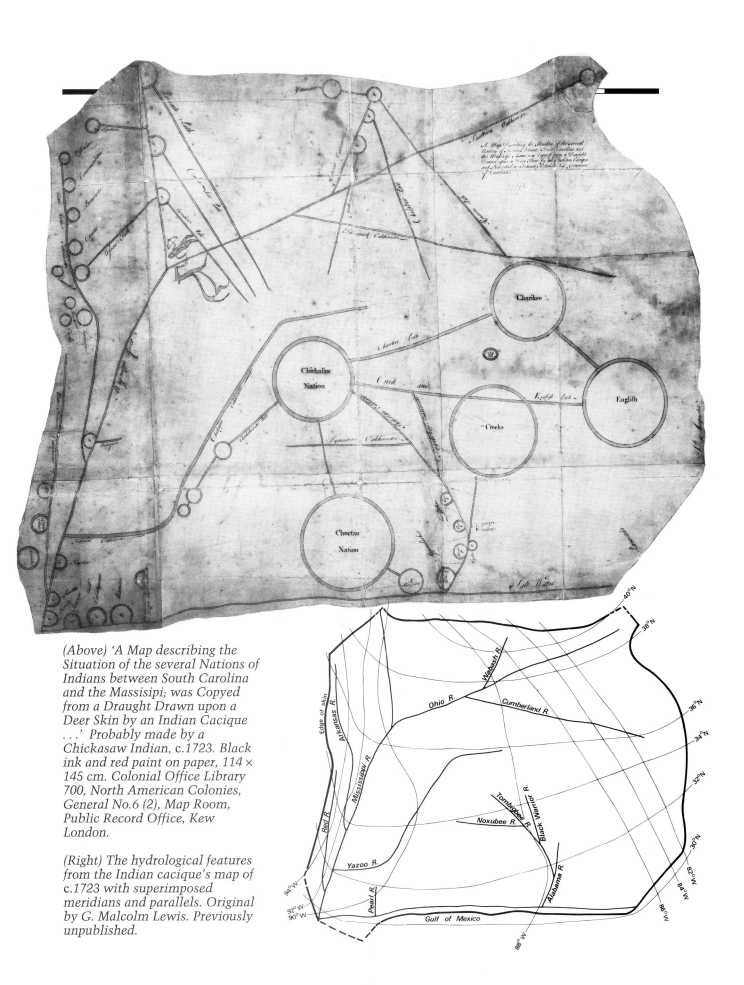

(Above) 'A Map describing the Situation of the several Nations of Indians between South Carolina and the Massisipi; was Copyed from a Draught Drawn upon a Deer Skin by an Indian Cacique . . .' Probably made by a Chickasaw Indian, c.1723. Black ink and red paint on paper, 114 × 145 cm. Colonial Office Library 700, North American Colonies, General No.6 (2), Map Room, Public Record Office, Kew London.

(Right) The hydrological features from the Indian cacique's map of c.1723 with superimposed meridians and parallels. Original by G. Malcolm Lewis. Previously unpublished.

MAPS OR TAXIS?

When travelling abroad it is often easiest to rely on the taxi and its driver to take you to your destination. However, this leaves the unsuspecting stranger at the mercy of an unscrupulous taxi driver. Even Japanese visitors to Tokyo would find it hard to estimate the cost of cross-city taxi travel, but armed with the map shown here they stand a much better chance of not being grossly overcharged. Of course, to be able to use this guide to taxi fares properly you would have to be able to read the map, with its network of railway and metro lines, sprinkled with monuments and landmarks and economically labelled with the names of localities.

How much lighter and more convenient this is than the guide to hackney carriage (taxi) fares based on distances between places in London a century ago: some 400 hundred pages weighing 2¾ lb (1.25 kg)! Cab travel was rapidly revolutionized by the taxa- or taxi-meter (hence the word taxi), invented in Germany in the 1880s and introduced in London only in 1899 where, as on the Continent, it rapidly helped to reduce overcharging.

Even if the traveller could benefit from a map, most taxi drivers do not need one because they pride themselves on knowing their own cities. Whether in Tokyo, New York, Paris or London, most trained and experienced taxi drivers rarely have to consult maps, except perhaps to find some obscure back street, but London's taxi drivers are recognized as the true professionals, even in New York. Sometimes well established maps in the mind are affected by planners and traffic managers when they introduce new routes or block off old ones. Most of us, including taxi drivers, can remember instances where our previous knowledge of the structure of a well-known town or city was completely destroyed by a new one-way system.

The French psychologist, Jean Pailhous, observed that taxi drivers navigating across Paris showed that they knew the city through a primary network of boulevards and a secondary network of narrower streets. He recommended that training taxi drivers should concentrate on knowing the major axes, the boulevards, and that

there was little point in learning street names by heart especially in the secondary network.

Cab drivers in London have been examined on their geographical knowledge of London for at least a century. In 1906 a parliamentary select committee investigating cabs and omnibuses in London uncovered the case of a very competent driver who repeatedly failed this examination. He

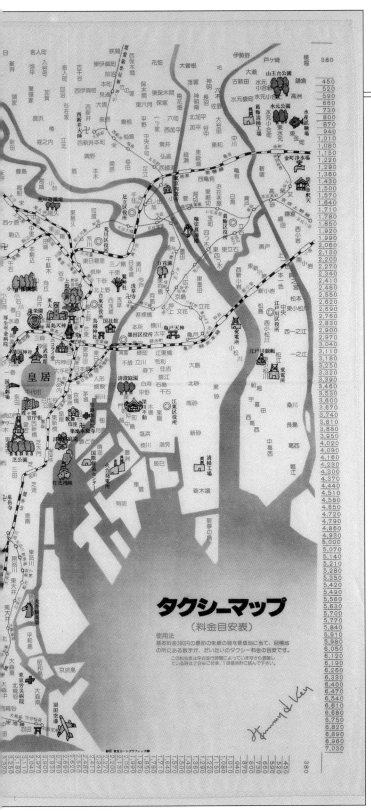

Japanese fabric map showing scale of taxi fares in Tokyo.

knew the way but could never remember the names of particular streets and was told to go away and study the map, then the accepted method of learning about London. In recent years learners have followed a series of prescribed routes, learned them thoroughly, and have then been subjected to questions about them. Becoming literally street-wise is perhaps the reason why they so rarely have recourse to maps. A 1978 tourists' handbook prepared by the Japan National Tourist Organization says: 'Do not be disconcerted if your driver has to stop several times asking for directions. Japanese addresses are often difficult to find.' Whilst maps are an insurance or backstop for the taxi driver they do give reassurance to the taxi passenger.

CHRISTOPHER BOARD

TRAVELLING THROUGH THE AGES

When planning a trip there are certain things you will always need to know, whether you are a Roman soldier, a medieval pilgrim, a seventeenth-century traveller or a modern motorist. There are also things, such as information about places far distant from one's route, that will always be irrelevant. As a result, route maps through the ages have tended to have the same long, thin strip appearance and to convey much the same information in much the same way.

The fragmentary map (below) was found at Dura Europos on the Euphrates in 1923. It must have been created shortly before AD 260 when the fort was abandoned by the Romans. It was originally a decorative covering for a Roman shield but is based on a utilitarian map. A military itinerary of the sort described by Vegetius (see p.102), it has west-southwest at the top and shows the major towns lining the west and northwest shores of the Black Sea (the detailed shape of which is ignored) extending from Bizone near Varna (Bulgaria) to the Crimea. Each staging post, indicated by a building with courses of pale green stonework, is named in Greek with its distance from the previous staging

posts (in both directions) given. Its original owner was probably a Roman soldier.

The second map (p.45 left) dates from almost exactly 1000 years later and is the work of Matthew Paris, a Benedictine monk of St Albans. It shows the first stage of the route that pilgrims could take from London (shown with its walls and most prominent buildings bottom left) to the Holy Land. Like the shield it emphasizes the sequence of towns (potential resting places) and their distances (given in terms of travelling time in days) at the expense of the detailed depiction of the geography and orientation, even if it is more sophisticated in its symbols and content. Thus in Canterbury (left strip), the important abbey of St Augustine is pointed out and on the right strip alternative routes from Boulogne to Beauvais and from Calais to Rheims are given.

Four hundred years after Matthew Paris, John Ogilby, an enterprising Scot who turned map-maker in old age, brought out a large book of routes as part of an intended multi-volume atlas (top right). Once again his emphasis is on the sequence of staging posts and distances (given in miles from

(Above) Detail of the right hand side of the map on the Dura Europos shield, c.AD260. Bibliothèque Nationale, Paris. Mss suppl. gr. 1354. No. 5. (Left) Redrawn with Latin names on page 120 of O.W. Dilke's Greek and Roman Maps, London; Thames & Hudson, 1985.

the starting point). He does, however, indicate orientation and a lot else too, from the nature of the track (continuous lines: hedged; dotted lines: open), miniature town plans, hills and their gradients, streams, wooden and stone bridges and land-use (like Combe's common or Lord Herbert's park near Montgomery) to places of refreshment and landmarks like the Rose and Crown Tavern near Bucknell or Clun's 'demolished' castle.

Ogilby had made his plan with horsemen and pedestrians in mind. Modern motorists have no time or need for such detail and the modern motorway map (far right) is as simple as its Roman ancestor, giving only the sequence of exits and the distances between them, oblivious of wider geographical considerations. PETER BARBER

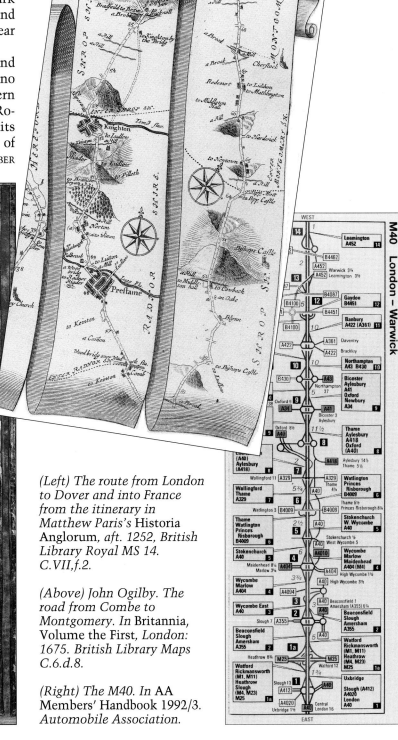

(Left) The route from London to Dover and into France from the itinerary in Matthew Paris's Historia Anglorum, aft. 1252, British Library Royal MS 14. C.VII,f.2.

(Above) John Ogilby. The road from Combe to Montgomery. In Britannia, Volume the First, London: 1675. British Library Maps C.6.d.8.

(Right) The M40. In AA Members' Handbook 1992/3. Automobile Association.

A MODERN LABYRINTH

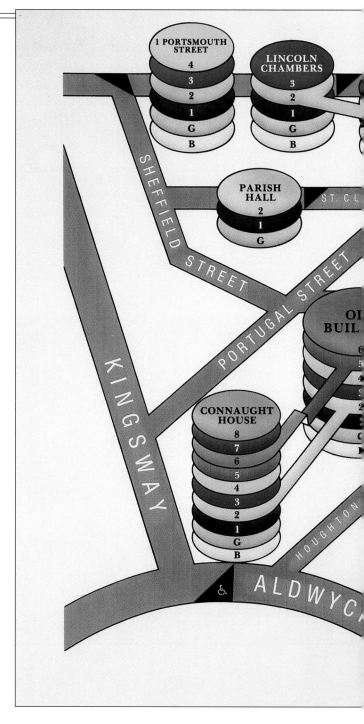

Designing guides for visitors to move around buildings is one of the most difficult problems facing the map-maker. Many universities, large libraries, museums and galleries are not well signposted. The problems facing the London School of Economics are compounded by the piecemeal accumulation of buildings over nearly a century on a site intersected by public streets.

The LSE visitors' map shown here is intended to help people find their way around its buildings. The map shows the whole LSE site, with each building represented as a stack of discs which represent floors and are colour and number coded. The map also shows links between buildings and street access points including suitability for wheelchairs. Two versions of the map have been produced, a poster-sized wall map (shown here) which appears at various locations throughout the complex, and a folding pocket-sized version.

Although attractive, the map fails as a practical aid to navigation around the School. It is too abstract and people have difficulty in relating the representations of the buildings to the reality as they try to find their way around. Some people think the discs look like sweets, and a resemblance to a pinball machine has also been suggested. The abstract representation causes problems because navigation involves a variety of mental processes including reasoning, which becomes more difficult as the subject matter becomes more abstract. However, reducing abstraction by adding more detail will only confuse the user who will not be able to cope with a large amount of information.

Because the map is abstract it gives no detail of the complex floor layouts within the buildings. These cause great navigational problems for visitors and staff alike. The School's buildings are a labyrinth and it is easy to lose one's sense of direction in the twisting corridors. The map is no help at all and may even be misleading. For example, it suggests that the bridges from the fourth floor of the Old Building to the East Building and to the St Clement's Building are very close

to each other. In fact, to cross the Old Building from one bridge to the other is a complex journey involving six sets of double doors, numerous left and right turns, stairs up and down and a walk the length of a restaurant. Nor is this an isolated example. To solve the problems of navigating around such buildings, floor plans are needed at strategic places with 'You are here' indicators.

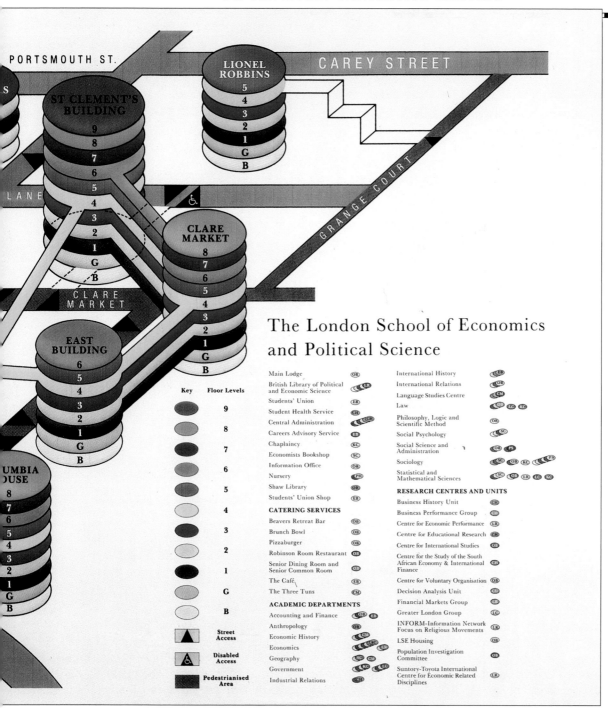

The London School of Economics and Political Science

Main Lodge	OB	International History	CLB	
British Library of Political and Economic Science	LR	International Relations	OB	
Students' Union	EB	Language Studies Centre	CM	
Student Health Service	CH	Law	OB LC KC	
Central Administration	CH	Philosophy, Logic and Scientific Method	OB	
Careers Advisory Service	EB	Social Psychology	SC	
Chaplaincy	KC	Social Science and Administration	OB PS	
Economists Bookshop	SC	Sociology	SC OB KC PS	
Information Office	OB	Statistical and Mathematical Sciences	SC OB LR LC KC	
Nursery	PH			
Shaw Library	OB	**RESEARCH CENTRES AND UNITS**		
Students' Union Shop	EB	Business History Unit	CH	

CATERING SERVICES

Beavers Retreat Bar	OB	Business Performance Group	CH
Brunch Bowl	OB	Centre for Economic Performance	LR
Pizzaburger	OB	Centre for Educational Research	CH
Robinson Room Restaurant	OB	Centre for International Studies	OB
Senior Dining Room and Senior Common Room	OB	Centre for the Study of the South African Economy & International Finance	CH
The Café	EB	Centre for Voluntary Organisation	OB
The Three Tuns	CM	Decision Analysis Unit	CH

ACADEMIC DEPARTMENTS

		Financial Markets Group	LR
Accounting and Finance	OB EB	Greater London Group	LC
Anthropology	OB	INFORM-Information Network Focus on Religious Movements	LR
Economic History	CM	LSE Housing	OB
Economics		Population Investigation Committee	OB
Geography	SC OB	Suntory-Toyota International Centre for Economic Related Disciplines	LR
Government	KC EB		
Industrial Relations	CH		

Key Floor Levels

9, 8, 7, 6, 5, 4, 3, 2, 1, G, B

Street Access
Disabled Access
Pedestrianised Area

Even the information which the map does provide is of dubious value for navigation. A visitor is unlikely to need to know that the Central Administration occupies six floors of Connaught House, but might very well want to know the location of the Undergraduate Registry, one part of the Central Administration.

So the LSE map may be a pretty piece of

Poster map of LSE buildings, 1990: Design House, 120 Parkway, London NW1 7AN.

artwork, but it is not suitable for navigation, because it does not offer the right sort and level of information. Maps such as this one must be designed carefully if they are to be of practical use and not merely decorative. ANDREW WELLS

IN ALL DIRECTIONS

The map shown here (right) was one of the most popular in late seventeenth and eighteenth-century Britain, and it owes its inception to market research – and fish.

Its creator, John Adams, a Shropshire-born lawyer with a passion for mathematics and surveying, had a friend, Mr Lloyd, who wanted to establish a fishery on the coast of Wales. But where could he do so most profitably? He consulted Adams who, as he later recalled, 'endeavoured to compute what sale he might probably make in the neighbouring markets, by projecting a specimen, wherein making Aberdovey, a village on the coast of Merionethshire, the first landing place, I set down all the markets within a hundred miles and entered the distance between them in figures, and shortly after, coming to London, I made a draft of all England and Wales in like manner, which being seen and approved by several knowing and judicious persons, I engraved upon copper plates and finished a large map of England in Trinity Term 1677 with computed and measured miles entered in figures.' The enormous wall map on twelve sheets proved so popular that Adams produced a reduced two-sheet version within two years. Well over thirty further derivatives were to be published before 1800.

Despite the beautiful engraving displayed in the royal arms and the borders (note the depictions of Neptune and Ceres, the gods of sea and land, at the right and left), the popularity of the map was due to its scientific precision and simplicity (see detail – far right). Adams used sophisticated mathematics to establish the correct positions for the towns and villages. He placed the town and village names in rectangles and roundels respectively and joined them with straight parallel lines giving (with varying degrees of accuracy) the direct distances between them. Everything else – roads and even, originally, rivers – was omitted. Though actual distances by road would normally have been a little longer, the map did enable its users, as Adams intended, to gauge distances without needing rulers or compasses. A few years later, anticipating the work of the Ordnance Survey by over a century, he unsuccessfully tried to produce a large-scale map of the

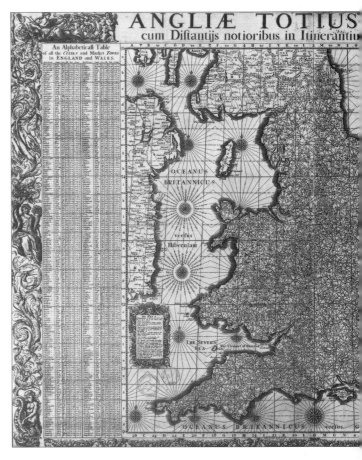

(Above) John Adams, 'Angliae totius tabula . . .', London 1679. Bibliothèque Nationale, Paris. Ge.DD.2987 (1968).
(Opposite top) Detail from 12 sheet map (1699 edition) showing surroundings of Aberdovey. British Library K. Top.5.82.
(Opposite below) The 'Gough Map' of Britain of about 1360. Bodleian Library, Oxford.

whole country on mathematical principles.

For all its mathematical precision, Adams's idea was not new. As early as the 1250s the St Albans monk, Matthew Paris (see pp.44–5), had used a matrix of itineraries to create oddly-shaped but essentially reliable maps of Britain. A century later similar methods were used to create a larger-scale map of England and Wales, the surviving example of which, known as the Gough Map (right), is now in the Bodleian Library in Oxford. If Adams's map originated in entrepreneurial market research, the Gough Map may well have been inspired by the needs of Edward III's tax gatherers. Both benefited from maps stating the distances between towns in all directions.   PETER BARBER

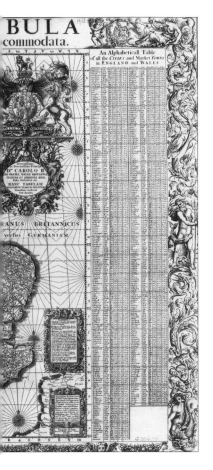

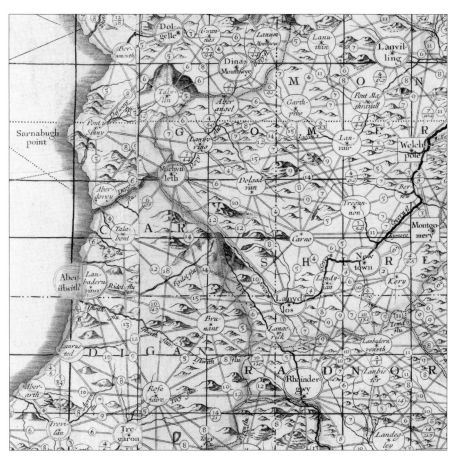

THE ROAD TO ROME

Many maps, modern as well as historical, carry lines representing routes. These lines connect places but do not portray the actual course of roads or any features on the ground. In the days of horseback travel, when the pace of movement was slow and road surfaces (and political conditions) notoriously unpredictable, travellers expected to ask local people what was the best and safest way to get to the next place. Road maps, in the modern sense, therefore, were scarcely relevant: a list of places in their correct order was all that was necessary. A map with routes on it is a rather different matter, as it suggests a direction of movement rather than telling you exactly where to walk or drive. A route on a map is simply some way of identifying a sequence of places or of enabling such a sequence to be drawn up – an itinerary, in other words.

Routes on early maps tend either to record a journey actually taken (perhaps by a famous person) or to have suggested to a specific group of people (such as pilgrims) the places to aim for. In 1500, when many people were thinking of going to Rome to celebrate the half-millennium, one map was made to help them plan their journey. The German map-maker, E. Etzlaub, used lines of dots, spaced to represent one-mile intervals, to suggest the way to Rome from various starting points in northern Europe.

Etzlaub's map contained several innovations and was copied by Georg Erlinger in 1515 and again in 1525, which version is shown here. The major physical features are represented by amassed hill-shapes. Although it is often described as a road map, no roads are shown. Instead we see the network of routes, shown by lines of mile-dots, suggesting to intending pilgrims their way, from various starting points in northern Europe, over the Alps, down on to the northern plain of Italy and then on to the papal city of Rome. Towns are marked by a circle, in which a dot marks the exact point from which measurements could be taken with dividers like those shown on the scale bar bottom left. A short line points to the place-name. It was Erlinger who added the reference grid (by over-printing in red ink). Since Erlinger's map was printed long after demand for a route map to Rome from pilgrims going for the mid-millennium celebrations had died down, he omitted those sanctuaries that happened to lie on the major route that Etzlaub had included for the pilgrims' benefit.

All sorts of routes can be found on early maps. For example, the route followed by a hind running across the Isle of Thanet was shown on a map illustrating a fifteenth-century history of the abbey of St Augustine at Canterbury because, according to legend, King Edgar had promised the abbey all the land so delineated. However, it is not always easy to be certain why a route was picked out on a map, as with Nicholas Claudianus' map of Bohemia (1518), where lines of mile-dots, like Etzlaub's but overlain by colour, indicate routes across the country. Lazarus made things clearer on his map of Hungary (1528), which distinguishes Turkish-held territory from that still controlled by Hungary. No routes are actually marked on it, but the map as a whole was described by its maker as an *itinerarium*, meaning that Lazarus considered he had included enough places sufficiently accurately for his map to be used for plotting a route.

CATHERINE DELANO SMITH

Georg Erlinger, 'Gelegenheit Teutscher Lannd'. Bamberg, 1525. This is a version of Etzlaub's map of the route to Rome. British Library Maps C.22.cc.6.

MOBILITY MAP FOR A CANAL WALK

Maps are often used to help someone get from A to B. For many, navigation is the beginning of the remarkable variety of map uses described elsewhere in this book. For others, navigation may represent a significant achievement in itself.

Amongst this latter group we may count a significant number of blind and visually impaired people, especially those who were born with these disabilities, for whom the understanding of spatial concepts is an important attainment. Maps,

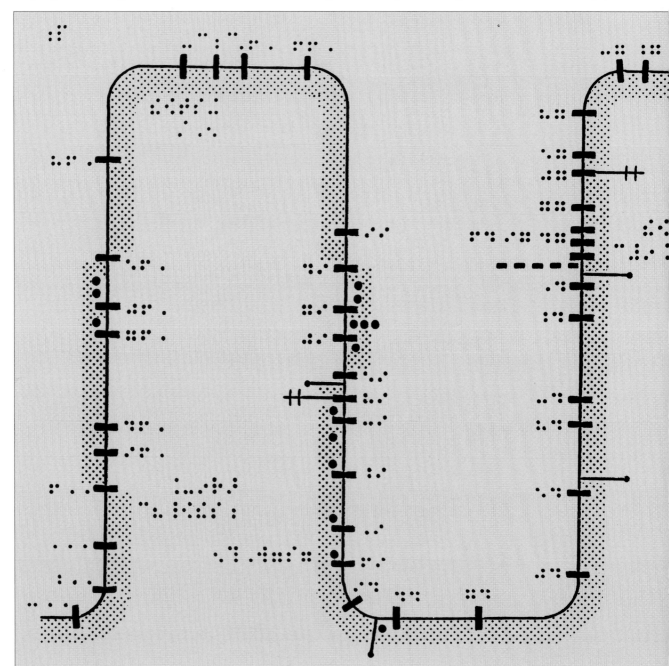

plans and diagrams can play an important role in this learning process, as well as providing displays of geographically distributed information, just as maps do for sighted users.

Maps for blind and partially sighted users therefore include statistical maps, maps of relief, of communications or of administrative areas. Each is carefully designed to be read by touch, rather than sight. A special category among these

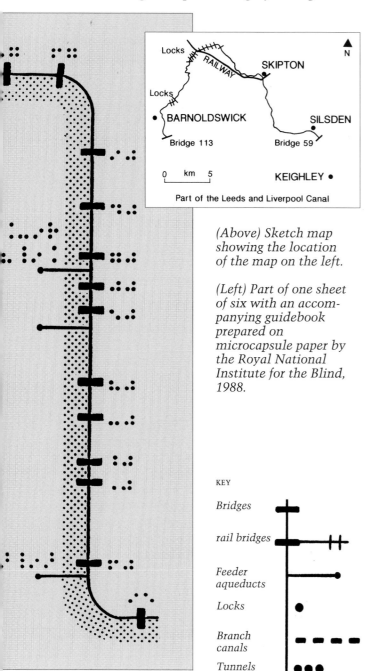

(Above) Sketch map showing the location of the map on the left.

(Left) Part of one sheet of six with an accompanying guidebook prepared on microcapsule paper by the Royal National Institute for the Blind, 1988.

KEY

Bridges

rail bridges

Feeder aqueducts

Locks

Branch canals

Tunnels

tactile maps is mobility mapping, which gives the blind user the necessary information to enable him or her to navigate safely through a local area. This includes many features that would not be considered necessary on a map for sighted users, such as the position of shop doors along a street, of bollards, planters and other ground-level obstructions, of overhanging head-height features and of kerb-lines.

In addition to general mobility maps of town centres, shopping precincts and transport terminals, a number of mobility maps of specific routes are also produced. These are of particular use in training and in providing confidence to the user, allowing the route to the postbox or the bus stop to be undertaken unaccompanied. They can also provide an introduction to a new area, whether for business or pleasure. For the blind user, the advantage of such a route map is that it presents information in the same way that it is received, which is sequentially (a map for sighted people presents the information that can be taken in almost at a glance). This difference, and its great advantage to the blind user, is demonstrated by this extract of the route map of the Leeds and Liverpool Canal.

This map was prepared for someone who wanted to hike along the canal towpath and a number of features of the map were specifically designed for that person. Firstly, while distances along the canal towpath were true to scale, the orientation of the canal was ignored and the route shown in a serpent-like strip to save space. Secondly, the map is to be read from left to right, although, as the trip was to start from Leeds, this is actually east to west. Thirdly, the map displayed features of significance to the blind hiker and omitted confusing details next to the route. Thus it shows the canal and towpath on its correct side. Crossing the canal are numerous bridges which are numbered as in reality. Railway bridges are differentiated. Locks and feeder aqueducts are also marked, as are branch canals and tunnels. Towns and villages are named (from the left: Silsden, Kildwick, Skipton, Gargrave, East Marton and Barnoldswick).

With its accompanying booklet, this map provided a clear navigational aid to enable a blind user to enjoy the hike in safety and without the distraction of unnecessary information.

ANDREW TATHAM

MAPPING THE COUNTRY ALONG A ROUTE

As mapping became more comprehensive, travellers demanded more information than was shown on the relatively simple strip maps. Train travel for the tourist was the ideal method of transport, both to reach a destination and to explore the countryside on the way. There are many examples which informed railway users about the country they could reach by train. One of the earliest efforts specifically to satisfy the requirements of train travellers was the series *Rechts und links der Eisenbahn!*. These guides to the main railways in Germany were published in about 1900 by the famous map and atlas-making establishment, Justus Perthes of Gotha. The map, cover shown below, is one of a series of seventy, portraying a belt of country some 50–75 miles

(Left) Front cover of Justus Perthes of Gotha's 'Rechts und links der Eisenbahn! Ostseebäder (Travemünde, Heiligenhafen, Kieler und Flensburger Föhrde, Borby, Alsen)'. Hamburg, Lübeck-Berlin. Heft 68. Updated to June 1901.

(Opposite) BEA Passenger Amusement Map. London to Paris Picture Map, showing area between London and the English Channel. Francis Chichester (n.d. c.1950). Scale approx. 1:507,000.

(80–120 km) wide from Berlin to the Baltic Sea resorts between Lübeck and the Danish border. To make it easy to follow the train journey, this belt is re-oriented north west to south east on to a concertina fold. Apart from practical hints about how to travel by mainline train, light railway or boat, the guide includes historical notes and a description of noteworthy scenery visible from the train windows. The map allows one to identify places seen while on the move and to help one plan stays of varying length in places of interest.

When leisure travel once more resumed after the Second World War, ocean voyages were the usual method of intercontinental travel, but maps were of little use for these tourists, who were asked instead to guess the distance travelled each day! Some American airlines had produced maps of what could be seen in flight, but the growing popularity of air travel in the decade after 1945 produced this Passenger Amusement Map (right) published by Francis Chichester. There was some point in maps of the country visible from the aircraft since it flew relatively close to the ground and slowly enough to allow one to spot features as they approached. This map of the belt centred on the flight path from London (Northolt) to Paris (Le Bourget) of the early 1950s shows elevated land, major rivers, railways, built-up areas and woodland. Prominent landmarks appear as pictorial vignettes with comments. In this way the map adopts the principles already employed on pre-war air-navigation maps by emphasizing the features easily visible from the air, but the addition of pictures is a concession to the bored traveller. Now that intercontinental aircraft fly at 30000 feet (9140 metres) or so there is little point in providing such detailed maps because one cannot often see the ground. Nevertheless, an enterprising company might consider adapting satellite imagery (see pp. 154–55) for some flights undertaken during daylight, possibly projected on to the screen normally intended for in-flight entertainment and safety demonstrations.

CHRISTOPHER BOARD

LONDON TO PARIS

Flying routes may vary. This map shows the direct route between London and Paris.

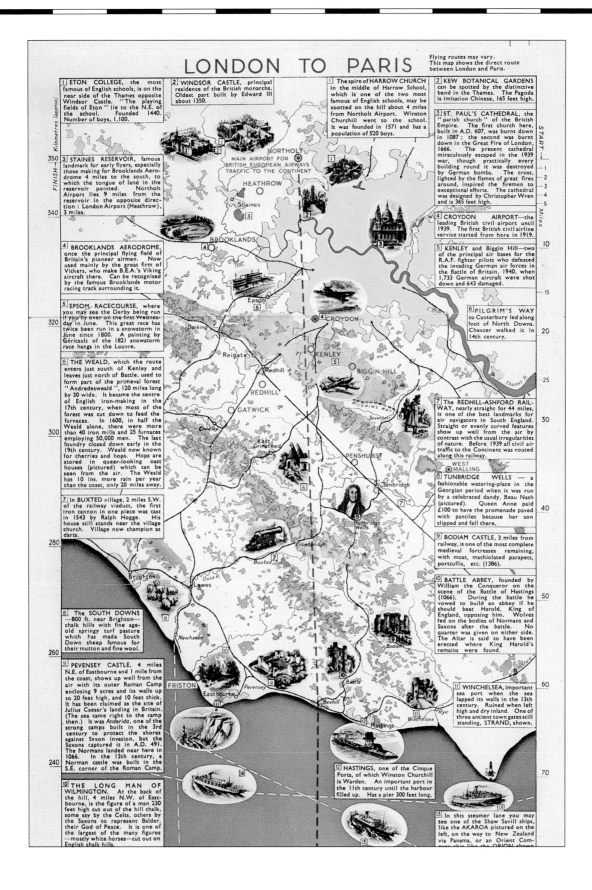

1. ETON COLLEGE, the most famous of English schools, is on the near side of the Thames opposite Windsor Castle. "The playing fields of Eton" lie to the N.E. of the school. Founded 1440. Number of boys, 1,100.

3. STAINES RESERVOIR, famous landmark for early flyers, especially those making for Brooklands Aerodrome 4 miles to the south, to which the tongue of land in the reservoir pointed. Northolt Airport lies 9 miles from the reservoir in the opposite direction : London Airport (Heathrow), 3 miles.

4. BROOKLANDS AERODROME, once the principal flying field of Britain's pioneer airmen. Now used mainly by the great firm of Vickers, who make B.E.A.'s Viking aircraft there. Can be recognised by the famous Brooklands motor racing track surrounding it.

5. EPSOM RACECOURSE, where you may see the Derby being run if you fly over it on the first Wednesday in June. This great race has twice been run in a snowstorm in June since 1800. A painting by Géricault of the 1821 snowstorm race hangs in the Louvre.

6. THE WEALD, which the route enters just south of Kenley and leaves just north of Battle, used to form part of the primeval forest "Andredesweald", 120 miles long by 30 wide. It became the centre of English iron-making in the 17th century, when most of the forest was cut down to feed the furnaces. In 1600, in half the Weald alone, there were more than 40 iron mills and 25 furnaces employing 50,000 men. The last foundry closed down early in the 19th century. Weald now known for cherries and hops. Hops are stored in queer-looking oast houses (pictured) which can be seen from the air. The Weald has 10 ins. more rain per year than the coast, only 20 miles away.

7. In BUXTED village, 2 miles S.W. of the railway viaduct, the first iron cannon in one piece was cast in 1543 by Ralph Hogge. His house still stands near the village church. Village now champion at darts.

8. The SOUTH DOWNS —800 ft. near Brighton— chalk hills with fine age-old springy turf pasture which has made South Down sheep famous for their mutton and fine wool.

9. PEVENSEY CASTLE, 4 miles N.E. of Eastbourne and 1 mile from the coast, shows up well from the air with its outer Roman Camp enclosing 9 acres and its walls up to 20 feet high, and 10 feet thick. It has been claimed as the site of Julius Caesar's landing in Britain. (The sea came right to the camp then.) It was Anderida, one of the strong camps built in the 3rd century to protect the shores against Saxon invasion, but the Saxons captured it in A.D. 491. The Normans landed near here in 1066. In the 13th century, a Norman castle was built in the S.E. corner of the Roman Camp.

10. THE LONG MAN OF WILMINGTON. At the back of the hill, 4 miles N.W. of Eastbourne, is the figure of a man 230 feet high cut out of the hill chalk, some say by the Celts, others by the Saxons to represent Balder, their God of Peace. It is one of the largest of the many figures —mostly white horses—cut out on English chalk hills.

1. The spire of HARROW CHURCH in the middle of Harrow School, which is one of the two most famous of English schools, may be spotted on the hill about 4 miles from Northolt Airport. Winston Churchill went to the school. It was founded in 1571 and has a population of 520 boys.

2. KEW BOTANICAL GARDENS can be spotted by the distinctive bend in the Thames. The Pagoda is imitation Chinese, 165 feet high.

3. ST. PAUL'S CATHEDRAL, the "parish church" of the British Empire. The first church here, built in A.D. 607, was burnt down in 1087 ; the second was burnt down in the Great Fire of London, 1666. The present cathedral miraculously escaped in the 1939 war, though practically every building round it was destroyed by German bombs. The cross, lighted by the flames of great fires around, inspired the firemen to exceptional efforts. The cathedral was designed by Christopher Wren and is 365 feet high.

4. CROYDON AIRPORT—the leading British civil airport until 1939. The first British civil airline service started from here in 1919.

5. KENLEY and Biggin Hill—two of the principal air bases for the R.A.F. fighter pilots who defeated the invading German air forces in the Battle of Britain, 1940, when 1,733 German aircraft were shot down and 643 damaged.

6. PILGRIM'S WAY to Canterbury led along foot of North Downs. Chaucer walked it in 14th century.

7. The REDHILL-ASHFORD RAILWAY, nearly straight for 44 miles, is one of the best landmarks for air navigators in South England. Straight or evenly curved features show up well from the air by contrast with the usual irregularities of nature. Before 1939 all civil air traffic to the Continent was routed along this railway.

8. TUNBRIDGE WELLS — a fashionable watering-place in the Georgian period when it was run by a celebrated dandy, Beau Nash (pictured). Queen Anne paid £100 to have the promenade paved with pantiles because her son slipped and fell there.

9. BODIAM CASTLE, 3 miles from railway, is one of the most complete medieval fortresses remaining, with moat, machiolated parapets, portcullis, etc. (1386).

10. BATTLE ABBEY, founded by William the Conqueror on the scene of the Battle of Hastings (1066). During the battle he vowed to build an abbey if he should beat Harold, King of England, opposing him. Wolves fed on the bodies of Normans and Saxons after the battle. No quarter was given on either side. The Altar is said to have been erected where King Harold's remains were found.

11. WINCHELSEA, important sea port when the sea lapped its walls in the 13th century. Ruined when left high and dry inland. One of three ancient town gates still standing, STRAND, shown.

12. HASTINGS, one of the Cinque Ports, of which Winston Churchill is Warden. An important port in the 11th century until the harbour filled up. Has a pier 300 feet long.

13. In this steamer lane you may see one of the Shaw Savill ships, like the AKAROA pictured on the left, on the way to New Zealand via Panama, or an Orient Company ship like the ORION shown

Map labels: NORTHOLT, MAIN AIRPORT FOR BRITISH EUROPEAN AIRWAYS TRAFFIC TO THE CONTINENT, HEATHROW, Staines, Brooklands, Epsom, CROYDON, Dorking, Reigate, KENLEY, Redhill, BIGGIN HILL, REDHILL, GATWICK, Crawley, East Grinstead, PENSHURST, Sevenoaks, PILGRIMS WAY, WEST MALLING, Tonbridge, Tunbridge Wells, Buxted, Crowborough, Brighton, Ouse R., Lewes, Newhaven, FRISTON, Eastbourne, Pevensey, Bexhill, Battle, Bodiam, Winchelsea, Rye, Hastings, Mole R., Thames R.

START, Miles (0–70), Kilometres (approx), FINISH, 350, 340, 320, 300, 280, 260, 240

Making Sense of Towns

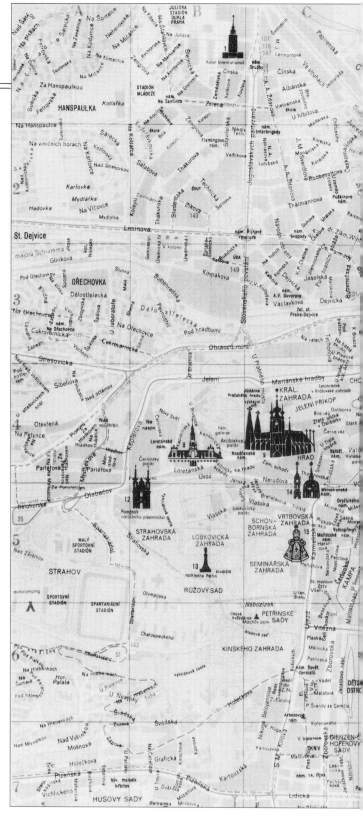

Many of us visiting a city or town for the first time on our own try to get a map of it before setting out to find someone or something in it. The intrepid urban explorer with plenty of time may boast at being able to do without a map as a guide, but people pressed for time can save it by employing the results of someone else's explorations and surveys preserved in map form.

There are many different approaches to mapping cities for the tourist unfamiliar with them. Many cities offer a wide-ranging choice of maps of varying clarity, attractiveness, usefulness, accuracy and interest. By their very nature cities present both problems and opportunities to the map-maker. Interesting and important features are closely packed into small spaces on many levels. The explorer can spend time reading the urban landscape: most of us will make do with a two-dimensional landscape visualized and then portrayed by a map-maker. One problem is that each map-maker, despite working more or less to a set of rules about how to achieve this, perceives the same city in a distinctive manner. For example, Leeds was one of the nastiest places Charles Dickens knew, but the modern historian, Asa Briggs, thought it one of the grandest 'poems' ever offered to the world. Extreme views like this rarely spawn nasty or poetic maps, but the look of city maps differs sufficiently to suggest that perceptions as well as style, knowledge, purpose or economics have some influence.

Newcomers to London are offered everything from ordinary A–Z street maps packed with names and numbers, to very elaborate, coloured pictorial maps, and recently three-dimensional maps whose buildings look like the ones on the ground, but are seen with bird's-eye perspective. Such maps often hide the streets, so they do have drawbacks. Visiting a new city involves unexpected problems, whatever the method of depiction and whether or not the scale is constant. How do you know whether all the streets and alleyways have been shown? Is the information on buildings trustworthy? For several decades town maps of former communist Eastern Europe often gave only a rough idea of land which was built up, whereas many town maps in Western Europe were faithful to detailed information on source plans and even show individual buildings. Typically, North American town maps, often provided by oil companies, give good information for

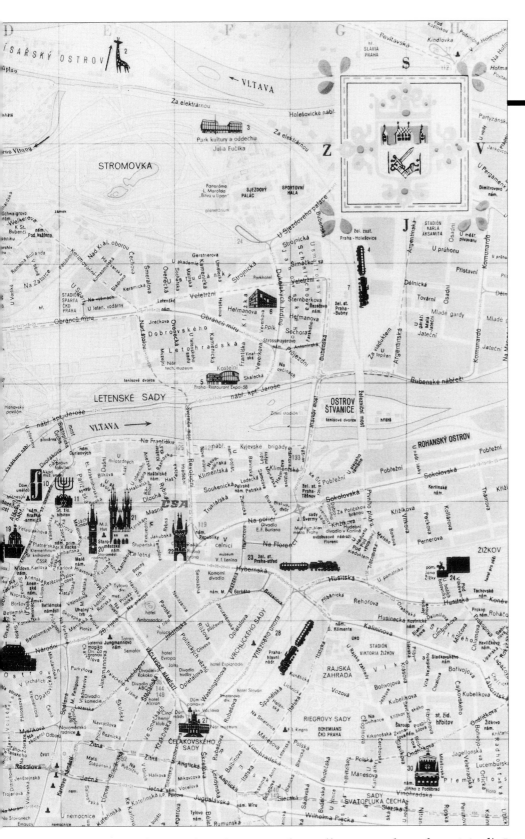

Praha Orientacni Plan – stred mesta. Vydala Kartograficke nakladatelstvi, 1968.

the motorist but not for other sorts of travellers.

This 1967 map of central Prague is an unusually good example of a city map. The buildings and streets have been simplified to an extent which helps the user to read it without destroying too much detail. The streets and their names stand out as do the public transport services (in red on the original). Landmarks are easily seen because their profiles pop up from the plane of the map. Open spaces and areas of water complete this visually harmonious production. For moving around Prague this map is an excellent compromise: not too much detail, but just enough for the stranger to 'read' the city. CHRISTOPHER BOARD

TRAVELLING THE OCEANS

Tradition has it that in the tenth century a Polynesian islander named Kupe, while on a fishing expedition in his canoe, was blown by adverse winds far to the south where he eventually made landfall. Returning to his homeland he told his people of the mountainous and afforested land he had discovered. It is claimed that the story of Kupe's discovery was handed down by the spoken word from generation to generation until, in the mid-fourteenth century, overpopulation in central Polynesia forced a number of chiefs to set out with their followers in seven great canoes to establish themselves in the land that Kupe visited.

The annual migratory flights of the shining cuckoo and the godwit southwards through Polynesia provided a direction for departure. The Polynesians' meticulous knowledge of the stars, their understanding of the direction of the ocean swells and their recognition of the nearness of land indicated by the presence of coastal seabirds and drifting weed provided the navigational aids to complete these ocean voyages of a thousand miles (1600 km) or more to reach the land we now call New Zealand.

Once the voyagers had arrived in their new homeland the easiest form of transport would have been by sea-going canoes. Sailing along an unknown coast and having found hidden reefs, dangerous rocks and safe anchorages, the travellers' verbal descriptions were all that were needed for others following the same route. The Maoris had no knowledge or need of charts.

Only when Tasman, Cook and other Europeans arrived were surveys made and set down as charts that others might follow. During his great Pacific voyages Captain Cook circumnavigated the two main islands of New Zealand, fixing his vessel by star sights and delineating the coastline and prominent landmarks by observing compass bearings as he sailed along, noting with care his ship's courses and speeds as the winds allowed. These 'running surveys', as they are called, provided the data for the production of the first chart of New Zealand dated 1772 which was published in the Admiralty's official account of Cook's first Pacific voyage.

In October 1969, on the two-hundredth anniversary of Cook's first landing in New Zealand in Poverty Bay, a gathering of naval vessels took place off Gisborne for the bicentenary celebrations. It was the idea of Commander W. J. L. Smith, the New Zealand hydrographer, to publish on this occasion a commemorative chart of New Zealand and the surrounding waters, which would replace the then current Admiralty chart. To quote from the memoir in chart N Z 11C, it 'serves to illustrate how the accumulated efforts of hydrographic surveyors, navigators and cartographers have been combined to produce a chart designed for modern navigational requirements and a record of achievement in man's increasing knowledge of the oceans' (bottom right).

Cook's original chart is shown as an inset so that two hundred years of cartographic progress may be noted. N Z 11C is a very beautiful chart produced before the advent of scribed contours as demanded by automated cartography. Manual hatching and hill shading were still being used to reveal vividly the tortured topography of New Zealand. As charted, the North Island of New Zealand portrays the writhings of the great fish that Maui had hauled from the deep, as it was killed by his brothers.

Polynesians made long ocean voyages across the Pacific without charts as we know them (though Marshall Islanders did have a form of navigational *aide-mémoire* constructed from bent sticks, representing currents, and shells, representing islands) at least one hundred and fifty years before Columbus crossed the Atlantic. Meanwhile, Mediterranean sailors had been using sea charts for over five hundred years. Only when Europeans entered the Pacific in the seventeenth and eighteenth centuries were charts developed for sailing the Pacific Ocean.

REAR ADMIRAL STEVE RITCHIE

Royal New Zealand Navy chart of New Zealand, 1969 [N.Z. 11C]. Reproduced by kind permission of the Hydrographic Office of the Royal New Zealand Navy, Auckland.

THE COMPUTER OBLIGES

Consider the problem of the motorist bent on getting the family to the sun and sand of the French Mediterranean coast as quickly as possible, only to find that a lorry drivers' dispute has frozen the entire French autoroute system. As the papers said, when this happened in 1992, 'motorists with a few good maps should have no problems getting through'. True, and it is also true that motorists without conventional maps but with a personal computer and the requisite route planning software would also have no problems, while ensuring at the same time a route which is as short and cost-effective as possible.

The motorist has requested a route to Nice from Calais avoiding the autoroute system, and two of the products of this request are illustrated below. On the screen below we see that the computer has found a route which closely shad-ows the autoroutes without actually using them. The *Routes Nationales* are not, however, neces-sarily the best way to go, and selecting a route which suppressed these, too, might have found a more interesting alternative using some of the delightfully empty 'D' roads which France has in abundance.

The map on the screen is a 'virtual map'. Until it is printed out it has no permanent form, and can be modified by the user. Initially the computer customizes the map to suit the request (and will take into account other considerations, such as expected driving speed and specified call-ing points on the way). The whole route between Calais and Nice will be shown at an appropriate level of detail, but if the user then wants to zoom in to a part of the route and to add more detail, as in the illustration, this is easily done.

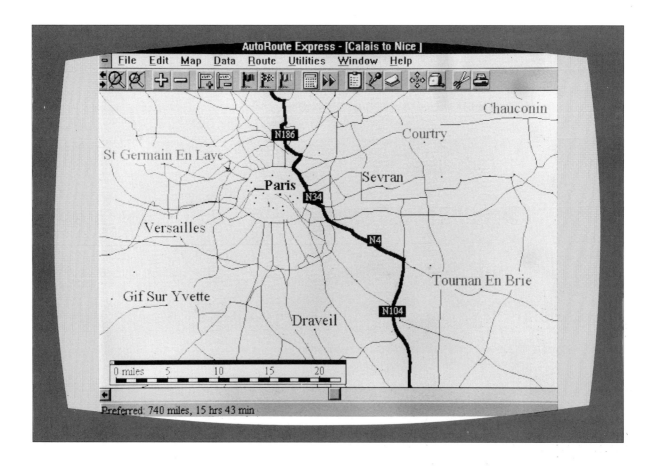

The illustration below shows a hard-copy print-out – and is not a map at all. Many people, when planning a route, prefer to transcribe their choice into a series of written instructions to be used on the road. Here the computer obliges.

At the heart of this computer package is a digitized map, in this case the French national survey's road map at 1:1 000 000 scale, a map the average motorist would use on a long journey. But the software has added intelligence to the map data, and has incorporated some of the map-reading processes normally applied by the user.

In some ways, electronic route planners are unsophisticated: they cannot yet weigh up all the factors a skilled map reader might consider when using a conventional map. Their advantage is in calculating the least distance, fastest route, timings and presenting the topology of the route in a choice of formats, all provided in seconds!

The map displayed on the screen is fundamentally different from a conventional road map. It is not a decision-making tool, but the decision itself – a map with a message, telling the motorist which way to go. To convey that message it uses another facility denied the conventional map: the route displayed on the screen flashes on and off, showing the correct way to go. In contrast, a conventional paper map provides a wealth of data but leaves the motorist to decide the route.

Computers are not only giving us new ways of dealing with navigational information, but also new ways of visualizing routes. With the further possibilities offered by three-dimensional views using digital terrain data there is much exciting new cartography in store for the route planner and navigator.

R. B. PARRY

(Opposite) A map which tells you where to go. A 'screenshot' of a proposed route east from Paris. The user can add or subtract detail.

(Below) The same route printed out. Many users will prefer to use this version for actual navigation. Maps provided by NextBase, part of their AutoRoute Express package.

AutoRoute Express - [Preferred]

File Edit Map Data Route Utilities Window Help

Time	Instruction	Road	Dist	Dir	Towards
11:42	Turn right onto	N17	2 miles	S	[Pte De La Villette]
11:44	At Pte De La Villette turn off onto	Plriphlrique	1 mile	SE	[Pte De Bagnolet]
11:45	At Pte De Pantin stay on the	Plriphlrique	1/2 mile	S	[Pte De Bagnolet]
11:45	At Pte Des Lilas stay on the	Plriphlrique	1 mile	SE	[Pte De Bagnolet]
11:46	At Pte De Bagnolet stay on the	Plriphlrique	2 miles	S	[Pte De Bercy]
11:48	At Pte De Vincennes turn off onto	N34	2 miles	E	Chelles
11:50	Turn right onto	N186	2 miles	S	Creteil
11:53	Turn left onto	N4	8 miles	E	Pontault Combault
12:02	At Pontault Combault stay on the	N4	1 mile	E	[Lesigny]
12:03	Turn off onto	N104	7 miles	S	[Brie Comte Robert]
12:11	Turn off onto	N105	3 miles	SE	[Moissy Cramayel]
12:14	At Moissy Cramayel stay on the	N105	8 miles	S	[Vert St Denis]
12:23	At Vaux Le Penil stay on the	N105	6 miles	SE	[Thomery]
12:30	At Le Chatelet En Brie stay on the	N105	11 mile:	SE	[Montereau Faut Yonne
12:44	At Montereau Faut Yonne turn right on	D403	1/4 mile	S	
12:45	Turn right onto	N105	2 miles	S	[Varennes Sur Seine]
12:47	At Varennes Sur Seine turn left onto	N6	13 mile:	E	Chalon Sur Saone
13:02	At Pont Sur Yonne stay on the	N6	6 miles	E	Chalon Sur Saone
13:09	At Courtois Sur Yonne stay on the	N6	1 mile	SE	Chalon Sur Saone
13:10	At St Clement stay on the	N6	4 miles	SE	Chalon Sur Saone
13:15	At Paron stay on the	N6	17 mile:	S	Chalon Sur Saone
13:35	At Joigny stay on the	N6	6 miles	S	Chalon Sur Saone
13:42	At Charmoy stay on the	N6	10 mile:	E	Chalon Sur Saone
13:54	At Perrigny stay on the	N6	2 miles	E	Chalon Sur Saone

Preferred: 740 miles, 15 hrs 43 min

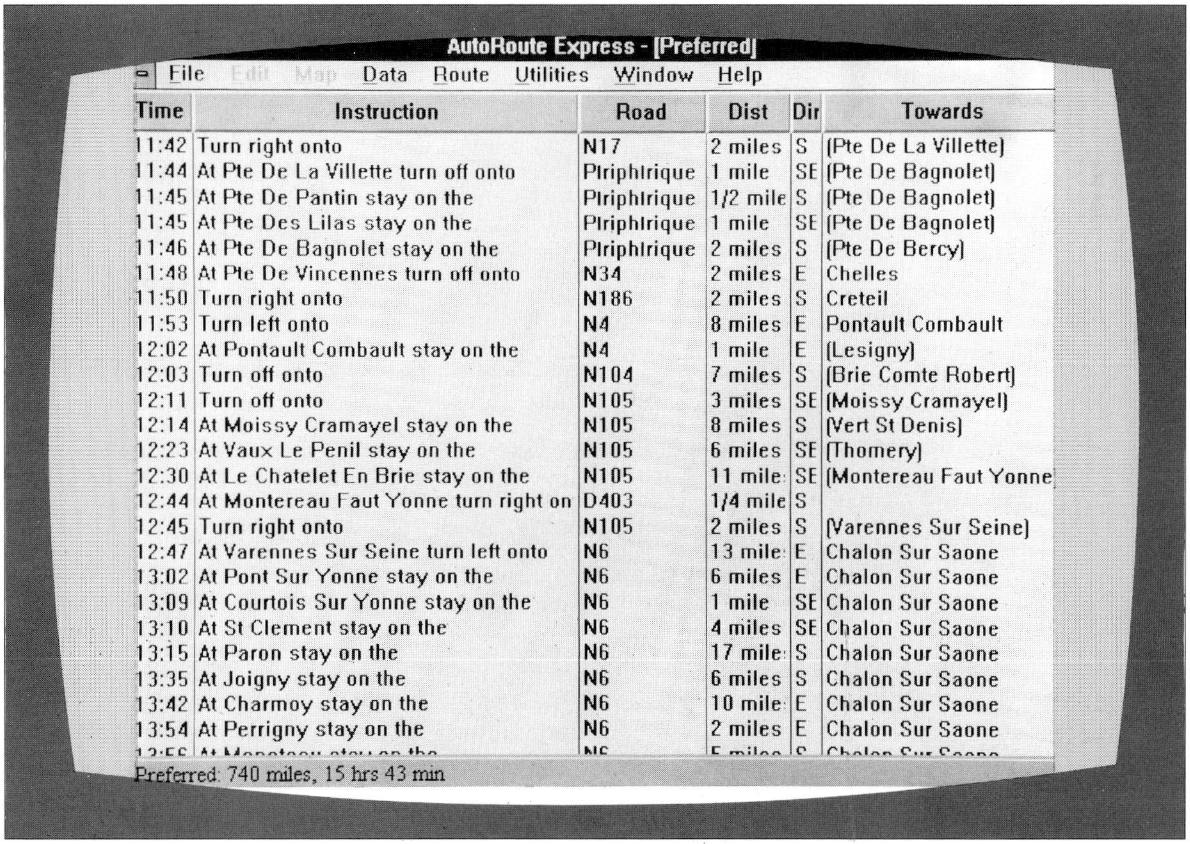

PACKAGED TO APPEAL
TO THE TRAVELLER

In the years between 1801, when Ordnance Survey published its first map, and the end of the First World War in 1918, the reputation of this military-cum-scientific department rested largely on the quality of its maps as aids to the British Army. While its products were generally available to the public throughout this period, there was little enthusiasm for aggressive selling, and map sales figures made dismal reading.

Once the First World War was over, things changed quickly and dramatically at Ordnance Survey. The inter-war years in Britain saw a greatly increased leisure activity among the working and middle classes: people were leaving their desks and factories to get out into the countryside with cycling, walking, bus and rail excursions – or motoring, if they could afford it. Ordnance Survey harnessed the public demand for maps of the country's favourite tourist attractions, and a professional artist called Ellis Martin was engaged to put an enticing face on the covers of the rather stolid maps.

Martin's brief was to 'design map covers and promotional material which will sell maps'. The choice of Ellis Martin was a particularly fortunate one for Ordnance Survey, for here was an artist with a topographical surveyor's eye, able to create realistic landscapes from impossibly lofty vantage-points: his Ordnance Survey Christmas card for 1919 (now a collector's item), and his dazzling Aviation Map of 1929 are prime examples of his art. His sense of time and place, his impeccable calligraphy and his range of media were qualities which marked his map cover art as something special. Martin's first cover designs appeared in 1919. By 1921, the department's annual progress report was recording the highest map sales in Ordnance Survey's history, and Martin's covers were acknowledged in the report to be the cause of this remarkable turn of events.

The two map covers shown here partially demonstrate Martin's range of skills. The manly young hiker consulting his trusty one-inch map is set in a realistic landscape in which the artist

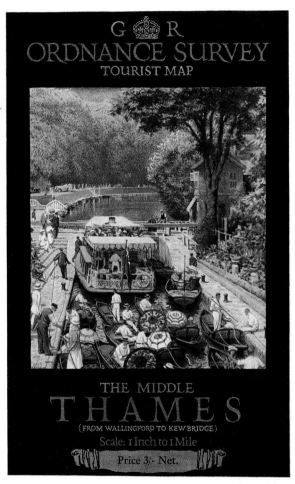

cleverly targets three other potential map-user groups – cyclists, motorists and day-trippers. The cover has been described as 'the high art of map selling', and was used as a series cover for a range of District and Tourist Maps from 1932.

Martin's cover for the Middle Thames Tourist Map displays a different technique. Here the style is neo-Impressionist: a peerless summer's day at Boulter's Lock on the Thames is shown, with all its bustle and colour, while in the distance a peaceful, verdant countryside beckons the tourist. It is probably Martin's most distinguished Ordnance Survey map cover design from a career that spanned the twenty years between the two World Wars.

ORDNANCE SURVEY "ONE-INCH" MAP

Hertford & St. Albans

Mounted on Linen
Price Three Shillings Net.

Published by the Ordnance Survey Office, Southampton.

The high art of map selling. (Opposite) Ellis Martin, cover design for the Tourist Map of the Middle Thames, 1923. It shows Boulter's Lock at Maidenhead.

(Left) Ellis Martin, cover design for District and Tourist maps, 1932.

Although map cover art was not a new sales technique when Martin joined Ordnance Survey in 1919, he was the artist who raised it from a crude and primitive art form to a plane imitated by other map publishers, not one of whom ever matched his skills as illustrator or calligrapher. His art was not that of the cartouche artists of earlier days, employed on sometimes sycophantic blandishments to their patrons, but his purpose was not all that different. He, like the earlier map publishers, had to sell maps and he did so by creating an attractive, more broadly cultural, complementary image to the map. Where earlier publishers used the body of the map and later the cartouche for their purposes, he used the cover and, in doing so, created a type of commercial, domestic art unique to Britain and unique, even, to his era. With his departure Ordnance Survey map cover art declined, to be replaced in due course by photographic covers, leaving the work of Ellis Martin a cherished reminder of a golden age when Ordnance Survey maps were perceived as 'old friends who led you to unknown places'.

JOHN PADDY BROWNE

MAPS FOR THE TOURIST IN SWITZERLAND

There is a long tradition of map use by tourists visiting Switzerland, and walking trips in the Alps are well served by official and commercial touring maps. The official topographic maps of the Swiss Federal Survey are world-renowned for depicting the nuances of the mountainous landscape of the country, but they make no concessions for the tourist. One has to be able to read and interpret the detail of the landscape in order to anticipate where there are good views of the scenery, but there are no distinctions between pretty and ordinary, or ugly, villages.

For France the Michelin maps have long indicated scenic roads, good viewpoints and interesting places. Some discerning tourists of course will spurn such help, choosing instead to work out routes for themselves. Others are content to wander as the mood takes them, deriving pleasure from the chance discovery of an attractive view, and extra pleasure from having discovered it for themselves.

Not everyone has the leisure and time to explore in this fashion. Both the growing popularity of limited package holidays and of cameras persuaded Agfa to launch a series of Swiss touring maps specially aimed at the photographer. Part of one of these, featuring the valleys leading down to Locarno, is illustrated here. The red, numbered diamonds indicate where good photographs can be taken and what direction to look in. Where there are many photopoints along, say, a valleyside path, they are marked by a sequence of red dots. These are easily located in the landscape by reference to rivers, forests, roads, settlements and a pictorial representation of valleys using classic techniques (see pp.14–15). There are plenty of place names, too. Two town plans appear on the back of the main map, each with photopoints. Accompanying the folded map is a detailed guide to the numbered photopoints, sensibly grouped to help the traveller who wishes to maximize photo-

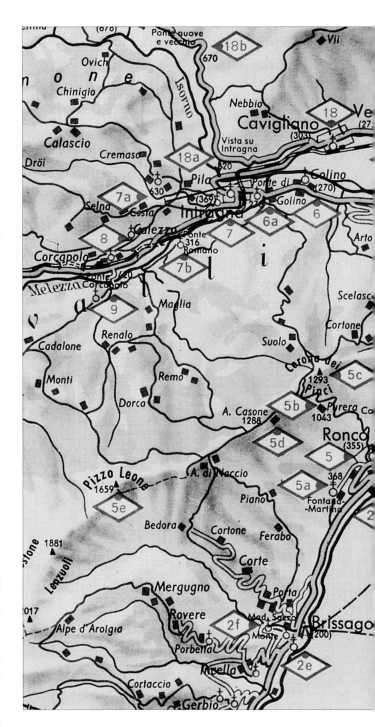

opportunities. Ideally suited to the needs of the walker who perhaps has to rely on public transport, this map and its guide serve both as a route planner and as a way of finding one's way from point to point. Usually walking times and the existence of train and bus lines are mentioned.

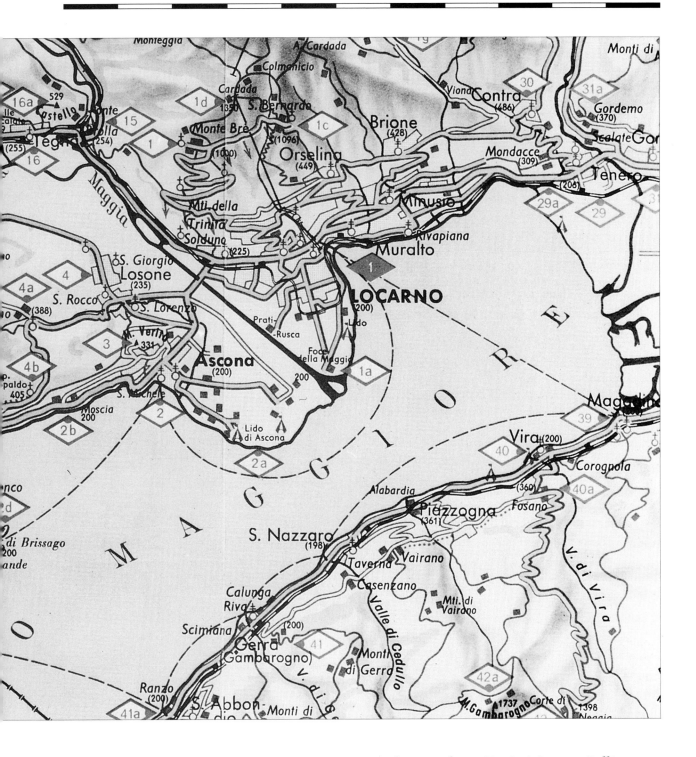

For the sheer quantity of useful and relatively long-lasting information these maps can scarcely be bettered. If they have not been produced for many other parts of the world, it is probably because they require much painstaking survey work – on foot, of course.   CHRISTOPHER BOARD

Agfa Tourenkarte: Tessin 1, Locarno-Bellinzona. Sheet A7. Scale 1:75 000. No date, but based on the Swiss Federal topographic map of February 1957. Gesamtherstellung Joh. Roth sel. Ww., München.

CADS ON CASTORS

The bicycle was the great liberator of the more modest end of the Victorian middle class, and the road map was the guide to freedom. Before the 1870s the clerk, the shopkeeper or the school teacher earning £2 a week could not – unless they walked – afford the liberty of the open road, which belonged to those who could buy or hire a carriage. After the arrival of the practical bicycle from France in 1869, Jack with £10 in his pocket could be as free, if not as good, as his master. A fall in the cost of living, the coming of Bank Holidays for all and the rapid growth of hire purchase, which offered a bicycle for four or five shillings a week, helped to put about 200 000 cycles on British roads by 1882. At this date most were penny-farthings essentially suited to the young, fit and male, whose exuberance earned them the name of 'cads on castors'.

As the craze for cycling grew, a market for maps aimed at cyclists opened up, and publishers enthusiastically exploited it from the 1880s. The cheapest way was to buy in defunct publishers' old printing plates and stock, or simply to pirate the products of up-market publishers such as Edward Stanford or Ordnance Survey. George Washington Bacon, notoriously the most entrepreneurial of the breed, did both.

One of his earliest maps was a Cycling Road-Map of England, in seven sheets on a scale of five miles to the inch, first published around 1883. It was derived from John Cary's *New Map of England and Wales* of 1816. It did not matter too much that the roads shown were still those of Regency England, for the highway network had scarcely changed. It was much more important for a map publisher, however mercenary and unscrupulous, to keep railways and railway stations up to date, since urban cyclists bound for a day in the country usually put their machines on the train. One of Bacon's maps, dating from about 1887, is basically of this sort, but it also emphasizes better class roads in yellow and is provided with ten-mile squares for calculating distances. By 1904, however, Bacon's maps (far right) were showing symbols identifying hills that had to be ridden with caution (arrows with one feather pointing down the slope) and those that were

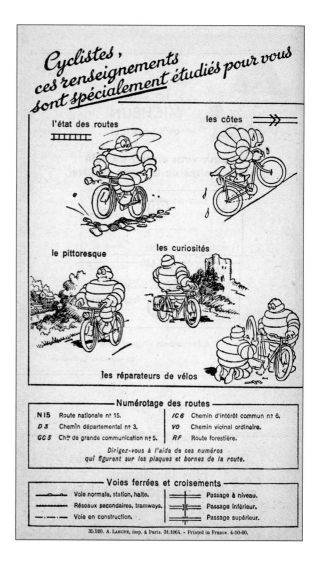

(Above) *Pneu Michelin,* Carte Cycliste l'état des routes, les côtes, les curiosités, le pittoresque, les réparateurs de vélos, 50 km. autour de Paris, *1950. Scale 1:100,000.*

(Opposite) *Bacon's Cycling Road Map – 30 Miles around London, 1904. British Library 3479 (101).*

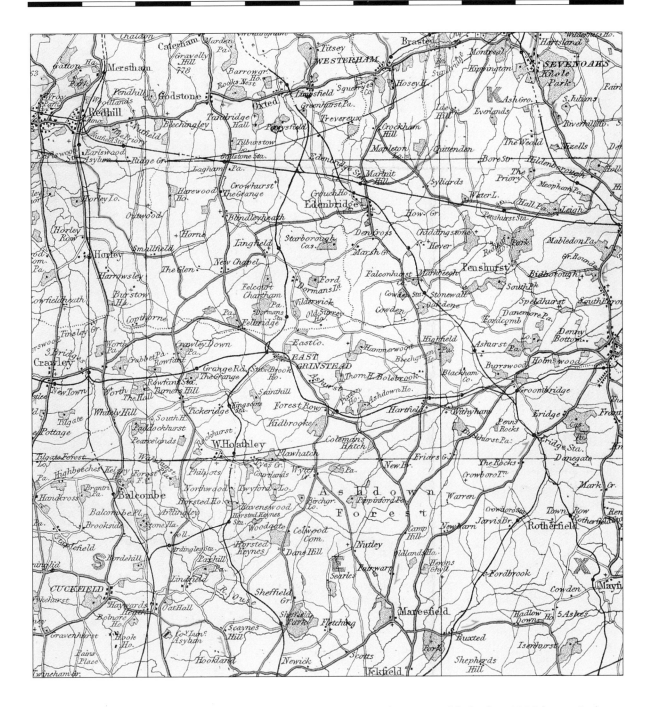

dangerous (arrows with two feathers). Good cycling roads were still indicated in yellow but, as this map shows, some routes did not follow the highways already marked in black on the base map, but instead used cyclable field tracks.

In this century, mapping tailored to the needs of cyclists also flourished on the near continent, sometimes serving the requirements of motorists too. Perhaps the Michelin *Carte Cycliste 50km* *autour de Paris* published in 1950 (opposite) represents the high point of specialization with lavish use of colour to show hard climbs (brakes had long since removed the need for dangerous hills to be shown). Cycle paths and their condition are specifically indicated and special attention is drawn to the dreaded *pavé*, still allegedly retained in parts of northern France and Belgium for the Tour de France!

CHRISTOPHER BOARD

HIGHWAYS AND BYWAYS

It must be every motorist's dream to be able to drive through the British countryside without encountering significant traffic. In the 1950s, when car ownership began to grow again after the Second World War, the new-found freedom of taking that 'extra room' with you on holiday was already causing frayed tempers from nose-to-tail driving along the main roads. There were then only 3 million cars, 1.25 million motorcycles and 1.1 million buses and commercial vehicles altogether. (In 1991 there were about 19 million, 750000 and 500000 respectively.) The editor of *The Autocar*, with help from *The Motor Cycle*, teamed up with the weekly magazine *Everybody's* to produce a guide to their favourite routes recommended for drivers and riders to avoid the bottlenecks and congestion on the trunk roads.

In the course of four weeks in May 1956 a set of sixty-four maps and a route guide describing a selection of the most popular holiday routes was included free with the magazine, assembling as *Everybody's* 'Avoid-the-Traffic' Road Maps of Britain. One is illustrated here, showing how simple it was to follow the thick black lines instead of the thin double lines which were the crowded main routes. Plenty of place names are given, but road numbers do not appear except in the route book, which also gives detailed instructions on how to avoid the most congested towns.

The map is almost the reverse of the normal road map. Instead of main roads creating the visible road framework, there is a network of minor roads linking country towns, villages and crossroads. Not all of the pet routes could be shown, but the editors hoped that the pleasure of enjoying the countryside would outweigh slightly longer journeys on which average speeds were not high. Especially steep or narrow sections of road were indicated by broken lines, and these were kept to a minimum. You can see how it was possible to drive to the Sussex and Hampshire coasts and not use the main Littlehampton, Portsmouth and Southampton trunk roads. However, avoiding Winchester and its notorious by-pass

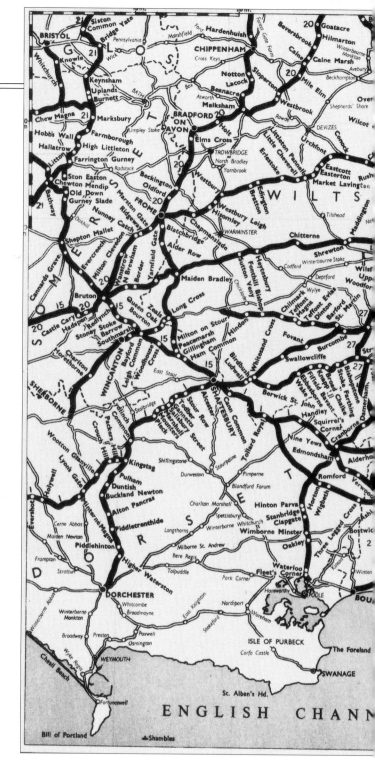

was rather complicated. Most of the alternative trunk route to the West Country across Salisbury Plain can be avoided, ironically by using some sections of the old coach road (the original A30) which passed through Overton and Whitchurch.

It might be thought that such an atlas would quickly prove to be self-defeating, as all the traffic switched to the quiet routes and struggled to cope

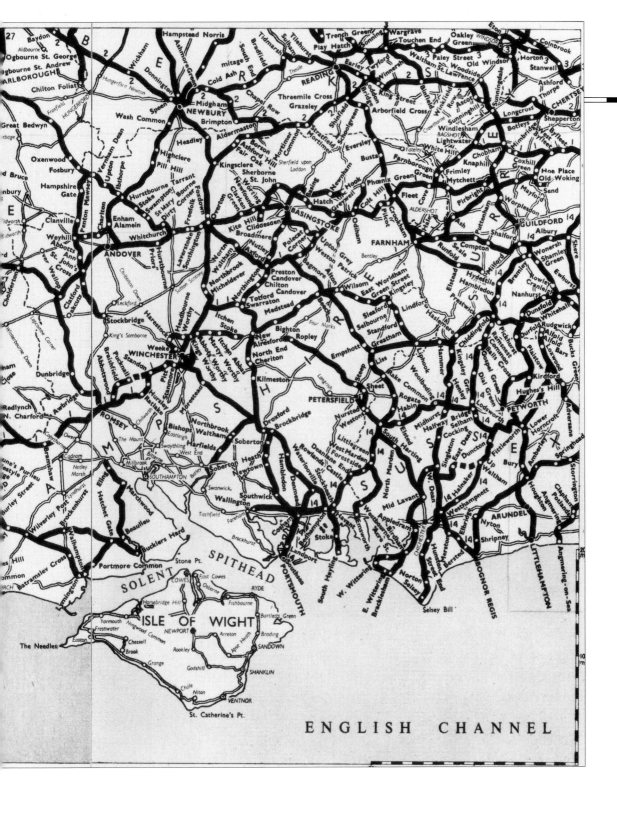

'Everybody's "Avoid-the-Traffic" Road Atlas of Britain' specially prepared by The Autocar, 1956. Scale 1:506 880.

with agricultural activities. However, that did not occur because even the clear instructions in this atlas had to be followed very carefully, with the route book sandwiched between the maps. What made the atlas harder to use is precisely the absence or lack of emphasis of the very roads you were meant to avoid. In practice, the main roads were, and still are, better signed, and so were more attractive to the drivers and riders who either didn't want to make the effort of following the atlas or were afraid of getting lost on the country roads.

CHRISTOPHER BOARD

THE PLUMB PUDDING IN DANGER: MAPS AND TERRITORY

Many behavioural scientists believe that a territorial sense is innate to many if not all animals, including humans. A robin knows and defends its territory and so has a mental map of it, the main outlines of which can be plotted on a flat surface by humans. In societies, such as medieval England, where large-scale maps were almost unknown, the boundaries of territorial units such as manors were defined in written charters or written surveys in terms that could, and sometimes can still, be followed on the ground and memorized through such ceremonies as the beating of the bounds. Drawn maps, whether they are of vast empires or small estates, are now the most familiar outward expression of these mental maps. Because they illustrate the human's innate territorial sense, and embody the profound emotions associated with land, maps and globes have become potent symbols of power and of national sentiment. In turn, because of the emotions they can arouse, maps have been much used, and continue to be used, as powerful instruments of satire and propaganda.

At the same time, since the second century BC in China and the Renaissance in western Europe, maps have assisted rulers in the more mundane tasks of defining territory culturally as well as legally, and of defending, increasing, organizing and managing it for the benefit of the owners and rulers if not always of the inhabitants. As the complexity of administration has increased, so the nature of the maps required by government has become more complex. It was realized as early as the seventeenth century that only the state had the means to finance the extensive, detailed, and accurate surveys necessary for the creation of such maps. Since then official maps have taken two principal forms: the topographical maps, at various scales, emphasizing relief, land use (where the scale allows), roads, rivers and political, judicial and administrative boundaries and used primarily for the purposes of defence, internal security and as a basis for the planning and management of public services and amenities; and

Prime Minister William Pitt and Napoleon divide the world between them. James Gillray, The Plumb Pudding in Danger *or* State Epicures Taking un Petit Souper. *Cartoon, 1801.* British Museum, Department of Prints and Drawings.

the large-scale cadastral, showing property ownership and land use and intended primarily for land management, settlement and taxation purposes.

The topographical map is epitomized by the original one-inch-to-the-mile British Ordnance Survey maps published from 1801 and by similar, but considerably earlier, official French and Austrian maps that covered much of western Europe. Before 1830, the compulsory, nationwide cadastral map was almost unknown in mainland Britain, though not Ireland, perhaps because the national government and administration were for centuries dominated by the private landowning classes who were vehemently opposed to central interference in this area. Instead, since about 1580, the English landowner had commissioned private measured surveys of his own lands. Like the larger national maps, they have served symbolic and very practical functions, expressing power and pride of ownership and facilitating the efficient exploitation and development of the estates portrayed.   PETER BARBER

MAPS TO IMPRESS

Amidst all the treasures in the Vatican, a modern visitor may pass through the *Galleria delle Carte Geografiche* (map gallery) with hardly a glance. When the gallery was first decorated in the 1580s by Egnazio Dante for Pope Gregory XIII, however, visitors to the Pope would have had to wait there for their audience in the next chamber.

They would have had plenty of time to study the paintings on the ceilings and the painted maps of the towns, districts and provinces of Italy that decorated the walls. They were based on the best and most up-to-date maps of the peninsula, and were revised in the 1630s to ensure they were still topical. Gradually visitors may have become aware of a political programme behind the decoration. An inscription on the north portal proclaimed Italy 'the most noble region of the entire globe', and the maps contain depictions of the great battles that had taken place there. The paintings in the vault show scenes from the Bible and from Italy's church history. In the very centre of the ceiling is the scene in which Jesus instructs his apostles to feed his sheep – the basis of the Papacy's claims to spiritual authority in the world.

Taken as a whole, the gallery is an expression of Italy's special place in the world of religion, and therefore of the Papacy's special position in Italy – one that found reflection in the Popes' claims to be overlords of all Italy as well as sovereigns in the Papal States alone. The latter claim is reflected in the inclusion of the Papal State of Avignon among the maps, even though it was in France, while the inclusion of the states of Naples, Milan, Florence and Venice must have given the envoys of their rulers food for thought as they waited to be presented to the Pope and to argue, perhaps, for some form of alliance with him.

Even in the sixteenth century, the public display of maps for propaganda purposes was not new; a building on one of the principal roads in first-century Rome contained a world map carved in marble (the probable prototype of the medieval world maps) and, in conscious emulation, Mussolini had a marble map of his 'empire' erected near the Roman Forum in the late 1930s. Nevertheless, using elegant maps in galleries to make territorial and political claims was particularly

typical of the sixteenth and early seventeenth centuries. Elizabeth I had a gallery in her palace at Whitehall lined with maps, some of which showed her realms and others which alluded to English discoveries and territorial claims in the New World. To this day some chambers and galleries

The Galleria delle Carte Geografiche, Vatican.

with painted maps survive in France (such as the *Galerie des Cerfs* at Fontainebleau) and Italy (the Palazzo Vecchio and the Uffizi in Florence), while guests at receptions in the mid-seventeenth-century former Town Hall of Amsterdam (now the Royal Palace) still sip their cocktails while standing on depictions of the world carved in marble on the floor and surrounded by statues representing Amsterdam's mastery of the world's trade.

PETER BARBER

A WHOLE WORLD IN YOUR HAND

The shape of a globe means it can bear a much more accurate representation of the earth's surface than a conventional map. For that reason it has for centuries been used as a teaching aid and, although to a much lesser extent, as an aid in navigation. It is also one of the most familiar of symbols. Sometimes it represents learning, as in pictures of seventeenth or eighteenth century gentlemen in their libraries, and sometimes it represents responsibility, symbolizing the weight of the world. More often, however, it has been

(Above) Augustus holding a tripartite globe as orb. Liber Floridus de St Omer c.1200. Bibliothèque Nationale, Paris. MS Lat 8865,f.45.

used as a symbol for power.

This is most obviously shown in the orb, derived from the Latin word for world, which has been carried by rulers since at least Roman times and is symbolic of their temporal power. The depiction of Augustus, in a French manuscript dating from about 1200 (above), shows him holding an orb in the form of a schematic 'TO' representation of the earth. In it the O represents the ocean surrounding the known world, with the Mediterranean forming the upright and the Don and Nile rivers the top stroke of the T, with Asia at the top, Europe on the left and Africa on the right. The picture as a whole (apart from disproving the oft-quoted statement that people in the Middle Ages believed that the world was flat) is one of majesty. The orb continues to be used in coronations and on royal great seals. However, it is only the Swedish orb, created in the middle of the sixteenth century, which is obviously a globe.

(Left) Queen Elizabeth II at her coronation – with orb – photographed by Cecil Beaton.

Jan Roettiers: Charles II medal commemorating the British colonization, 1670. Gold (reverse). British Museum: MI i 546/203.

Jean Warin: Louis XIV personal device, 1672. Gold (reverse). British Museum: George III Fr. Medal 28.

Globes, however, have been part of the panoply of power since the fifteenth century. In the 'Armada' portrait of about 1590 in Hatfield House, Elizabeth I is shown with her hand resting on a

George Bower: Louise de Quérouaille created Duchess of Portsmouth, 1673. Silver (reverse). British Museum: MI i 554/215.

globe. At the height of his power in the 1680s, Louis XIV commissioned one of the largest globes ever for his magnificent palace at Versailles. It was made by the most famous globe-maker of his age, the Venetian, Vincenzo Coronelli. Little more than a century later, Gillray showed Napoleon and William Pitt dividing the globe, or 'plumb pudding', as the artist called it, between themselves, while 250 years later Charlie Chaplin brilliantly satirized the association of megalomania with globes in his film, *The Great Dictator*, although it didn't put a stop to the habit as photographs of world statesmen regularly demonstrate.

Globes have also been used in smaller formats to make a variety of points relating to power. In the course of the 1660s and 1670s alone, Louis XIV used his personal image of a sun dominating the globe to warn that, in the words of his motto, he was 'not unequal to many' (above), while Charles II used the globe to remind contemporaries that the British – and their empire – were 'spread throughout the world' (above left). Most charmingly of all, however, a medal honouring Charles II's mistress, the Duchess of Portsmouth (left), proclaimed that love, personified by a cupid surmounting a globe, 'conquers all'!

PETER BARBER

MAKING A POINT

'Hail GEORGE! the Bulwarks of thy Realm survey
Both Land & Sea thy sovereign power obey!
What rival dares dispute thy lawful claim
Since they give strength to thee and thou to them!'

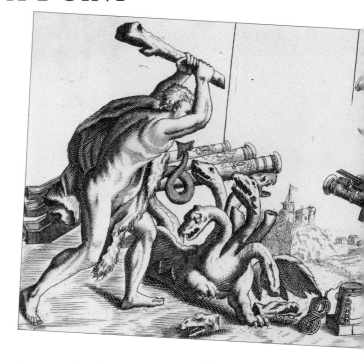

Map and detail from George Willdey's, '. . . Great Britain and Ireland', 1715 (1716). British Library Maps C.11.a.2.

So runs the inscription under the picture of the ship (far right) bringing George I to England in September 1714 following the death of Queen Anne. Although the map is not, as George Willdey claims under the King's portrait on the top left, 'corrected from the newest & most exact observations' (being instead a close copy of a map by one of Willdey's associates that was already about ten years old), it would have given the King a good idea of his kingdoms. In particular, it is one of the first maps to show the correct alignment for Cornwall (see pp.164–65). It has a charming advert at the bottom left for the clocks, snuff boxes, pistols, scissors, barometers and combs that were on sale, with Willdey's maps, at the Great Toyshop in Ludgate Street.

Essentially, however, this map is a political statement on behalf of the Anglican establishment of the day, which was celebrating the defeat of the Catholic James Edward Stuart, The Old Pretender, who had attempted to regain his ancestral thrones at the end of 1715. Despite being dated 1715, the map probably appeared in about February or March 1716, which still counted as 1715 under the Julian calendar that was in operation in England at the time. As befits a map produced for the political establishment, it singles out, with special symbols, important pillars of society such as the university towns and the Anglican archbishoprics and bishoprics as well as the counties and the towns that returned Members of Parliament. But it is the decoration which most clearly establishes the purpose of the map and would have helped its sales. Underneath the portrait of George (who is also given his main German titles) and the dedicatory cartouche which contains his British crown and sceptre and the symbolic horse of Hanover, there is a picture of Hercules (representing George's forces) slaying

the many-headed hydra of the Pretender, his French allies and the Scottish clans that supported him, with Edinburgh Castle in the background and Britannia trumpeting George's fame.

Between 1500 and about 1800, decorated panels or cartouches, far from being mere space fillers, were essential parts of the maps that they adorned. Often they imparted ethnographical, economic or social information that would have sat awkwardly in the body of the map (see pp.20–21), but they also acted as a channel for political propaganda and justified the appearance of the map at that particular time. Emperor Charles V, the first secular ruler in Christendom, was represented as king of the gods atop a world map by the Bavarian cartographer, Philip Apian, in the 1540s when his hold over Germany was being challenged by its princes. The opposing views of Louis XIV and his enemies can often be understood from the decoration adorning the maps of the same events, such as the siege of Luxembourg in 1684, that they both produced for the general public.

PETER BARBER

A PAPER LION

The notion of a united Netherlands of seventeen provinces remained an ideal for many of its citizens long after the split between the independent north and the Spanish south, which happened during the course of the war of independence from Spain. Because most provinces included a lion in their arms, the Leo Belgicus or Belgic Lion was the obvious symbol to choose for the country. The coincidence in geographic outline of the provinces with the shape of a lion made the cartographic Belgic Lion a particularly popular beast from his first appearance in 1583.

The lion shown here, a splendid example prepared by Jan van Doeticum, first appeared in 1598 at a time when peace between the Dutch and Spanish seemed imminent. At the sides were therefore shown the rulers of the Spanish-governed provinces and, underneath, the leaders of the northern provinces. In the bottom right-hand corner a miniature view of the capital of the southern Netherlands, Brussels, is coupled with a view of the northern capital, the Hague. In 1633–4 there must have been thoughts of republishing the map, because it was updated to include, in the top left corner, the then leaders, Philip IV of Spain's brother, the Cardinal-Infante Ferdinand, and Frederick-Henry, Prince of Orange.

This example was still being published, without further changes, as late as 1650. It demonstrates that the sense of cultural unity, which still underlies today's Benelux countries, had survived the final, formal separation of the northern and southern Netherlands under the terms of the treaty of Munster in 1648. The political fragmentation had already left its own cartographic mark, however: long before 1650 a purely Dutch lion had made its appearance, incorporating only the seven provinces and pointing in the opposite direction to the Belgic Lion.

Maps have been used as a focus for national loyalty since the sixteenth century. Spain was depicted as a Queen of Europe (Spain being the head, Sicily the orb and Italy the arm) and the German empire was shown as a double-headed eagle. The unadorned map has often played a similar, emotive role. In Commonwealth England a finely engraved map of England, Wales and

Jan van Doetecum and C.J. Visscher, 'Leo Belgicus', Amsterdam, 1633–4 (1650), Beudeker Atlas. *British Library Maps C.9.d.1. (6).*

Fifty-pence piece commemorating the UK's presidency of the European Commission in 1992.

Ireland replaced the image of the ruler on horseback on the Great Seal, which was used to seal important state papers. The Jacobites made repeated use of the map of Great Britain in the medallic propaganda that accompanied their attempts before 1750 to recover their thrones. In the

1980s the stamps, coins and banknotes of countries such as France, Brazil and Cyprus have all contained simplified maps of their countries. Nationalism has not quite had things all its own way, however, as is demonstrated by the fifty-pence piece (left) commemorating the United Kingdom's presidency of the European Commission in 1992, containing stars in the approximate geographical positions of the capitals of the twelve member states, although the British star is noticeably bigger than the others!

PETER BARBER

WRENCHED FROM THE HOMELAND!

After the First World War, Hungary lost more than half of its surface area under the terms of the treaty of Trianon of 1920. Having been one of the pillars of the Austro-Hungarian monarchy, it shrank to become a little, land-locked state in the middle of Europe with large Magyar minorities beyond its frontiers. Following the expulsion of the Habsburgs and the installation of Admiral Horthy as Regent, 'a kingdom without a king ruled by an admiral without a fleet', Hungary almost became the laughing stock of Europe.

Needless to say, these were traumatic happenings for all patriotic Magyars, and the Hungarian Women's National Association vented its anger through a map. At first glance the postcard below appears to show (historically inaccurately) the borders enjoyed by Hungary from the date of the conversion to Christianity of the leader of the Magyars in 896 until 1918. It spreads from the Adriatic in the west to Transylvania in the east and from the Tatras in the north to the Rivers Sava and Danube in the south. Turn a lever at the side of the card and the old Hungary collapses (right) along the lines of the Treaty of Trianon, with, it is claimed, over 70 per cent of Hungarian territory and over three million Magyars being torn from their homeland and joined to the successor states of Austria (Burgenland), Czechoslovakia (Slovakia), Romania (Transylvania) and Yugo-slavia (Croatia and Voivodina). It is powerful stuff although, as far as population figures are concerned, not necessarily accurate.

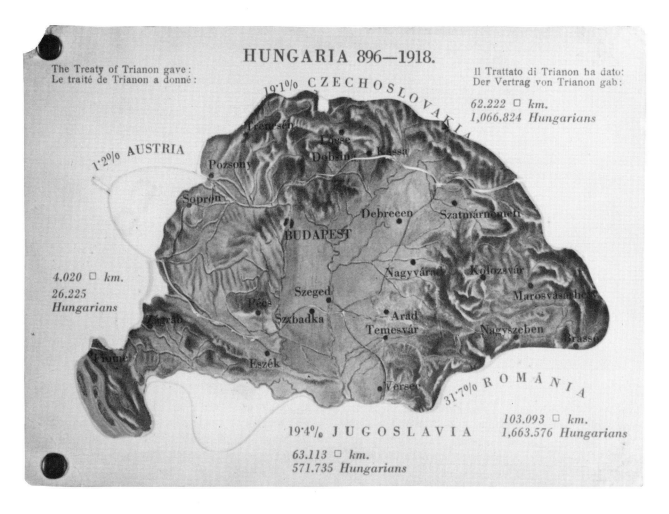

HUNGARIA 896—1918.

The Treaty of Trianon gave:
Le traité de Trianon a donné :

Il Trattato di Trianon ha dato:
Der Vertrag von Trianon gab:

19·1% CZECHOSLOVAKIA

62.222 □ km.
1,066.824 Hungarians

1·2% AUSTRIA

4.020 □ km.
26.225 Hungarians

31·7% ROMÁNIA

103.093 □ km.
1,663.576 Hungarians

19·4% JUGOSLAVIA

63.113 □ km.
571.735 Hungarians

Because of their emotive connotations, maps have long been excellent tools of propaganda. The trick of showing a map being dismembered in order to arouse horror at the proposed partition or destruction of a country is one of the most common ploys. It was used in popular prints and on cheap medals in the eighteenth century to stir up feeling against the intended partition of the Habsburg empire in 1740, the repeated partitions of Poland after 1772 and, early in the nineteenth century, French territorial losses in 1814–15 following the defeat of Napoleon. In a similar way after 1918, some German map-makers sought to arouse the indignation of their countrymen at the creation, at Germany's expense, of a Polish land corridor separating Germany proper from East Prussia – they showed the Polish corridor as a flaming red overlay, on a black and white pre-First World War map of Germany. In the 1930s, the supposed 'Jewish Menace' was illustrated in the German film, *Ewiger Jud*, by the depiction of rats scurrying in a westerly direction, from Poland, across a map of Europe.

Since 1945 maps on coins and stamps have been used to make propaganda for, among many others, Argentina's claim to the Falkland Islands, or the association of the Greek ruling family, which stemmed from Denmark, with Greece (on a thirty-drachmai coin of 1963). A stamp produced in 1949 commemorating the Communist victory at the end of the Chinese civil war showed a fist, clenching a triumphant Communist hammer, emerging from a map of China. In themselves maps may not cause wars, but they can certainly inflame the passions of the people involved in them.

PETER BARBER

Two views of the same postcard. 'Emich', 'Hungaria 896–1918', Budapest, Hungarian Women's National Association, c.1920. British Library Map Library, Cave Collection.

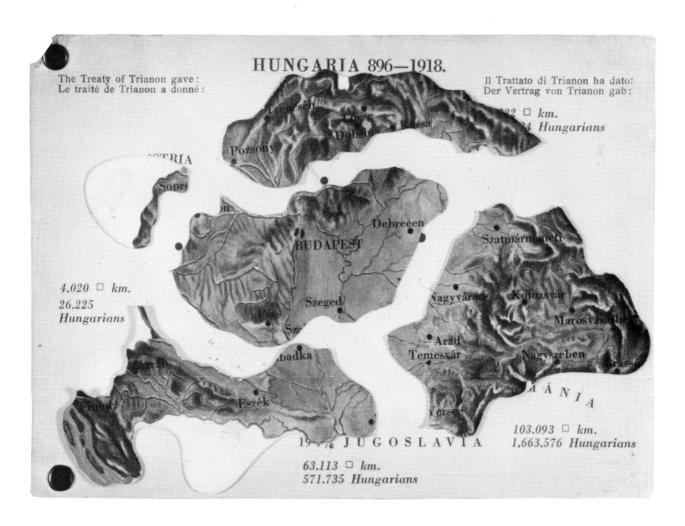

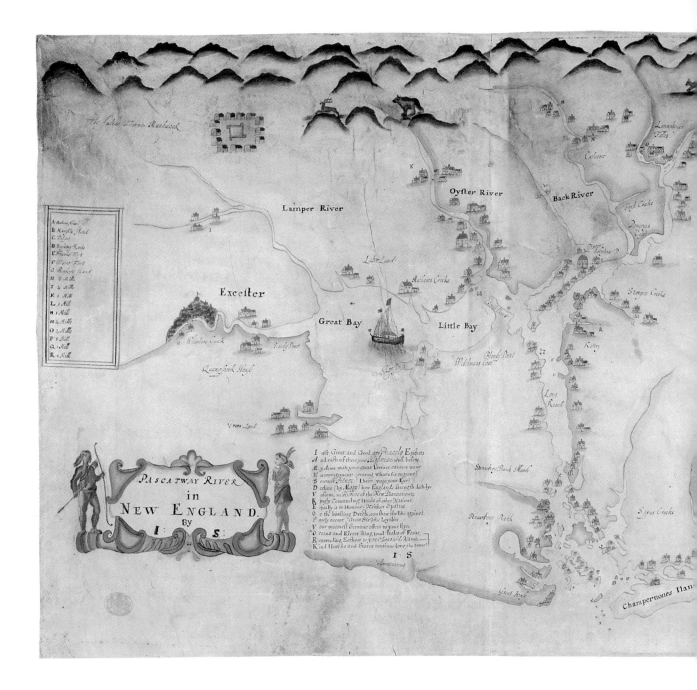

Within the map image:
- Lamper River
- Oyfter River
- Back River
- Exceſter
- Great Bay
- Little Bay
- PASCATWAY RIVER in NEW ENGLAND. By I S
- Champernoones Ilan

CARTOGRAPHIC COLONIZATION

'Serene Prince I heer unto your eye declare (by Mapp) how Englands strength doth lye unseene in rivers of the new plantations . . . Neither Spaine or the boasting Dutch can shew the like againe . . . Oceans and Rivers ring loud peals of fame, resounding echoes to your honour'd name.'

It was with these words that 'I.S. Americanus' (possibly the adventurer John Scott of Long Island), introduced the above map of British settlements in New Hampshire, in about 1680. He was presenting it to James, Duke of York, later James II, whose name is indeed echoed in York Town to the right of the map. The loyalty and patriotism extend to the images on the map itself. There are, it is true, a few slightly exotic touches: Indians guard the title cartouche, and the Indian village of Manhadok is shown and named at the top left. A few other names, such as the Pascatway River itself, are Indian and the bears may also be a North American touch. Essentially, however, the Duke of York would have been excused for

(Opposite) 'I.S. Americanus' (John Scott of Long Island?), 'Pascatway River in New England by I.S.'. Manuscript, c.1680. British Library K. Top. 120.27.

(Right) A German map of Czechoslovakia, c.1943: detail showing the area around Mirowitz/Mirovice. Landesvermessungsamt Böhmen und Mähren (Protectorate of Bohemia and Moravia). Scale 1:75 000, 24 Ausgabe (1943), sheet 4152 (Pribans/Pribram).

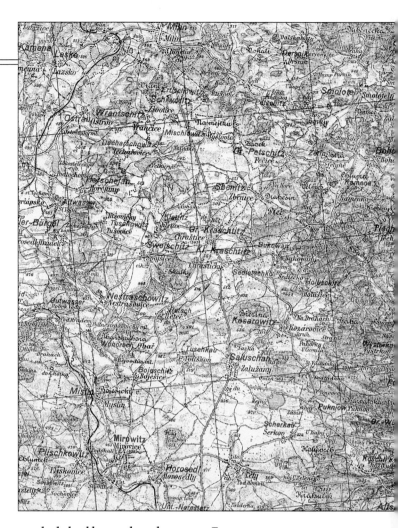

thinking that New England was little different from old England. For example, there is a view of Exeter as seen from the sea. Dover, Pomgrey's Castle, Strawbery Bank and Welchmans Cove increase the English feel, while the symbols used for settlements, the hills and the rocks around the coasts are those that would have been found on local maps produced in England at the time. Even the deer would not have been unfamiliar.

Whether the reality was quite as European as the image implies is another matter, but by 1680 it had become standard practice to 'Europeanize' America on maps. From the first map to name America (Waldseemüller's printed world map of 1507), European names, shields and cartographic symbols had been placed on most European maps of America, while inconvenient American realities, such as its native population, their settlements and the actual nature of the terrain had been relabelled understated or even totally ignored. Although unthinking convention sometimes led to such mapping, it could also be caused by a conscious intention – settlers would be deterred if the image on the map appeared too harsh. In a few cases there was genuine detestation of the reality and a determination to change it.

Such cartography was not confined to the New World. Perhaps the ultimate examples are the maps derived from the pre-war medium-scale surveys of Czechoslovakia which, in the course of the Second World War, were overprinted by the Nazis in red with German names (see above example), whether or not the districts had ever had German-speaking inhabitants. Stamping out the reality of the time, these maps sought to anticipate a new reality. They bloodlessly implied expulsion, misery, cultural and probably eventual physical genocide.   PETER BARBER

ANGLING IN TROUBLED WATERS

During the closing thirty years of the last century, Fred Rose specialized in creating 'Serio-Comic maps', which transformed maps into satirical commentaries on world (which meant European) affairs.

The best-known is probably the 'Octopus' map of 1877 which portrayed Russia as an octopus putting out tentacles throughout northern and eastern Europe. By November–December 1898 when the above cartoon must have been drawn, attention had switched to fishing in the troubled colonial waters outside Europe (see pp.86–7). Russia continued to cause concern. Despite the peaceful protestations of its young Czar, Nicholas II, it is shown strongly armed (see Finland), is still trampling the Poles and menacing the Turks and has caught fresh fish (colonies) in the Far East and China. John Bull in Britain, well supplied with ships, money and men, has landed an excellent colonial catch and is currently fishing in Egypt, while his ally, Portugal (Carlos I), has managed to retain its 'fish' of Delagoa Bay in southern Africa in the face of German acquisitiveness. Leopold II of Belgium has the Congo, but also the stigma from the numerous casinos on his soil. Other colonial powers have done less well. Italy (represented by Umberto I) has got fish from eastern Africa, but is weighed down by debt. Spain, menaced by civil war instigated by the pretender, Don Carlos (to the right of the bullfighter), has just lost Cuba, the Philippines and Puerto Rico to the United States, while France, divided against itself by the Dreyfus affair which paralysed the army (note the Jew fighting the soldier), has lost the 'fish' of Fashoda on the Nile to the British, though it retains Indo-China and Tunis. Despite their own weakness and emaciation and the 'stain' of the Armenian and Bulgarian massacres (skulls),

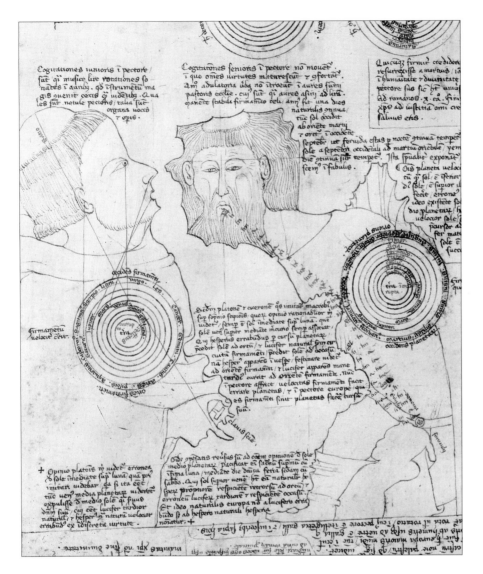

(Opposite) Frederick Rose, 'Angling in Troubled Waters', London 1898–9. British Library 1078 (38).

(Left) Opicinus de Canistris (The Mediterranean), early 14th century. Vatican Library Codex Palatinus 6435, c.69, recto.

the Turks continue feebly fishing in Crete: King George of Greece has had his finger pinched while trying to snatch it. Of the non-colonial powers, Franz-Joseph of Austria-Hungary and his peoples are mourning the assassination of the Empress Elisabeth in Geneva in September 1898 and are putting pressure on the Swiss to expel the anarchists who perpetrated the deed. The German Kaiser in the meantime is trouble-making generally. His country's industry gives it growing influence, particularly in the Ottoman Empire. In the north, the federation of Sweden and Norway is threatening to tear itself apart, while Denmark's ruling family prepares to give monarchs to other nations. The youthful Balkan states of Romania and Serbia, recently liberated from the Turks, are still infants on the international scene as is the young Queen Wilhelmina of the Netherlands.

Artists have been tempted to bring maps to life in this manner for centuries. The Pavian cleric, Opicinus de Canistris, used the Mediterranean coastlines for his political and religious critique of the world in the 1330s (above), which may have been the first map to show Italy as a boot. By the late sixteenth century early cartographic cartoons showed the Belgic Lion fighting the Spanish 'Queen'. Similar techniques were used to satirize the squabbling within the European Community on the eve of an EC summit in the late 1980s, and no doubt other satirical maps are yet to be made.

PETER BARBER

DRAWING BORDERS

During the 1890s the partition of Africa by the European powers reached its final phase. The extent of possessions and spheres of influence had grown to the point where international agreements were necessary if military conflict between European states was to be avoided (see pp.84–5). The process of establishing political control and commercial advantage was already subject to the hazards of native peoples hostile to political change and of an inhospitable natural environment: it was clearly in the interests of the Europeans to avoid further difficulty arising out of conflicts of interest between themselves.

The first map below illustrates one stage in the process of international agreement to settle the boundaries between the European powers' possessions and interests in West Africa. Specifically, it documents the agreement of 1898 between Great Britain and France on the boundary dividing the

Niger Territories from French Sudan (present-day Nigeria and Niger). The other boundaries shown on this map indicate the position as it had been agreed in 1892. British territory is outlined in brown, French in mauve and German in pink. The map was produced as the second of two maps illustrating the text of the Convention of June 1898 (the other map, not shown here, documents the Anglo-French boundary in the territories to the north of the Gold Coast). It is overprinted on a German map of 1892: Germany had no direct interest in the particular boundaries covered by the Convention so this provided an impartial base. The map was printed by lithography at the Intelligence Division of the War Office in August 1898.

The process of boundary alignment did not end with the signatures on a map. From about 1750, after due ratification, a Boundary Commission, usually comprising military survey officers

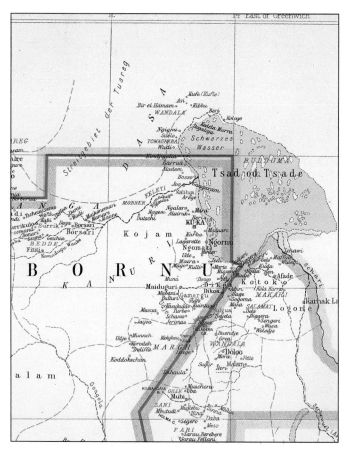

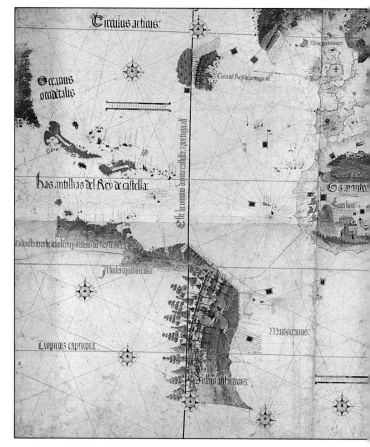

from each country, would be established so that the precise line could be fixed on the ground and definitive maps produced at a relatively large scale. The Commission usually had considerable control over boundary problems caused by inaccurate and incomplete maps. In the final stage, the boundary would be marked on the ground with stones or pillars, duly numbered and incorporated into the definitive map.

The flat surface of maps seems to invite people to draw lines over them, regardless of the underlying physical and cultural realities. The drawing of boundaries outside Europe by agreements of this kind took little account of ethnic distribution, and even less account of existing patterns of property ownership and rights than would have been the case in western Europe, where boundaries were historically influenced by dynastic and feudal rights. To this day European borders reflect this. They tend to be tortuous and still include some enclaves of foreign territory. In Africa, by contrast, borders usually run straight. The European powers' immediate commercial interests were paramount and native rulers and kingdoms only affected the drawing of boundaries where they possessed sufficient military strength to challenge the colonialists (such as the kingdom of Ashanti in present-day Ghana). In every case they were ultimately overcome. Note how, on the map below left, the new, straight boundary line runs through the middle of tribal lands marked by dotted red lines.

It is reasonable to draw an analogy between the often arbitrary straight-line boundaries agreed between European states when dividing Africa among themselves and the Line of Tordesillas drawn by Pope Alexander VI some 400 years earlier (see the 'Cantino' World Map below), which divided the world beyond Europe between Castile, the major Spanish kingdom, and Portugal. This line, although influential on subsequent political and cultural history, has not survived as a political boundary: whether the lines drawn 100 years ago in Africa will prove more durable remains to be seen.
A. CRISPIN JEWITT

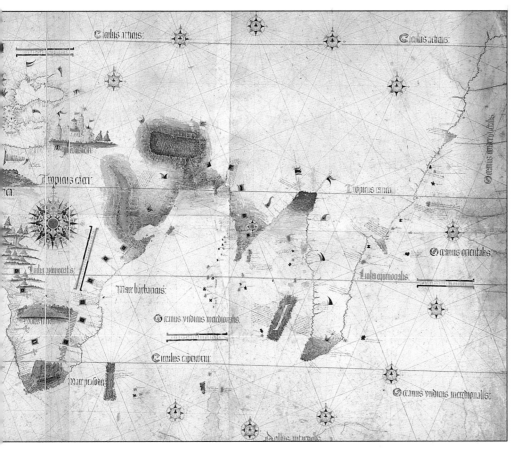

(Opposite) Detail showing Anglo-French border in the region of Lake Tsad (Chad) from Map No.2, (I.D. W.O. No.1355(b)). Lithographed at the Intelligence Division, War Office, August 1898. In: Convention between the United Kingdom and France . . . Signed at Paris June 14 1898. Together with a Declaration completing the same. Signed at London March 21, 1899. *British Library Maps Z.12. (1355).*

(Left) The anonymous, 'Cantino' World Map, 1502. Biblioteca Estense, Modena. Note the Line of Tordesillas: 'this is the mark between Castile and Portugal'.

THE MINISTER LEAVES HIS MARK

William Cecil, Lord Burghley (1520–98), was Elizabeth I's chief minister for almost the whole of her long reign. Throughout that period, whenever confronted by a problem with even the most remote geographical connection, he sought to clarify it by consulting a map. If there was no available printed map for him to annotate, Burghley took an existing manuscript map (even if it meant denuding the royal library) and wrote over that. If there were several maps, but they conflicted with one another, he took them all on the assumption that collectively they would approximate the truth. Maps that came as enclosures to letters were separated, identified on the back and put aside for future reference. If there was no map, Burghley seems to have commissioned one and, if he could not do this (perhaps through lack of time) he would draw a sketch map himself.

With maps he plotted the course of trade routes and military campaigns, but above all the maps were used for administrative purposes. What were the most densely populated and flat (and therefore the richest and most fertile) parts of the country, from which the highest tax returns could be expected? Which members of the gentry should be appointed Justices of the Peace, to ensure an even distribution and loyalty to the Queen? (Sketchy genealogical tables were also useful here.) Where might the enemy land most easily, how good were the defences and were the families in the vicinity Catholic and therefore possibly disloyal? Which families could be relied on to take action against them and how many men could they raise? Were there parks with woodland and animals to feed the levies? How many beacons were there to transmit important news to court and where were they positioned?

Not surprisingly, Burghley was the person ultimately responsible for the appearance of the first printed atlas of the counties of England and Wales, surveyed by Christopher Saxton and published in 1579. Burghley got hold of the map of Hertfordshire shown here before the engraving had been completed. It is coloured to highlight

the hills (shown in profile), parks (trees shown within circular railings) and the towns. To this, in his characteristically spikey hand, Burghley has added, sometimes incorrectly, names of places, such as Barley, that were of importance to the Crown; and, most important of all, he has inserted the names of landowners – 'Lytton' under Knebworth, 'Mr Capell' under Hadham Parva and

Christopher Saxton, 'Hartfordiae comitatus . . . descriptio . . . 1577. Christophorus Saxton descripsit. Nicolaus Reynoldus Londiniensis sculpsit'. Proof state. British Library, Royal MS 18.D.III,ff.33v–34 (detail).

'B(ishop) of London' under Hadham Magna. With this information to hand Burghley could ensure that the Queen's writ ran throughout the land and was able to contemplate danger from Spain with something approaching equanimity. After Burghley's death, James I felt he could have no better source of reference and the atlas from which this map comes passed to the royal library.

Equivalent maps to this are known to have existed in the well-run Roman and Chinese empires. However, as society and the responsibilities of government grew more complex such relatively simple maps became insufficient and, by the nineteenth century, governments throughout Europe had created official mapping organizations to meet their needs.   PETER BARBER

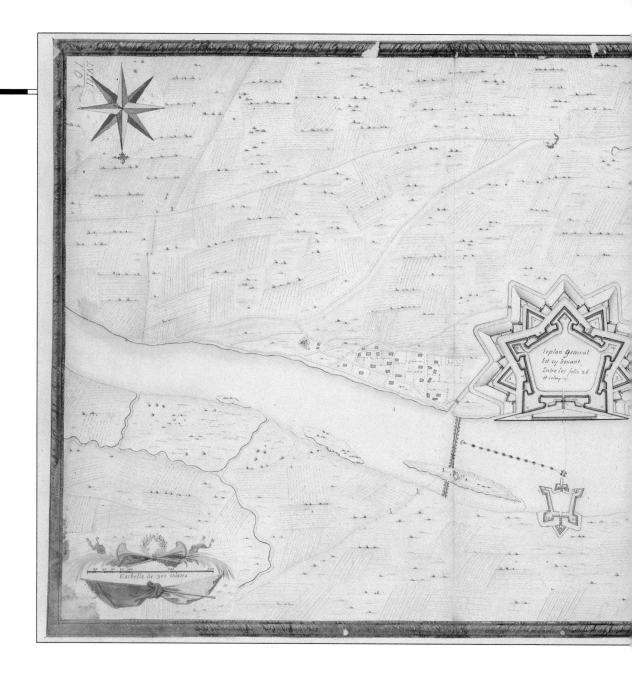

Eschelle de 300 thoises

le plan General
Est cy deuant
Entre les folio 26
et celuy cy

ESPIONAGE!

Colbert, Louis XIV's leading minister before 1683, was convinced of the importance of good maps for government and administration. In the late 1670s and early 1680s he instigated the first scientific measurement of France by the *Académie des Sciences*. At the same time he and Louvois, the minister for war, arranged for all the best manuscript surveys of fortresses inside and outside France, official and unofficial, by engineers or spies, to be gathered together. They were then copied by the best court draughtsmen and artists, at a standard size, into handsome volumes for the personal use of the King and his ministers.

French military engineering and map-making were at that time the best in Europe, but security at court left much to be desired and plans in varying states of completion were soon floating fairly freely around Versailles. By August 1683, the English ambassador was able to write to Charles II offering 'the plans of some fortified places which I believe are very exact. If Your Majesty . . . approve of them, I do not question but to have draughts of all the other fortification of France in a little time.' Within a couple of weeks the ambassador was informed that Charles had received the plans and 'carried them to his closet: where . . . he perused them . . . commended the fortification of some [of] those towns extremely . . . appeared extremely

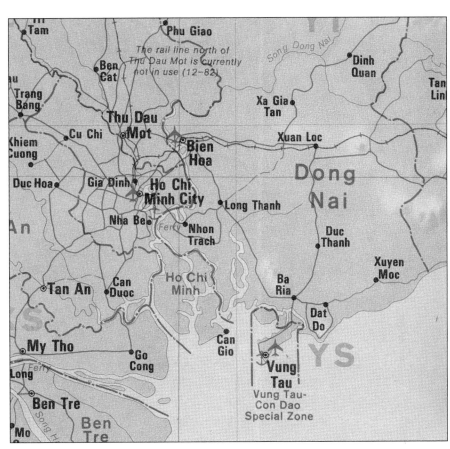

(Left) Manuscript plan of Huningue (Huningen) prepared for Louis XIV in about *1683 probably in the artists' workshop in the Invalides. British Library K. Top. 58.10.* *(Above) Detail showing area around Ho Chi Minh City and Cambodian border from 'Kampuchea', Washington: CIA (1983). Scale 1:1 500 000.*

well pleased and . . . desire [d] you would goe on & procure as many as you could.'

This plan (above left), from King George III's Topographical Collection, which incorporates what remains of Charles II's map collection, is almost certainly one of the plans that the ambassador sent over. Its elegant finish and the fine portrait of Louis XIV as Hercules (see pp.76–77) betray its source. It shows Huningue, an important fortress on the Rhine near Basle that had recently been occupied by the French. As one of Louis's allies, Charles would not immediately have been interested in Huningue itself. The plan would, however, have provided a model of the latest theories of fortification for Charles's own engineers and it could be copied for Louis's Ger-

man enemies if and when he changed partners.

As was acknowledged even in classical antiquity, a map or picture can say more than a thousand words, which is why both have always been star prizes for spies. Few are as elegant as this example, and today they are as likely to be plans of factories as of defence installations (see pp.104–5). Even so, they are still appreciated by those called on to guide the fortunes of the state and today, in the case of the 1:1.5 million (about 1 inch to 24 miles) maps derived from photographs taken from spy planes and issued by the CIA (see example above), they provide relatively accurate, if generalized, maps of regions of the world for which maps by national agencies have not been readily available.

PETER BARBER

THE SAVOY CADASTER, 1728–38

The spa town of Evian along the southern shore of Lake Geneva (Lac Léman) is today in France but, in the 1720s, it was part of the tiny but cartographically influential Duchy of Savoy. Its Duke, Victor Amadeus II, who also ruled Piedmont on the other side of the Alps, had recently proclaimed himself King of Sardinia.

The map shown here is taken from a mapped survey of every parish and commune in the Duchy. This was begun in 1728 to provide a detailed inventory or cadaster of the King's territory, so he could both maximize the tax revenue that it yielded and also share out these dues fairly among his dependent land-owners. Each piece of prop-

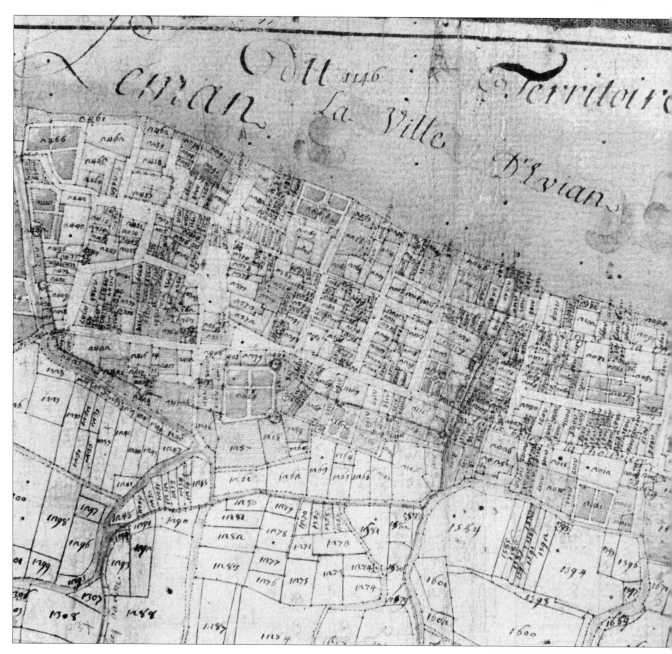

erty was surveyed in the field and valued in one of three categories of agricultural productivity, its boundaries were established and then drawn on large-scale, 1:2372 (about 1 inch to 66 yards), maps. In common with most such cadastral maps, these from Savoy are functional and stripped of ornamentation, although exquisitely coloured contemporary copies were also made. The original maps, despite being carefully drawn, are quite

(Above) Detail from the Savoy Cadaster, Tabelle alphabétique.

(Left) Detail showing Evian from the Savoy Cadaster, 'original' manuscript map, c.1728. Scale 1:2373.

plain; watercourses and roads are tinted in blue and green, but there is little other detail beyond land parcel boundaries and reference numbers. These numbers relate to a second part of the cadaster, a written schedule, known in Savoy as the *tabelle alphabétique définitive*. This is a list of land parcels in alphabetical order of the proprietors. Each parcel is identified in its parish *tabelle* by its map reference number, it is described and named, its quality is assessed according to the three-category scale, and its area and its taxation assessment are recorded.

Cadastral maps came to serve many purposes for government administration. When calculating land taxation they provided a fair and rational basis on which to assess and apportion tax liability, a precise record of that liability and a record of land ownership. In colonies or conquered lands, such as Ireland, they provided the basis for land redistribution. This Savoy cadaster was indeed a product of Enlightened Despotism, instituted to identify those minor aristocrats who were avoiding dues, and also to extract fair taxes from all land-owning peasants.

The Savoy cadaster was not just important in this little Duchy. The imagination and effort that had been expended were much admired by contemporaries, especially by writers in neighbouring France. The physiocrat movement, which regarded agricultural land as the only true resource from which all material wealth flowed, saw maps as a means of highlighting the importance of land and its effective management. What is more, the accuracy with which large-scale maps could record precise boundaries appealed to the increasingly scientific minds of administrators in Enlightened Europe. Though pre-dated by some seventeenth-century Swedish mapping and by that in Piedmont from 1718, the Savoy mapping system proved very influential, not least in France where, after the Revolution of 1789, cadastral maps were used as one instrument with which to extinguish the rights of the old aristocracy and to bring in a new, and more equitable, land tax. No lesser figure than Napoleon Bonaparte was a convinced advocate of such maps as tools of effective statecraft. Mapped cadastral surveys in the style of the Savoy cadaster became common accompaniments to the effective government control of land over much of continental Europe by the middle years of the nineteenth century. ROGER J. P. KAIN

PRIDE OF OWNERSHIP

Visitors approaching the entrance of Long Melford Hall in Suffolk may pause to admire the handsome Elizabethan red-brick building, its turrets, two-storeyed porch and Renaissance ornamentation. Greeting them on arrival in the great hall is a masterpiece of late-sixteenth-century cartography – a map of the estate. Such a local plan is as much a statement of power and prestige as globes and painted mural maps (see pp.72–3).

The map in Long Melford Hall, shown here, is magnificent, over 8 feet (2.4 metres) high, 6 feet (1.8 metres) wide, and drawn on nine pieces of parchment. It shows land and buildings in great and colourful detail, at about 1:4500 or 1 inch to 125 yards. Long Melford and neighbouring churches are drawn in perspective with blue roofs; red is used to colour the roofs of houses, farms and cottages, mills, barns and a dye house; houses of important neighbours are shown in exaggerated perspective; and Long Melford Hall has pride of place in the centre. While symbols depict many buildings, the individual characteristics of the larger and more important ones are shown. Many have gilt windows and flags flying from their chimney pots. Each field is given its name and acreage; yards, gardens and a hop garden, trees, hedges, rivers, the village cross, two conduits, woods, deer parks and a warren, complete with rabbits, are shown. The map is of Long Melford manor and rectory, not the parish, so parts of adjacent parishes are included, while the land of neighbouring owners, even in Long Melford itself, is either shown only in outline or is excluded. At the bottom are tables listing the tenants, their fields and acreages. Orientation is roughly indicated by words in each border.

The lord of the manor of this thriving market and textiles town from 1545, and patron of the living, was Sir William Cordell, Master of the Rolls to Queens Mary and Elizabeth. Sir William rebuilt the Hall and in 1578 he entertained Queen Elizabeth there. In 1580, he employed Israel Amyce, a gentleman from Barking in Essex, to map his land. Amyce was one of the first estate surveyors to practise: his career ran from 1576 to 1607 and took him to six counties in East Anglia and nearby. The estate was mapped partly to show Sir William his lands, their layout and tenants. It also demonstrated to his visitors his power over his land and tenants (with the manor house carefully drawn in the centre) and his influence and prestige with his peers, and showed that he was a patron of the developing art of local map-making. Had the map been drawn simply for administrative purposes, it need not have been so decorative (it is interesting to compare it with the later cadastral map of Evian, on pp.92–3).

This is an early example of an estate map; before the mid-sixteenth century, written surveys were made and there were few local maps. Many owners came to follow Cordell's example and commissioned maps, often highly decorated in contemporary styles with coats of arms, for similar reasons. Indeed today, the new Ordnance Survey Superplan (see pp.131 & 157) can be little different. Custom-made, like the example recently produced to commemorate a visit to Ordnance Survey's Southampton headquarters by the Lord Mayor of London, it can centre on a particular property or area, show it at an appropriate scale and orientation and even include a coat of arms. Here, then, is a twentieth-century estate map for a twentieth-century parlour.   A. SARAH BENDALL

Detail showing the middle section from Israel Amyce, 'A Plotteforme of all and synguler the Mannors Lands Tenements and other hereditaments percell of the possessions of the right worshipfull Sir William Cordell Knight Master of the Rowles . . . within . . . Longe Melforde . . . sett downe by the Scale of an Inche deuided into Twentye partes by the Industrye and Trauayle of Israell Amyce of Barkynge in the Countie of Essex gentleman in the yere of our Lorde God 1580 and in the Twentye and one yere of the Reigne of our souereigne Lady Elizabeth by the grace of God Quene of England Fraunce and Irelond defender of the Faith &c'. Sir Hyde Parker, Long Melford Hall, Suffolk. The map is slightly faded through prolonged public display.

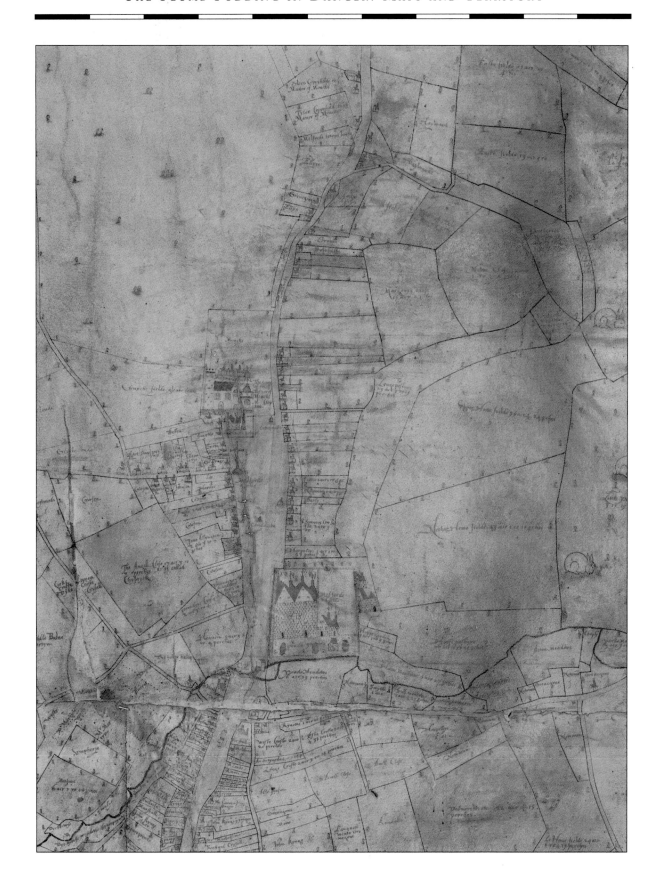

MAPS FOR THE LANDLORD

This map of the 'Castle of Exon' is one among several others in a bound volume of surveys of manors belonging to Charles, Prince of Wales, the son of King James I. The surveys were undertaken by John Norden (c. 1548–1625) during the summer of 1617. On his accession James I had re-appointed Norden as one of the surveyors of Crown lands and, in particular, of the territories assigned to the Duchy of Cornwall. It was in that latter capacity that Norden was commissioned to survey the castle of Exeter which had been part of the Duchy since its inception in 1337. John Norden's particular strength as a surveyor was to search for pieces of land which had been lost or encroached upon.

The castle at Exeter was formed by enclosing a volcanic knoll. The inner ward was entered through an imposing gatehouse. The inner bank was crowned with an equally formidable curtain wall. These two prominent features, along with the Roman walls, are perhaps the first to attract the eye on Norden's map, drawn in a cartographic style which attempts to depict the townscape as it would have been seen from an elevated viewpoint. The real purpose of the survey was to show explicitly the extent of the Duchy property, so several reference letters and a table were added. By the early thirteenth century the outer ditch had been filled in and several encroachments (C–K) had been made on to what formerly had been the outer bailey. Norden failed to locate the actual course of the outer ditch but established two points on it which he indicated on his map with two pictographs of a hand. To remedy such territorial losses for a lord, Norden in his book *Surveyor's Dialogue* (1607) advocated 'due plots and descriptions'; in doing exactly that at Exeter he was more than generous to Prince Charles, who may not have had any right to the land shown as C. Though Norden found early documents to support his case, an even earlier one, such as Domesday Book, could have informed him that King William had removed no fewer than forty-eight houses belonging to the citizens of Exeter to

build his castle in the first instance.

This type of dynastic jurisdictional map constructed to establish ownership or to illustrate some issue that was in dispute has a long history, dating from Roman times. Nearer to the time of John Norden, a series of charts of English coastal jurisdictions, that date from 1604, was created

CITIE OF EXCETER

John Norden, 'Castel of Exon'.
British Library Add. MS 6027
ff.80v–81.

Transcript of the explanatory
table (on f.80).
A the place of the olde Draw-
bridge of the Castle over the
ditch
B the house where the assises
and sessions are helde
C the outer ditch of the castle
which the Citie usurpeth and
have lately made a payre of
Butts in the same, being the
Prince's Demesnes
D the inner ditch of the Castle,
now made into severall gardens
E A garden which the Patentee
hath lett to him that keepes ye
Prison
F The Prison common for the
Shire, builte upon the Castle
grounde and caried away with
divers other howses by one
Master Southcote as is sayde by
what right is not knowne.
G are contain orchards and
gardens, which I thinke owghte
to belong in right to the Castle,
which with manie howses
seeme to be also caried away,
by some citizens; compare the
lyinge of G. with H. and it will
playnlie appeare, lying upon the
side of the Castle Ditche on the
Brow of the hill towardes the
Citie.
H Belongeth to the Castle and
the Patentee hath graunted his
estate therof unto Master
Manwayringe whose orcharde
adioynes it, and hath buylte
upon the Castle lande a row of
some 8 tenementes
I Master Manwayrings new
tenementes
K the Castle hill, the Banck and
fall of the Castle ditche, wherof
with the Ditch itselfe, the
Citizens take the profit
contayning about 4 acres of
Pasture upon part wherof they
have rayled in a bowling greene
being the Princes Demense
Land'.

to define the 'King's Chambers' within which
James I claimed territorial sovereignty. Ever since,
surveys have been undertaken specifically to provide evidence in courts, and other maps, designed
for more general purposes, have been used in
similar circumstances.   WILLIAM RAVENHILL

MANAGEMENT AND PROFIT

Until very recently, colleges in Oxford and Cambridge have depended on their land-holdings to provide most of their income. They held estates throughout England and Wales, in arable and pastoral areas, in market towns and London. Each property was surveyed and valued from time to time as the need arose. From the mid-eighteenth century, colleges took an increasing interest in the active management of their land, and maps came to be used as tools of estate management.

In 1770, Queens' College in Cambridge employed a local man, Joseph Freeman, to survey and map its property at Drapers and Lancelets Farms in Bumstead Hellions (Essex) and Haverhill (Suffolk). The map (shown here) is drawn on parchment at a scale of about 1:3000, or 1 inch to 250 feet. It shows the farm buildings in bird's-eye view and just over 274 acres (110 hectares) surrounding them. Roads, verges, watercourses, hedges, fences, gates, arable land, pasture, an orchard, a hop ground and acreages of each field are included. Woods are drawn too, pollards indicated, and the numbers and species of trees in hedgerows are given: elms, oaks, ashes and poplars. The map is coloured and decorated, and a gold symbol identifies the land which was occupied by the tenant of Lancelets Farm.

At about this time, Queens' College was much concerned with the management of woods on its properties on the Cambridgeshire, Essex and Suffolk borders. The estates were surveyed, valued and mapped so that the College knew exactly what land it owned, what income it could expect from it, and whether the tenants were acting in the College's best interest. The maps were used over a long period – on the example described here, red ink is used to show those woods which were to be grubbed up, or uprooted, at Lady Day 1800, thirty years after the survey. Estate income depended on more than woods, and the College needed to improve its knowledge of its property before the renewal of leases, during boundary disputes and after enclosure. Maps were

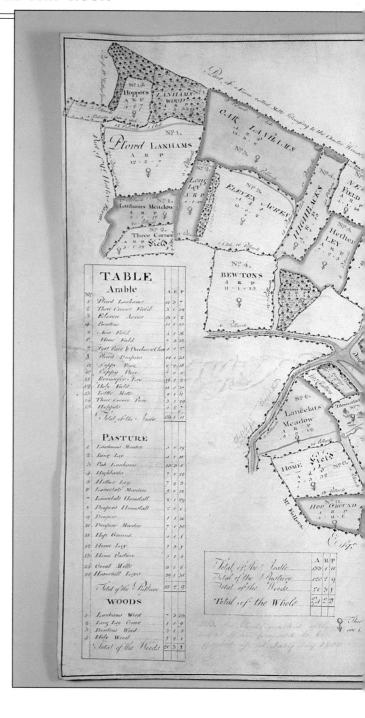

not drawn in every case, but they became increasingly common as aids to maximizing revenues.

Other owners have also used maps for estate management in Britain since the sixteenth century. At Laxton in Nottinghamshire in the 1630s, for example, Sir William Courten recognized the need to increase his rents and consolidate his property to maximize his income. He commissioned a detailed map and survey of his estates but

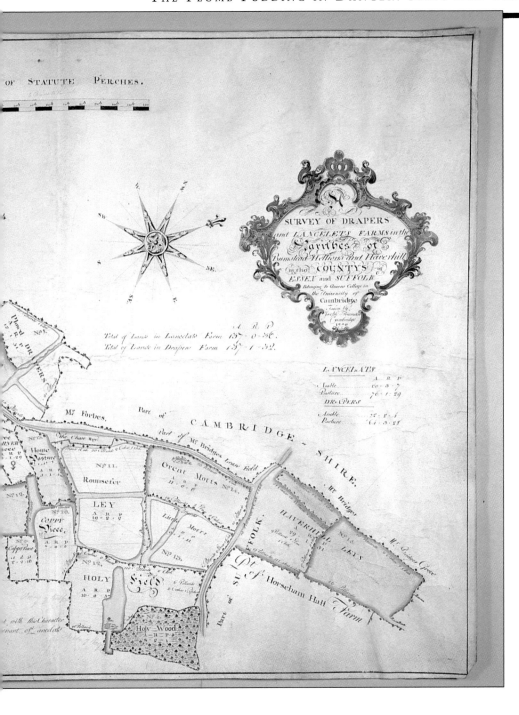

Joseph Freeman, 'A Survey of Drapers and Lancelets Farms in the Parishes of Bumstead Hellions and Haverhill in the Countys of Essex and Suffolk Belonging to Queens College in the University of Cambridge Taken by Joseph Freeman Cambridge 1770'. Cambridge University Library: Queens' College Archives 328.

unfortunately, despite his efforts, he was bankrupt by the end of the decade. Maps were increasingly drawn when land was to be reorganized: the enclosure movement in the late eighteenth and early nineteenth centuries led to much mapmaking. Whole parishes were plotted, showing how land was to be redistributed. After the 1836 Tithe Commutation Act, titheable lands were valued and mapped. This enabled rent-charges tied to particular plots of land to be substituted for tithes in kind, and so eased the Church's problems of collecting its dues. From 1940, the Ministry of Agriculture commissioned maps of agricultural land, graded according to quality, in order to make England as self-sufficient as possible: a twentieth-century example of the use of maps as an aid to economic development.

A. Sarah Bendall

THE FOG OF WAR

'By the feat of portraiture or painting a captain may describe the country of his adversary, whereby he shall eschew the dangerous passages with his host or navy; also perceive the places of advantage, the form of embattling of his enemies, the situation of his camp for his most surety, the strength or weakness of the town or fortress which he intendeth to assault'. Sir Thomas Elyot, The Boke named the Governour (London: originally published 1531. Everyman edition, 1962), pp. 23–4.

The popular image of the general of yesteryear, sword at side, telescope in hand, consulting his map in the midst of battle while giving his troops orders, was rarely more than a romantic fiction. Conventional two-dimensional maps were difficult to use and were not particularly helpful in the confusion and movement of the battlefield.

However, maps have long been used strategically for planning national defence and foreign campaigns and there are records of maps being created and used for these purposes by Alexander the Great and Julius Caesar. During campaigns maps have been used for planning and recording marches, billets and encampments and, if time allows before the outbreak of hostilities, for sketching the terrain of the future battlefield. Tactically, maps have also been used for taking decisions on the course of sieges and trench warfare, because their more leisurely tempo gave time for map-making and consultation.

During campaigns, maps were created for the information of commanders

in the field and the national leaders at home, and to inform and encourage the public. Nor did the end of battle lead to any pause in mapping: on the contrary, maps were needed to help those caught behind enemy lines to escape, to commemorate victories, to instruct future cadets on the rules of war and to provide geographical and tactical information for the planning of national defences and future wars and battles. Continuing military necessity also meant that certain

(Opposite) Military training, 1726. From H.F. von Fleming, Der Vollkommene Teutsche Soldat. *Leipzig: Martini, 1726. British Library 8825 h.35.*

(Left) Information 1944. George Horace Davis, Panorama Map of the Normandy Landings, 6 June, 1944, created for the Illustrated London News, *17 June, 1944. British Library Maps c.c.5.a.24.*

isolated but strategically important areas were mapped in detail, often in the lull between wars, before more 'civilized' but safer areas. Such defence considerations led to the detailed eighteenth-century mapping of Scotland and the border areas between the Austrians and the Turks in the Balkans.

In many countries mapping is still considered too important to be left in the hands of civilians: even in Britain, until recently, a soldier was always the head of Ordnance Survey. For similar reasons of national security, good official mapping can be withheld from the public and intentionally misleading mapping is sometimes produced – as much in the West as in the East.

Today virtually instantaneous communication means that battles are controlled from afar. The cartographic back-up, however, remains much the same, as was shown by the British army's sudden search for relevant maps of all kinds (to augment its own extremely extensive map library), that coincided with the outbreak of the Falklands and Gulf Wars. Moreover, the sad incidents of deaths from so-called friendly fire in both wars confirm that battles can be as chaotic as ever and reveal the limitations even of electronic mapping techniques and gadgetry in a swiftly evolving battle.   PETER BARBER

The Eyes of the General Abroad

'In the first place,' wrote the author Vegetius in his book on military matters in about AD 390, 'a commander should have itineraries of all the war zones very fully written out, so that he may thoroughly acquaint himself with the intervening terrain, as regards not only distance but standard of roads, and may study reliable descriptions of short cuts, deviations, mountains and rivers. In fact, we are assured that the more careful commanders had, for provinces where there was an emergency, itineraries that were not merely annotated but even painted, so that the commander who was setting out could choose his route not only with a mental map but with a constructed map to examine.'

This manuscript map seems to meet Vegetius's specification. It was drawn up in France in about 1708 and shows the border country between France and Savoy. Since 1701 this had been much fought over, with the French enjoying the upper hand until 1706. Afterwards there had been a stalemate, punctuated by annual Savoyard raids and French menaces.

Exceptionally for would-be invaders, the French were able to compile the map from detailed surveys of their own and the enemy's terrain, roads, fortified towns and coastlines without having to use Savoyard maps or rely too much on the work of spies. Past experience was also noted, particularly that the enemy actually landed near Hyères in 1707. The map shows provincial French boundaries (red), the *de facto* Savoyard-French border (blue), plus the lands of the Duke of Savoy and others, such as Genoa and Mantua, that were neutral and had to be avoided or handled carefully. Distinctions are made between the tracks that were passable with cannon (red-lined and shaded), passable only on foot or horseback (dotted) or impassable in the snow (continuous black parallel lines). Also shown were harbours where a larger naval force could anchor, disembark and stay (red double anchor), only anchor and disembark without staying (black double anchor), where a smaller naval force could anchor and disembark (red single anchor) or only disembark (black single anchor), and where a fleet could take on water (barrel). In addition, soundings of depth are given in figures for the most sensitive coastal areas and the lines of rivers and mountains are indicated as accurately as was possible at the time. Lastly, there are vignettes of the fortifications of the more important towns. In short, the map shows almost everything that a commander planning for attack or defence would need to know for his purposes, though with varying degrees of accuracy.

The existence of such explicit maps as this was usually a closely guarded secret. Most remained in manuscript to prevent diffusion, and were used until they fell apart. Few survived the end of the war for which they were made, though some sixteenth-century ones are still intact. The survival of this example may be due to the continuing military importance of the area it depicts: there were to be French invasions of Italy in the 1730s, 1740s and 1790s.

Peter Barber

Detail of the land and coast around Monaco from an anonymous manuscript map of Dauphiné, Provence and Savoy, c.1708. British Library Add. MS 71065.

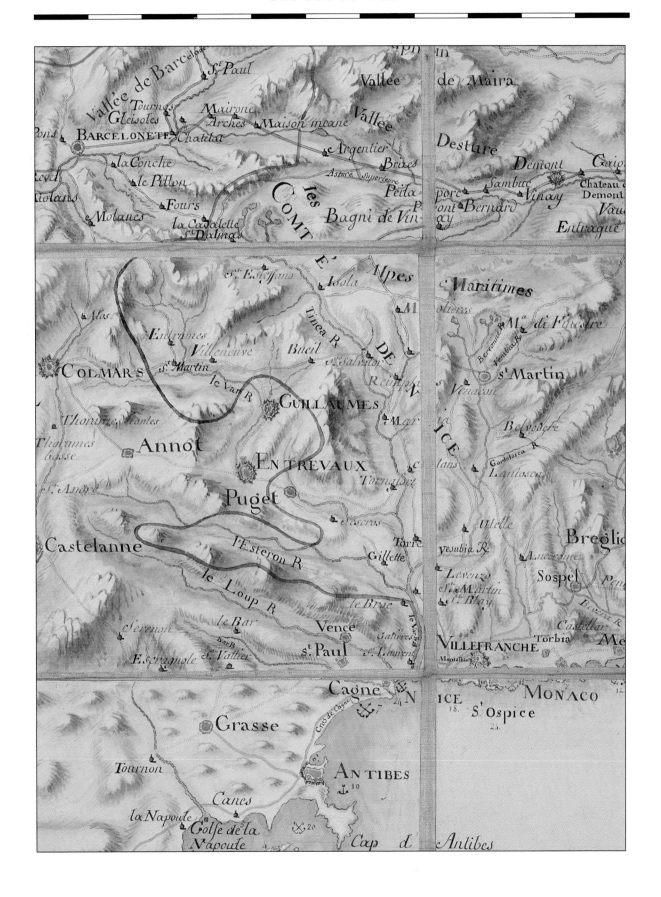

SUPPRESSING AND DISCOVERING SENSITIVE INFORMATION

Information about foreign countries in map form has long been regarded as valuable intelligence. In the 1630s, the French first minister, Cardinal Richelieu, began the collection of military maps and atlases of foreign countries which is now housed in the Château de Vincennes. States which have official map-producing agencies are very aware of the value of their maps to foreign powers and so exercise careful control over what appears on their maps. Since the middle of the last century the British War Office has enforced rules about what information can be shown on civilian maps and what should be suppressed.

Before the Second World War the German military authorities were busy acquiring and using British and Irish Ordnance Survey maps, ready for the military operations that would take place once war broke out. Many of these maps were captured by the Allies as they retook Belgium from the retreating German Army in 1944. A few copies of the 'Militärgeographisches Stadtplan von London' at the scale of 1:20 000 (or 3 inches to the mile) fell into British hands. These plans are sometimes referred to as 'bombing maps' because they identify targets or military objectives, but they also highlight buildings of architectural significance such as Westminster Abbey, St James's Palace and Charterhouse. They were reproduced from the civilian, or 'sales', edition of the Ordnance Survey 3-inch Map of London published in 1933. Both the German and British maps were published in four sections: part of the north east

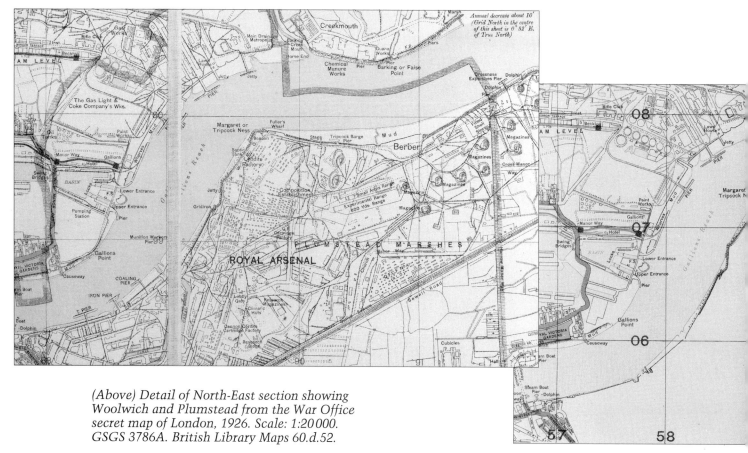

(Above) Detail of North-East section showing Woolwich and Plumstead from the War Office secret map of London, 1926. Scale: 1:20 000. GSGS 3786A. British Library Maps 60.d.52.

section is shown here. The copy in the British Library is the second, special edition revised by the Germans in December 1941, presumably using air reconnaissance.

Large areas of the Ordnance Survey map, such as Plumstead Marshes and Woolwich Dockyard, are devoid of detail because they contain sensitive military buildings and structures. On the German map, a cartographer has drawn in all the buildings visible from the air and noted in the margin that this is a very important research and testing establishment for artillery with a prohibited flying zone of a 2.5-km (1½-mile) radius and a balloon barrage around it. The German map indicates how many people worked there, how that number increased from 1936 to 1938 and what tasks they had.

From the British point of view, suppressing military information on civil or sales editions worked because the German authorities never had access to the source for the 3-inch map of London. This was the military map specially prepared for the Forces and emergency services

during the General Strike of 1926 (GSGS 3786A), and it contained all the detail of the Woolwich Arsenal and Plumstead Marshes. All remaining stocks were destroyed and the plates were wiped off in 1932, but the new sales edition was produced from the War Office drawings updated by Ordnance Survey. The Barking by-pass (A 13) was added, but by 1941 the German revisers had found several new housing developments to add to their map as well as several buildings, some of which may have had a military significance (for example, a new estate called Hameway, and storage tanks, all situated north of Beckton station). The obvious care with which the Germans' revision was carried out is a testimony to their map-making abilities and the use of intelligence sources to counteract British policies designed to keep such information secret. In recent years the widespread use of satellite imagery has made such security omissions less plausible, but the names and uses of particular buildings can still be suppressed if thought desirable.

CHRISTOPHER BOARD

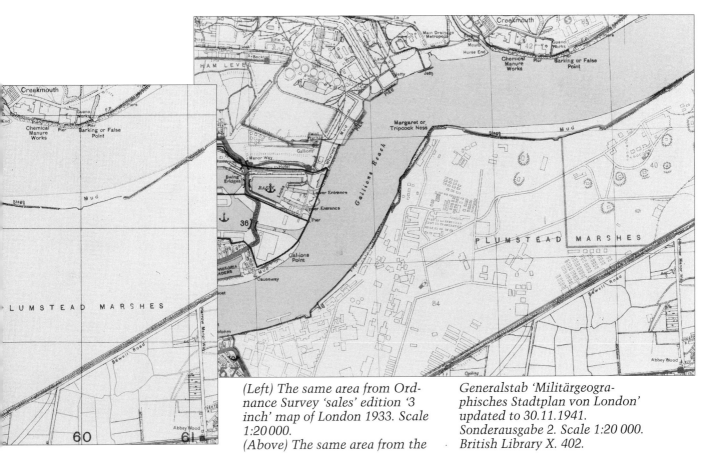

(Left) The same area from Ordnance Survey 'sales' edition '3 inch' map of London 1933. Scale 1:20 000.
(Above) The same area from the Generalstab 'Militärgeographisches Stadtplan von London' *updated to 30.11.1941. Sonderausgabe 2. Scale 1:20 000. British Library X. 402.*

FALSIFICATION AND SECURITY

Map-users who know an area very well are sometimes puzzled by obvious differences between the map and the landscape. Their first thought is that the map is out of date, although its date of publication and subsequent revision may give the lie to that. Working with an air photo mosaic of South Buckinghamshire (5107NE) I was struck by the absence of an aircraft factory near Langley. In its place was what looked like a farmstead surrounded by market gardens typical of the area. The mosaic was dated by a reference to RAF photography of 1948 from which it was prepared, and clearly showed buildings put up during and just after the Second World War. Why was the factory not shown? The obvious answer lay in matters of national security, but why were

authorities so sensitive in 1948 unless it had something to do with the Cold War? Not even the road I cycled along was in the right place. Close inspection revealed that the market gardening, the farmstead and some of the roads had been painted in. This proved to be an example of one of two ways of obscuring sensitive detail, the other being to paint clouds over the offending features. Public Record Office files later revealed the extent to which these mosaics had been modified before putting them on sale to the public, replacing undoctored original mosaics which had been for official use only. Some of the latter, including 5107NE, are still secret.

In a Public Record Office file on security deletions on Ordnance Survey maps, opened only

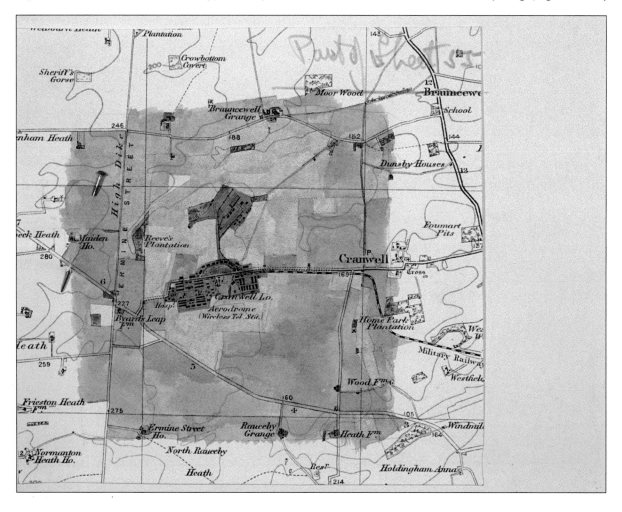

in 1990, considerable attention is devoted to aerodrome security. In the early 1930s Dr Christie Willatts of the Land Utilization Survey of Britain raised the question of how to show land use within Cranwell Aerodrome in Lincolnshire. He had been told that the Air Ministry would object to the publication of a land use map showing aerodrome buildings, and even to indicating in colour the land use classes 'in such a way that it would suggest desirable targets to a hostile power' although no actual buildings were shown. He was expected 'to commit academic perjury' to obliterate all indications of such properties, under some innocent looking colour such as light green (pasture) or brown (arable). A sketch of the proposed land use map was appended. It shows detail of aerodrome buildings and a military railway as it existed when the map was first published in 1920, plus the appropriate land use classification. The second map, published in 1935, demonstrates

how the Air Ministry and Ordnance Survey resolved the problem at a time of growing threat of German rearmament. It shows none of the building detail connected with the aerodrome and therefore none of the red colour for that class of land use. Two patches of new houses with gardens are plotted, but the airfield is shown as pasture. Only the word 'Aerodrome' provides any clue to what might be present.

The falsification of maps for security has a long history – evidence for it has been found at the beginning of the eighteenth century during the War of the Spanish Succession, and its extent has varied with the degree of insecurity felt by the mapping authority. Until recently official maps of the Soviet Union went so far as to mislocate cities on small-scale maps, though it is now widely accepted that the advent of spy satellites renders such subterfuge pointless.

CHRISTOPHER BOARD

(Opposite) Small hand-coloured extract of the unpublished Ordnance Survey 1:63360 Land Utilization Survey sheet 55 (Grantham), 1934. Public Record Office OS 1/250 89a.

(Right) Extract of the published colour-printed Ordnance Survey map, 1:63360 Land Utilization Survey sheet 55 (Grantham), 1935.

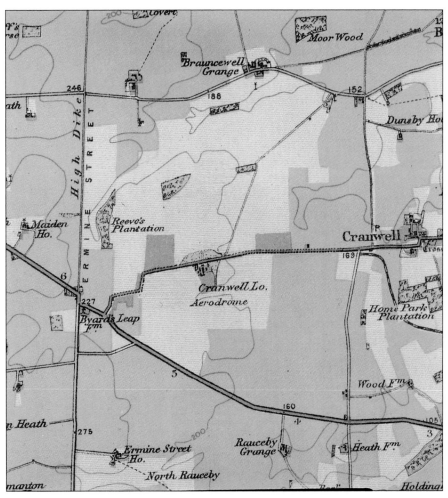

PLANNING A CAMPAIGN

During his visit to Vienna in November 1705, the Duke of Marlborough, the supreme commander of British and Dutch forces during the War of the Spanish Succession, was obsessed by the problems of the Italian front. The armies of Britain's allies, led by Marlborough's close friend, the Austrian general, Prince Eugene of Savoy, were short of men and money and seemed to be facing imminent expulsion across the Alps by the army of Louis XIV of France. A big British loan would go some way to solving the problem. The dispatch of Prussian mercenaries to Eugene would help even more – if the Prussian King agreed to send them. But how were they to be sent to Italy? And, emulating the epic march that had preceded his victory at Blenheim in the previous year, might the Duke himself not march his troops from the Netherlands, through Germany and across the Alps to sustain his comrade in arms?

The spots that Marlborough added (originally in red ink) to this map reflect his ruminations. It is not a purpose-made military map, however, but a separately published item from a book on the Habsburg lands, published some four years earlier, that the Duke may have come across in a Viennese palace. One of the earliest maps to depict mountains realistically, it emphasizes the good hunting that was to be found in Tirol rather than marching routes or (with any great accuracy) terrain, but it was sufficient. The spots indicate staging posts on the two routes that an army could follow. One led directly from Bavaria and across the Brenner down Lake Garda; the other westwards through the Inn Valley to the Valtelline (which is not shown) and Lake Como. The Brenner route was shorter, but the hazardous terrain made it suitable only once the snows had melted. The Inn Valley/Valtelline route was easier and had been much used by Austrian, French and Spanish forces in previous centuries. However, it was longer and would involve negotiations with, and probably concessions to, the Valtelline's masters, the Grey Leagues (Graubünden) – a miniature federal state – whose relations with the Austrians were notoriously bad.

From Vienna, Marlborough went on to Berlin where he discussed the problem with the Prussian King, perhaps using this map. His pleadings for troops met with success. In the spring of 1706, after the snows had melted and without any need for special concessions to the Grey Leagues, Prussian forces crossed the Brenner into Italy. With

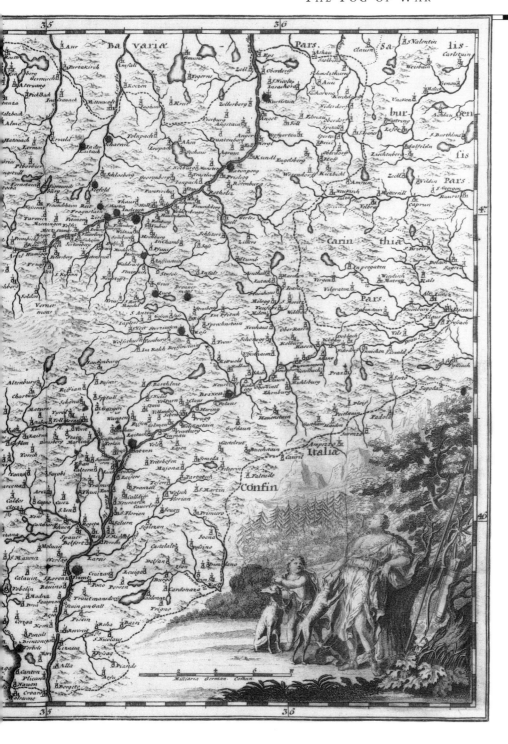

Ignaz Reiffenstuehl, Christian Engelbrecht and Johann Andreas Pfeffel, 'Tyrolis' from Wenzel Karl Purgstall and Ignaz Reiffenstuehl, Germania Austriaca. Vienna, 1701. British Library Add. MS 61342, ff.111v-112.

their help, Eugene was able to beat the French at Turin in the early days of September and to expel their forces from Italy (see pp.102–3). The Duke, in his turn, was able to stay in the Netherlands where his great victory at Ramillies in May led to the French loss of what is now Belgium.

Generals often have to make do with what they have to hand. As recently as 1944, the Allies used postcards and air photographs to create the maps for the Normandy landings. Yet even relatively small-scale maps made primarily for civilians, like this example, can be quite sufficient for sketching the broad lines of a campaign.

PETER BARBER

PREPARING AGAINST INVASION

Contrary to its appearance this map is not about commemoration but about prediction. It was probably a response to the crisis of 1539 when, threatened with invasion by Francis I of France and the Emperor Charles V, Henry VIII and his minister Thomas Cromwell sent orders to certain 'sadde and expert men of every shire in Ingland beyng nere the see . . . to viewe all the places alongest the secost [sea coast] wher any daunger of invasions ys like to be and to certifie the sayd daungers and also the best advises for the fortificacion therof.'

The order resulted in a series of pictorial maps of the English shores, pinpointing areas of particular danger. This one is typical – it is a 'show' map, prepared at court for presentation to the King on the basis of locally supplied drafts. Utilizing, by way of example, a serious raid that had actually taken place in 1514, the map demonstrates how French galleys could land on the shingle beach and burn the lower town before advancing to the upper town to wreak havoc there. Inscriptions elaborate further on the dangers. 'These grete shippes rydeng hard aborde shore', reads one, 'by shoting into the hille and valeis over the towne so sore oppresse the towne that the Countrey dare not adventure to reskue it.' At the end of the road on the left is the possibly exaggerated warning that 'upon this weste parte may lond 100 000 persones unletted [unhindered] by any provision [defences] there.' The Hove area (left) was 'all daungerous and without cleves' [cliffs], but the east, the site of modern Kemp Town, was safer from invasion because it lay 'on cleves [cliffs] high'. The only defences were the stone towers of Hove and Brighton churches and 'the towne fyre cage' (right) and 'the bekon [beacon] of the town' (left) which could alert the militias of Poynings and Lewes. These, however, even if they had braved the naval bombardment, would have had their road blocked before they reached Brighton, as the plan shows, by some enemy detachments at the mouths of the narrow valleys along which they would have had to pass.

Pictorial and innocent of scientific measurement though it is, the map serves its purpose, although adequate defences were not created until 1559, following another, lesser, French raid in 1545.

Central section of an anonymous map of Brighton of about 1539–40. British Library Cotton MS Augustus I.i.18.

The modern descendants of this map are immeasurably more sophisticated. Nonetheless, the map of Brighton and its contemporaries (for instance, in China) were precursors of a type that has continued to be created, using different artistic styles and improved degrees of precision, whenever and wherever a government has the time and means to take precautions against a foreign or sea-borne threat – whether from foreign armies or piratical fleets.

PETER BARBER

FAST MAPS

After France had declared war on Great Britain, Spain and the Habsburg Emperor Francis II in 1793, a British officer was heard to comment that 'when the first campaign opened in Flanders in 1793, if the whole British army had been searched for a means of laying down [surveying] a range of country with a view to military operations, we are convinced that not a dozen officers would have been found in our ranks who were capable of reading a survey, not one individual who could have assisted in its compilation.'

But by the time the Peninsular War began in 1808, a revolution was underway in British military cartography. It was the first time that regimental officers, trained in surveying (ironically by an émigré French general) at the newly formed Royal Military College at High Wycombe, provided a co-ordinated mapping force. It was also the first time that cartographic reports of war had been printed by the new and quicker method of lithography, which used the technique of drawing on, and printing from, stone, instead of laboriously engraving on copper. The new technology was quickly appreciated by Wellington who employed a mobile lithographic printing press in the field – the forerunner of the field printing presses of the First World War.

The immediate advantage of swift reproduction was offset by the crude appearance of the coarse linework of early lithography (the first lithographed map was printed in 1808) which is apparent in this map of Corunna. Nevertheless, an earlier version was printed in London only ten days after the action it portrayed. If we consider the time taken to draw the original sketch in the first place, and then to transmit it to London, we can see that the response time was relatively fast.

The value of reliable mapping was readily appreciated by Wellington, who confessed himself to be no 'draughtsman and but a bad hand at description', because in retrospect he wrote that if he had been able to turn the enemy position from the lines of Torres Vedras, he could have brought the army 'into a country of which I had an excellent map and topographical accounts ... and the battle which it was evident would be fought in a few days would have had for its field a country of which we had a knowledge.' Even so, an engineer writing in the War Office in the 1870s referred to some of the maps as 'the old smudges you will find upstairs here, on which the Duke of Wellington based some of his most important movements.'

In its day, the Peninsular War was unique for its range of cartographic coverage: geographically, in variety of scale and fast production methods. These meant that many copies of each map could be produced relatively easily, although maps at that time were used only by officers, who were responsible for acquiring their own copies. Map reproduction technology was still a long way from the print runs of several thousands, achieved in the field within one-and-a-half days, for issue to the troops during the two World Wars.

YOLANDE HODSON

'Plan of the Action near Coruna January 16th 1809. Quarter Master General's Office Horse Guards March 27th 1809'. Scale 1:23000, 484 × 359 cm. British Library Maps C.18.m.1. (10A).

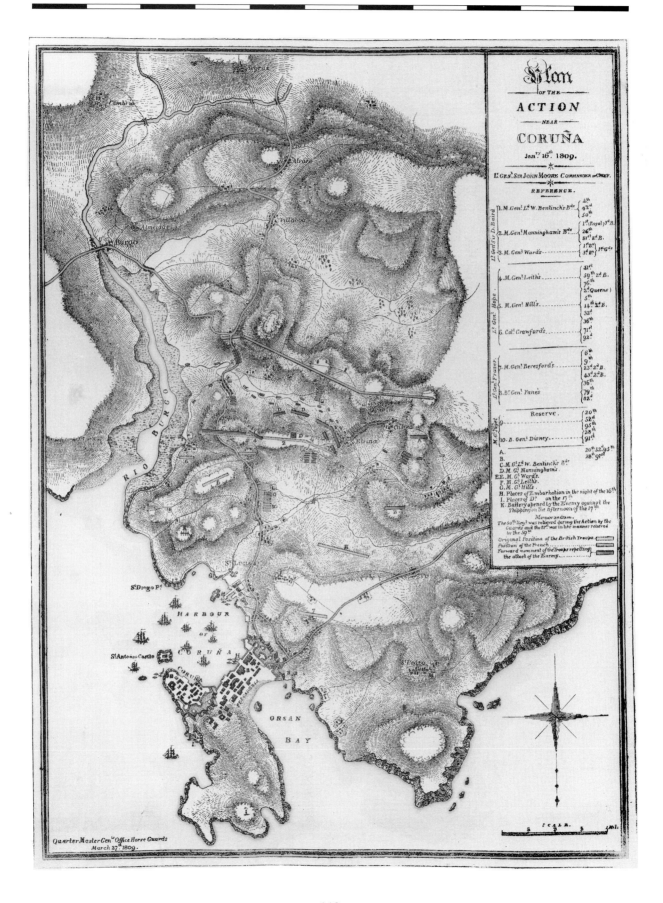

MAPS IN THE FIELD

Eighteenth-century warfare was marked by the laborious movement of thousands of troops across vast tracts of the European continent, and by prolonged sieges and battles fought by conventional rules. Commanders spent more time on logistical exercises than in offensive action: men and horses had to be fed, therefore a knowledge of the land-use of the terrain through which they had to pass, and the length of time it would sustain an army, were important factors in military management. Surveyors, who were not always trained engineer officers but were often officers of the line regiments who either had a rudimentary instruction in map-making or who could just draw well, would be sent ahead of the main body of the army to examine and sketch the ground with three purposes in mind: movement, encampment and engagement with the enemy.

A commander could expect to have at least three groups of graphic documents to consult. Most importantly, he would have acquired maps

(Below) Detail with manuscript annotations by F. Hancko, from 'Carte des Provinces des Pays Bas . . . Dressée sur les Mémoires de Eugene Henri Fricx et augmenté sur les observations les plus nouvelles, à Paris chez Crepy . . . 1744'. Scale 1:110 000. Royal Library, Windsor, K. Mil. IX.60. © Her Majesty the Queen.

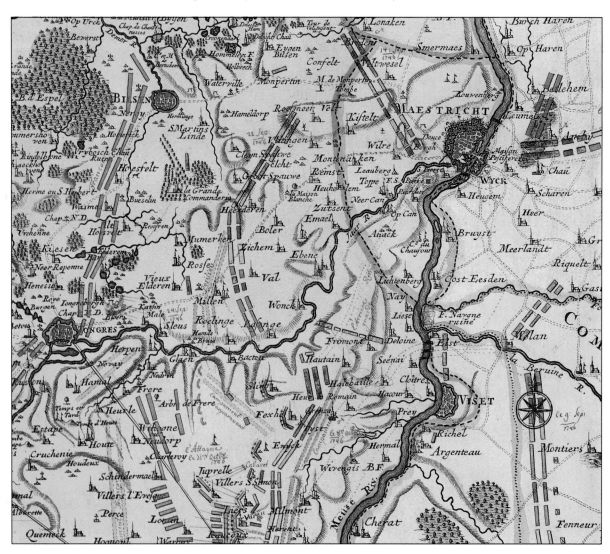

and reports from earlier campaigns in the same area. These would give him a general idea of the lie of the land and its advantages and disadvantages.

The second group of maps would be the most up-to-date available. Civilian in origin, and very small in scale, the detail, such as relief (necessary not only for planning troop movements but also for discovering the best areas from which to observe and shoot at the enemy) and land-use, was always inadequate for military purposes. However, they did show settlements, rivers and main lines of communications. These would be traced or enlarged by the surveyor who then took this skeleton framework into the field, corrected it where necessary and filled in the required information using simple graphics or eye sketching. The resulting maps, together with any others made in the field, provided the third group of cartographic material (below).

The larger map shown here is an example of the second category of map that was available to a commander. Originally published in twenty-four sheets by Eugene Henry Fricx in 1704, it was reissued with minor corrections between 1744 and 1747. Drawn to a scale of about 1:110 000 (just under 2 miles to the inch), it covered virtually the whole of modern Belgium, Luxemburg and parts of northern France. George II's younger son, the Duke of Cumberland (1721–65), possessed at least seven sets of this map, which he used on campaign to plan operations and to record, as here, the progress in this area of the War of the Austrian Succession (1740–8). He had some copies edged in red silk and fitted with rings so they could be hung up and displayed in his headquarters. This map became the standard source on which more detailed military field surveys were based at this time.

Although Cumberland had bought this map, which was widely available to the public, he also relied on maps captured from the enemy, which provided graphic information on such objectives as fortifications (see pp.90–91). In the same way, two hundred years later, the Allied armies relied on captured data in the Second World War to provide greater positional accuracy for their artillery, for instance in Italy.   YOLANDE HODSON

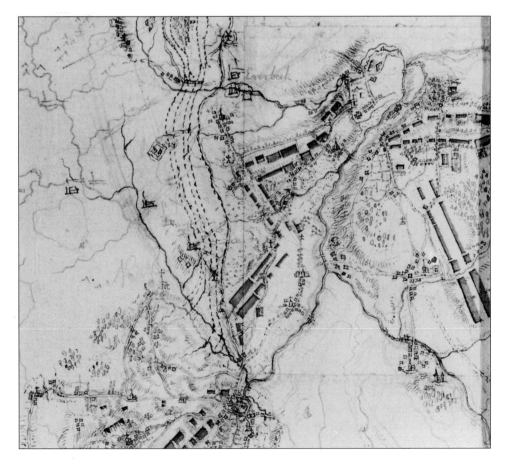

(Left) Tracing, by Schultz, c.1745, from Fricx's map showing the pencilled outlines of roads, rivers and settlements which is in marked contrast to the greater detail which has been filled in for the areas of encampments. The squaring would have been drawn for copying the map at a larger scale. Royal Library, Windsor, K. Mil. IX.62. © Her Majesty the Queen.

IN THE HEAT OF BATTLE

In 1978 a large and decaying map, suspended perilously from a wooden roller, was offered to the National Library of Scotland by a dealer. Heavy varnishing could not disguise the finely lithographed and hand-coloured detail lurking under the grimy surface. The map turned out to be of the ill-fated Crimean campaign and, according to information printed on it, to have been surveyed by four military officers between 1854–5, and published in 1856, the year in which the campaign ended.

The map covered the south-western part of the Crimean peninsula lying between Sevastopol and Balaklava. Military encampments of the armies involved in the conflict are shown, together with trackways and other details of particular interest to the British forces and their allies. Topographic detail showing the nature of the terrain uses the thin black hatched lines typical of military draughtsmanship of that period. Also included are the principal skirmishes and battles of the campaign, particularly the notorious and tragic episode immortalized by Tennyson in his poem 'The Charge of the Light Brigade'.

Nothing about this sad-looking map suggested that this particular copy was special but, pandering to hunch rather than to logic, the curator was drawn to the Scottish surname of one of the named surveyors, Brevet Major Ewart. The hunch paid off. After a little investigation it emerged that Ewart was not only the surveyor but had also owned this particular copy of the map. As an added bonus, it was found that he had recorded his experiences during the Crimean campaign in his autobiography, *A Soldier's Life*, published in 1881.

Born in 1821, and educated at Sandhurst, John Alexander Ewart was appointed to the Quarter Master General's Department as a surveyor on 26 September 1854. Indeed, in October 1854 he described himself as 'the only officer on the staff employed surveying'. His life was busy. 'I was out surveying every day from morning to night, General Airey [the illustrious Quartermaster General] having ordered me to make a sketch of the whole country between Balakclava [sic] and Sebastopol. Lord Raglan [Commander-in-Chief of the British Army] was very anxious to have it finished as soon as possible, so I worked as hard as I could; but being quite alone, and on foot.' Ewart's role was to provide a record of the lie of the land where the campaign took place, providing as much significant military detail as possible in the event of future skirmishes and for future record. It was not for immediate use on the battlefield, though Ewart could not avoid seeing action. 'On the 6th November [1854] I was out sketching in the neighbourhood of the 2nd Division, and was for some time on the field of battle [Inkermann] which presented a fearful spectacle.'

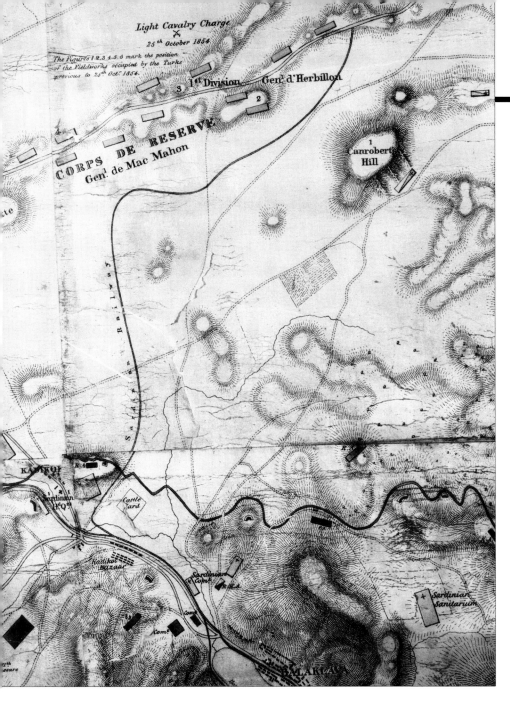

Within the map image:
Light Cavalry Charge
25th October 1854
The Figures 1.2.3.4.5.6 mark the position of the Fieldworks occupied by the Turks previous to 25th Oct.r 1854.
1st Division — Gen.l d'Herbillon
CORPS DE RESERVE.
Gen.l de Mac Mahon
Canrobert Hill
Sardinian Railway
KADIKOI
Sardinian H.Q.s
Cattle Yard
Kadikoi Bazaar
Sardinian Com.t
Com.
Com.
Sardinian Sanitarium
BALAKLAVA

Detail from 'Military sketch of the southwestern part of the Crimea, Surveyed . . . in the years 1854–5 . . . by Lieut. Col. Hallewell . . . Brevet Major Barniston . . . Brevet Major Ewart, etc. Quarter Master General's Office', London, 1856. National Library of Scotland, Map R.1.a.

By 11 February 1855, Ewart commented, 'the large plan I had been working at was now finished, and there was no more surveying then required.' His association with the Quarter Master General's Department ended the next day when, he records, 'I accordingly sat down and wrote out my resignation.' Ewart was not to know that his map was probably the last one to be produced by the Quarter Master General's Office before its mapping responsibilities passed to the Royal Engineers, ending a tradition that stretched back for centuries. After a further distinguished military career, ending as a Lieutenant General, he retired to the house in the Scottish Borders where this map was later to resurface.

As an official document, the original manuscript map which Ewart produced is now located in the Public Record Office at Kew, but Ewart, obviously wishing to keep some reminder of his part in the Crimean campaign, must have held on to the printed version. His experience mirrors that of other military officers who, while required to regard their work as purely official, nonetheless kept some personal mementos. Sir George Murray, the Quarter Master General during the Peninsular War (see pp.112–13), also held on to many manuscript maps and sketches made during the War, and these too eventually entered the National Library of Scotland with his papers.

MARGARET WILKES

CONTROLLING CIVIL UNREST

On the evening of 2 June 1780, orderly demonstrations led by Lord George Gordon in London, against a proposed bill to lift some restrictions on Catholics, degenerated into an orgy of rioting and looting. In the following days, the London mob, wearing the distinctive blue cockades of the Protestant Association, burnt down gaols, Catholic chapels, the homes and property of Catholics and their sympathizers and even attacked the Bank of England. It was a week before the 10 000 militiamen and troops, who had been summoned to London from far afield, succeeded in quelling the riots. The experience was so traumatic for the authorities that detailed records were kept for reference in a future emergency.

This one-sheet map of London and its environs by John Rocque, which first appeared in 1754, was owned by Major-General George Morrison (1704?–99) who, as Quarter Master General at the time and for some time afterwards, was responsible for accommodating, feeding and arming the troops and for mapping their encampments and progress. It is annotated to show encampments (red and yellow), stations (red circles), the positions of cavalry (red squares) and infantry (red rectangles), the locations of detachments (red crosses) and the route of patrols (blue lines).

Tradition and practicality dictated that the largest concentration of forces should be encamped in the open spaces of Hyde Park and St James's Park. Further troops were posted in smaller open spaces such as the gardens of the British Museum, and in Lincoln's Inn Fields which were closer to the centre of the trouble: the legal quarter of London, the City and the poorer St Giles, Seven Dials and Covent Garden districts. The cross over Kenwood House, the suburban home of the Lord Chief Justice, the Earl of Mansfield, indicates that it was guarded by a detachment of 100 infantrymen of the Cambridgeshire Regiment, based in Hampstead.

The mob suspected Mansfield of being a secret Catholic and his town house with its large library (containing many medieval and classical manuscripts) in Bloomsbury Square had been set ablaze on the evening of 6 June. On the next day Kenwood House itself was saved from destruction only because the publican of the nearby Spaniards' Inn, with assistance from the Earl's steward, plied the rioters with unlimited amounts of drink, rendering them paralytically drunk by the time a detachment of Light Horse arrived from Whitehall to round them up.

Because commercial map-makers mapped large towns and their surroundings in detail earlier than the countryside, numerous printed maps of a sufficiently large scale to manage civil unrest were available at a realtively early date. Though this particular map was almost certainly annotated for record purposes after calm had been restored, there can be little doubt that the information it contains was taken from annotations made on similar maps in the course of the riots of June 1780. In much the same way, the War Office created special maps for use by the authorities at the time of the General Strike of 1926 (see pp.104–5), while Churchill was able to chart and control the campaigns of the Second World War from the Map Room that can still be seen in his bunker, the Cabinet War Rooms, beneath Whitehall in London.

PETER BARBER

Detail from 'Disposition of the Troops and General View of the Patroles in and about London on account of the Riots in 1780': an annotated copy of John Rocque, 'A Plan of London on the same scale as that of Paris'. London, 1754 (1762 edition). Scale 1:48 000. British Library Add. MS 15533,f.39.

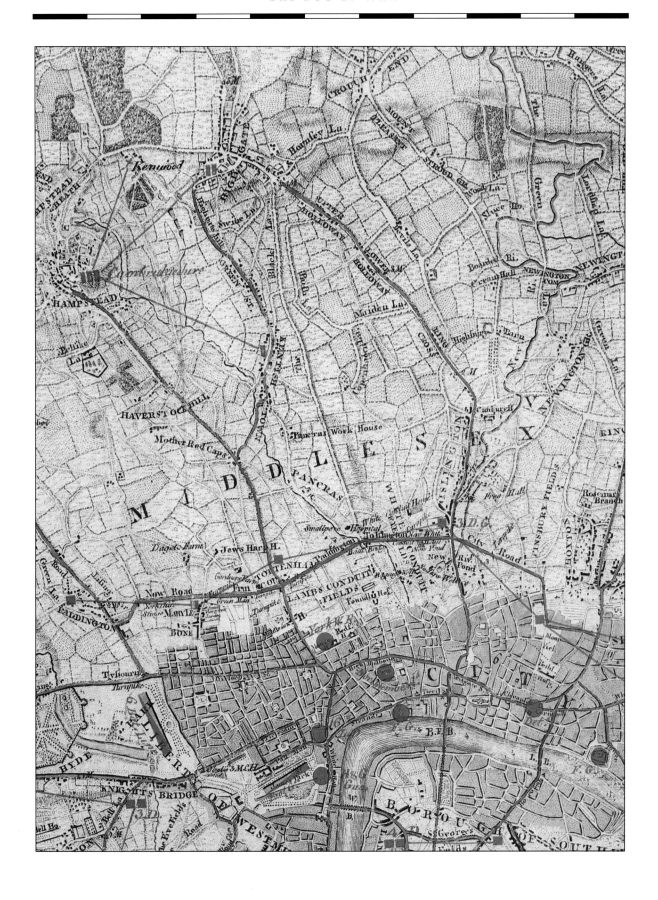

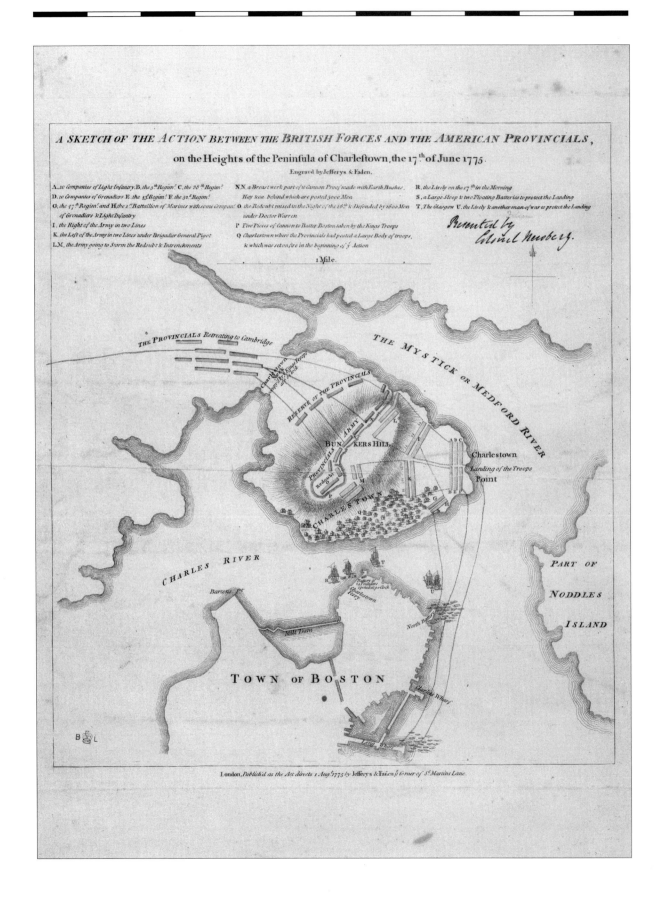

INFORMING THE PEOPLE
BACK HOME

It is said of the Romans that 'a map of the conquered country was always carried in the victor's triumph'. This must be one of the earliest examples of using maps to keep the public informed and raise the morale of the victorious power.

With the invention of printing and map engraving in Europe in the later years of the fifteenth century, news and scenes of military events could be quickly publicized. When the great Venetian empire in the eastern Mediterranean became engaged in a series of battles and sieges against the invading Turkish fleets and armies, the flourishing Italian map trade responded to the challenge. Many military maps, often accompanied by lengthy texts, were engraved and published by Antonio Lafreri and others at Venice, Florence and Rome for the information of the nobility and general public. The sieges of Famagusta and Nicosia in 1570, which ended in the fall of Cyprus to the Turks, and the Christian naval victory at Lepanto the following year, are depicted in a series of German and Italian maps. Contemporaries followed the episodes of the eighty-year-long Dutch struggle for independence from Spain and of the Thirty Years' War in central Europe almost as quickly as they occurred on news maps published in Amsterdam (see pp.136–7), while the siege of Vienna in 1683 was depicted in some of the finest siege maps of a city that were ever made.

War reporting quickly became a profitable activity for map publishers. With a public avid for news, and governments wanting to maintain public morale, publishers could market atlases of the theatres of war at little cost to themselves. They consisted of maps from minimally amended old plates, and depictions of the latest battles and sieges, based on official surveys 'leaked' to them by government officials. When the American War of Independence broke out in 1775, map publishers, profiting from the ignorance and curiosity of the British public, rushed out maps as quickly as possible as the war proceeded. One of the earliest engagements was the Battle of Bunker Hill between the British and American forces on the Heights of the Peninsula of Charlestown, on 17 June 1775, in which the British won a Pyrrhic victory. The first map was published in London by Thomas Jefferys and William Faden, who had close links with the British government, only four days after the news of the battle reached London. It was diagrammatic and the topography was not particularly accurate, but it conveyed the main features of the scene. In contrast, later maps of the same event included some of the finest topographical maps of their day, such as Henry Pelham's aquatint map of Boston and its environs, dated 1 June 1777.

The technical skills of cartographers in recent times have produced some innovative styles of military mapping. Computer techniques have opened up still more possibilities, though the welter of misinformation and partial information, which is now available in greater profusion than ever before, means that the resulting maps often prove to be inaccurate and misleading.

HELEN WALLIS

'A Sketch of the Action Between the British Forces and the American Provincials, on the Heights of the Peninsula of Charlestown, the 17th June, 1775. London 1 August, 1775'. London: Thomas Jefferys and William Faden, 1775. British Map Library RUSI A30/3.

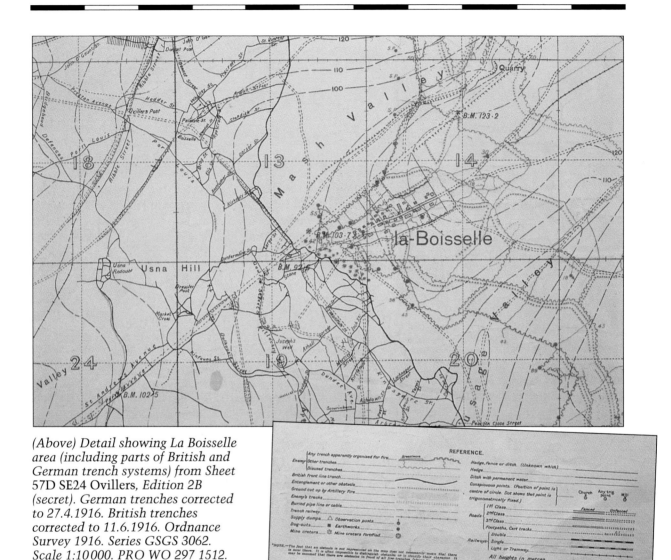

(Above) Detail showing La Boisselle area (including parts of British and German trench systems) from Sheet 57D SE24 Ovillers, Edition 2B (secret). German trenches corrected to 27.4.1916. British trenches corrected to 11.6.1916. Ordnance Survey 1916. Series GSGS 3062. Scale 1:10 000. PRO WO 297 1512.

IN THE TRENCHES

Large-scale trench maps were rapidly developed by all belligerents in 1914 when the stalemate conditions of siege or position war superseded those of open warfare. When the enemy dug in, it became necessary to plot all his defences – trenches, machine gun and mortar positions, observation posts, dug-outs, batteries, barbed wire entanglements – so that these could be destroyed by accurately directed artillery fire prior to an infantry attack. A crucial feature of these maps was thus their accuracy of plotting, and they were compiled with great care from national large-scale survey (Belgium), French fortress *plans directeurs* covering frontier areas, cadastral (land registry), mine, railway and canal plans. If these were not available, the old French 1:80 000 (about 1 inch to 1¼ miles) had to be enlarged and redrawn.

The area behind the British reserve line was surveyed on the plane table, then new or corrected detail taken from air photos was plotted on

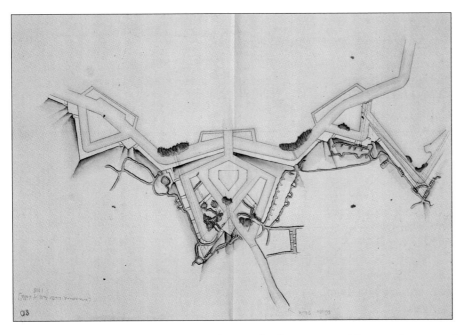

(Left) Anonymous plan of the Water Gate in Lille showing the progress of the siege of the town by English and Spanish forces in October 1708. The plan was sent by Prince Eugene of Savoy, who was leading the battle, to the Duke of Marlborough, who was providing cover. The plan uses standard colour conventions. British Library Add. MS 61245,ff.79v–80.

the outline, as well as enemy trenches and other defensive works. Pinpoint accuracy was essential, otherwise the artillery fire would miss its targets and might even hit friendly forces, though such a mishap was usually due to the artillery not knowing the position of its own and the enemy's forces rather than to inaccurate maps. Accurate positioning on maps was essential if the range and bearing of targets were to be properly calculated, but the contours on each map also had to be correct if the gunners were to set their weapons effectively and allow for the differences in relative height between the guns and the targets. As it was, in areas of France only covered by the old hachured 1:80 000 map, the contours of the trench map were often faulty and so artillery fire frequently fell short of, or beyond, the enemy. The trench map was used as a base on which to overprint data for specific operations, particularly enemy battery positions, barrage lines and timings. A grid or squaring system was used for reference and the calculation of relative positions.

This 'Secret' edition (opposite) showing British (blue) as well as German (red) trenches near Albert, was prepared for the Somme battle in 1916 (although the artillery bombardment did not prevent British casualties amounting to 57 000 on 1 July). Both sides, making good maps of the opposing trench systems from air photos, had an exaggerated view of the need for secrecy and did not show their own trenches on ordinary editions

until late in the war. The troops complained that they had to use captured enemy maps to find their way round their own trenches. Such caution was unnecessary and counter-productive. This sheet shows mine craters in the front lines and German trench mortars (dots), snipers' posts (SP), observation posts (arrows) and so on.

All British trench maps were drawn in the field but most were printed at Ordnance Survey, back in England, so they were always weeks out of date. Rapid printing in the field developed in 1914, and duplicated and lithographed maps were printed on hand presses to supplement the regular series sheets from England. By 1916 there were five Field Survey Companies with printing equipment on the Western Front, and in 1917 they were given power presses. In 1918 an overseas branch of Ordnance Survey was established in France.

Sieges or trench wars usually give enough time for detailed mapping to take place and for advice and information to be transmitted to and from home during the course of operations. Such maps are known to have existed from the sixteenth century and, by the eighteenth century, they had their distinct colouring conventions. They were often produced at great risk to the map-maker. Trench maps are a development from siege surveys and fortress plans (see pp.26–7 and 90–1), but contain many special and novel features and are so sophisticated as to be a *genre* in their own right.   PETER CHASSEAUD

ESCAPE

It was hell!

Edward Fisher's parachute opened with a jolt. His Lancaster bomber was falling away beneath him in flames, and where were his friends, the crew? As the pilot, he was the last out, but the aircraft's loss of control had delayed him and the others would now be well away in the distance. All the crew had got clear, but there was little chance of his meeting up with them now and it would have to be each man for himself. Fortunately, they had all been issued with the special escape maps for crashed aircrews printed on silk, and they had been well briefed on escape options.

But where was he? The bombs had been dropped on the docks at Ludwigshafen so at least the crew's task was complete, but the plane had been hit as they turned away to the north east. Fisher tried to calculate the distance and direction in his head, taking account of the time from target and the wind direction, but had to stop while he concentrated on his descent.

He landed on a quiet wooded hillside, normally forbidding on such a cold wet night, but now encouraging as it would help him avoid being captured while he planned his way back from enemy territory. As far as he could tell, his descent had been unobserved. He reached for his tightly rolled up silk map, which unfolded readily and quietly – something not possible with paper maps. At a scale of 1 to 1.25 million (about 1 inch to 20 miles), it covered the south east coast of England, all of France, the western part of Germany, the Benelux lowlands and much of Switzerland. On the reverse the area continued south west to cover all of Spain and Portugal. Fisher studied the map and calculated his position to be near Bensheim, allowing himself a brief recollection of a peacetime visit he had made to nearby Heidelberg some years before, but at this moment his situation was very different, and he considered again the options open to him.

Fisher studied the map once more. It had been printed in four colours and had an unusually clear appearance, with contours standing out well. The edges were reinforced to prevent fraying, and the map's scale and size meant that it covered anywhere he might need to go. He looked at the

lines of communication away from Bensheim and remembered his pre-mission briefing. He would have to choose carefully, for some routes would be very hazardous and the Rhine was a difficult obstacle. At this stage of the war, he could expect some help from partisans in France and Belgium, and had been briefed on this only a few hours earlier. He planned his escape route westwards accordingly.

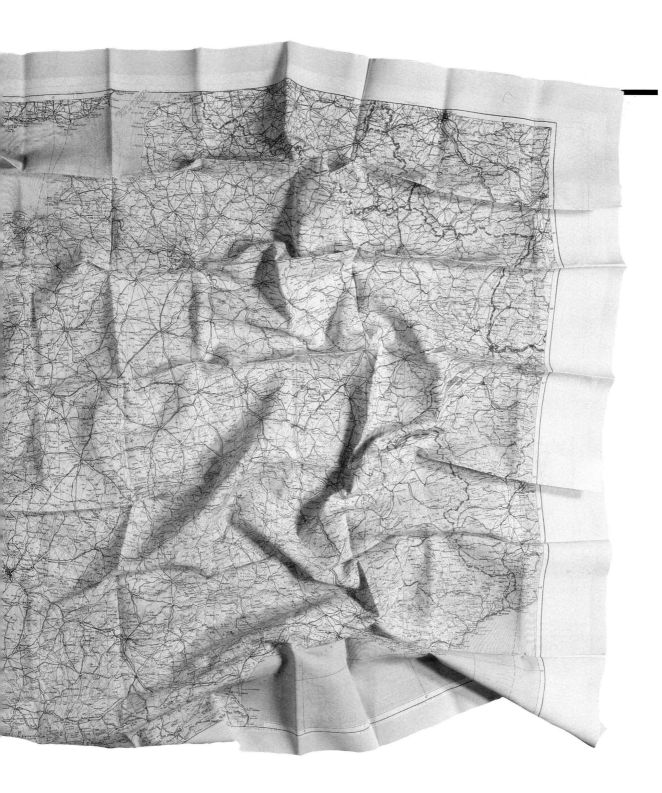

Confident in his navigation, he rolled up the already wet map and wound it round his neck to keep out the rain and to provide some welcome warmth. This map would be opened and rolled up many times on his journey, so the silk made it practical and durable and – after a good wash – he thought it would be a handsome present for his girlfriend on his safe return.

These silk maps were an essential aid to

Fabric Map of France and Spain. Scale 1:1 250,000. A GSGS Misc. map specially compiled from GSGS 2758.

aircrew during the Second World War. Since then, various alternatives have been considered and tested, including 35mm map slides and viewers, but none of them have been adopted. Silk maps were used again by aircrew during the 1990–91 Gulf War.   PATRICK FAGAN

WARTIME DIFFICULTIES – PEACETIME MAPPING

In the aftermath of the defeat of the Jacobite forces at Culloden on 16 April 1746 by William Augustus, Duke of Cumberland (the second son of George II), his officers found themselves 'embarrassed for the want of a proper survey of the country'. Less than a month after the battle, Major-General John Campbell wrote to Cumberland that 'by the map of the Country it appears very easy & a short cutt [sic] to cross over from Appin by the end of Lismore to Strontian. I have had it view'd and it is impracticable in every respect.'

This comment underlines the contrast which usually existed between the printed map and the reality on the ground. Cumberland's army was faced with the task of preventing the Jacobite clans from returning to their Highland strongholds and of maintaining civilian order. Although a number of maps had been made of General Wade's roads, which were built after the 1715 Jacobite uprising, there were no coherent maps of the Highlands as a whole, and so it was impossible to know where the troops should be placed.

It comes as no surprise, therefore, to learn that on his return to London, the Duke spoke of the 'Inconvenience and want of such a Survey to the . . . King his Royal Father.' The royal consent, given at a time when Cumberland was at the height of his popularity (Handel had composed *Judas Maccabeus* in his honour) was thus secured for what was to become the first comprehensive large-scale national survey of any country in the British Isles. Drawn at a scale of 1:36000, or 1 inch to 1000 yards, this map eventually covered the entire mainland of Scotland and was surveyed between 1747 and 1755. Today it is referred to as the Military Survey of Scotland, or as 'Roy's Map', after William Roy, its principal surveyor.

In later years General William Roy was to refer to his map as 'rather . . . a magnificent military sketch, than a very accurate map of a country', because surveying 'instruments of the common or inferior kind' had been used to create it. Nevertheless, Roy's map was a formidable undertaking: he surveyed the coastline himself, which involved a long-distance walk of hundreds of miles. Only one manuscript copy exists, and if all its sections were joined it would measure about 40 × 28 feet (12 × 8.5 metres). Fifty-seven people helped to make it, which is more than the forty-four staff members of the whole of the Ordnance Survey of Great Britain in 1834.

Before the second half of the nineteenth century, one of the main differences between civilian and military maps was the latter's need for more detailed information about the use and lie of the land. Different colours had to be used to satisfy these complex requirements, and to allow a commander to plan his strategy from the comfort of his tent. Artistic ability was therefore a decided advantage in a military draughtsman, and the Scottish survey was fortunate to have as its chief draughtsman the young Paul Sandby, who was later regarded as the father of English watercolour art, and who painted the Scottish mountains 'with a thousand graces'.

The onset of the Seven Years War in 1756 prevented the finishing touches being put to the Scottish survey, and in fact it was never used for its original purpose. Even so, it set a pattern for British military surveys of the second half of the eighteenth century, notably the Survey of Canada and the St Lawrence by George Murray (1760–1), the east coast of North America by Samuel Holland (1764–75), of Bengal by James Rennell (1766–77), and of Ireland by Charles Vallancey (1778–90). Roy's experience on the Scottish survey confirmed him in his belief that maps were essential for the defence of the realm and that they were best made at leisure in peace time. He campaigned for nearly thirty years for a national survey of Great Britain, and Ordnance Survey began in 1791, a year after his death.

YOLANDE HODSON

Extract from sheet 16 of the manuscript Military Survey of Scotland (1747–1755). Scale 1:36000. Pencil, ink and watercolour on paper. British Library K. Top. 48.25-b,c.

126

EVERLASTING FAME

In 1642, Louis XIII of France commissioned a much-wounded war veteran, the military engineer Sébastien de Pontault, Sieur de Beaulieu (c. 1612–74), to design and publish plans of his country's military triumphs. Perhaps in an attempt to rival the Dutch who had dominated this, as most other, areas of mapping since about 1590, Beaulieu secured the services of some of the leading European graphic artists, notably Stefano della Bella and Romeyne de Hooghe, to design the pictorial maps. As well as creating grandiose wall maps, from the late 1640s Beaulieu published folio-sized views of conquered towns and commemorative siege and battle plans which he sold separately. He planned to publish them eventually as an atlas but first his death, and then that of his successor and nephew by marriage, Jean-Baptiste Hamont, Sieur Desroches, thwarted the project.

This typical military map, engraved by Nicolas Cochin, illustrates the successful crossing of the Rhine near Speyer by French forces in June 1645. A beautifully observed portrait of an army on the march in the foreground, in the style of Jacques Callot, blends into a pictorial plan of the rest of the army, drawn up in formation, waiting to cross the bridge of boats next to the town of Speyer, which is shown in outline plan. The panels at the top and side identify the regiments involved and the fortifications of Speyer, with the country around it being depicted in an inset map on the bottom left.

The atlas was finally published in 1694. Supplemented with newly engraved plans of sieges of the 1640s that Beaulieu had neglected but which had been officially re-evaluated, and accompanied by politically correct texts by leading authors 'explaining' the plans and views, it became part of the effort by Louis XIV and his ministers to enrol the arts and sciences in the service of the French state. The culmination of the process was reached in 1727, twelve years after Louis's death, when the plans were republished as the five concluding volumes of a twenty-three volume printed series, the *Cabinet du Roi*, which eulogized the King's cultural and military achievements. It became the standard French diplomatic gift for foreign monarchs and distinguished foreigners.

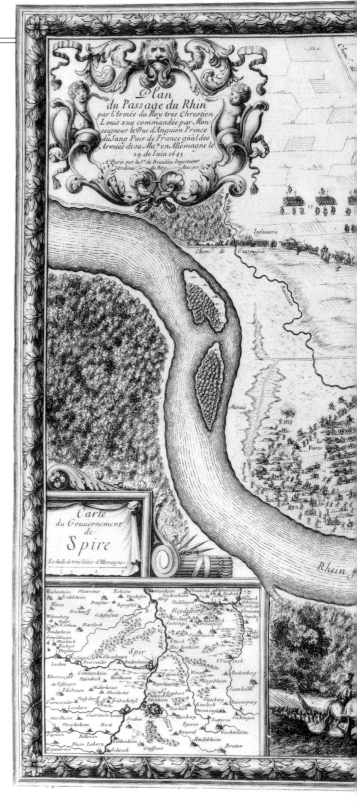

To this day, visitors to the Louvre can buy modern impressions of the plans taken from Beaulieu's original copperplates.

Since their first modern appearance in about 1500, commemorative siege and battle plans have

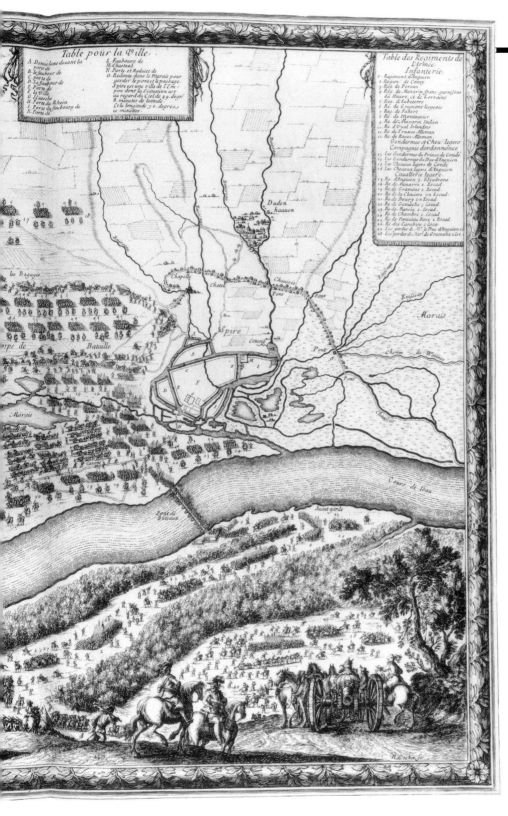

Sébastien de Pontault de Beaulieu, 'Plan du Passage du Rhin par l'Armée du Roy tres Chrestien Louis xiiii commandée par Monseigneur le Duc d'Anguien Prince du Sang Pair de France General des Armées de sa Majesté en Allemagne le 29 de Iuin 1645'. In Les Glorieuses Conquestes de Louis Le Grand Roy de France et de Navarre. *Paris: Reine de Beaulieu, 1694, vol i, plan 54 (cent vingt six). British Library 198.i.4.*

abounded on paper, on canvas, on plaster, on medals (see p.10) and in tapestries. Some served to raise popular morale, others to flatter old generals and to educate future ones. Many have been a speculation on the part of their publishers, but few have combined all of these features and played a role in a country's diplomacy to the extent of Beaulieu's *Glorieuses Conquestes de Louis Le Grand.*

PETER BARBER

LONDON: THE METROPOLIS MAPPED

Because they are so crowded and complex, cities present greater difficulties to the map-maker than the countryside does. We have chosen to illustrate metropolis with London, but the maps and themes selected could have been illustrated with other major cities in Europe or Asia.

The density and complexity of the life and fabric of cities present challenges that conventional maps cannot meet. Cities are not always best shown in plan form, but instead invite the use of bird's-eye views and panoramas. The traditional topographic map indicates the ground plans of buildings, streets and railways against a framework of visible water features. The historian gains much insight from these snapshots, but is handicapped by the absence of other information not conventionally shown on such maps. They are not so good at showing how high buildings are, whether they replace earlier ones, how many and what types of people live and work in them, or how busy, quiet or safe different parts are. Only indirectly can we guess what the inhabitants and visitors actually thought of the various parts of the city.

Many old maps, however, that were originally created for very specific and prosaic administrative or legal purposes, have now become invaluable sources of information on economic or social conditions in the past. Early detailed surveys of surrounding countryside are also an unrivalled source of information on what existed before the growth of London. It is surprising how often the streets of the metropolis can be traced back to the fields and villages of London's environs by studying maps.

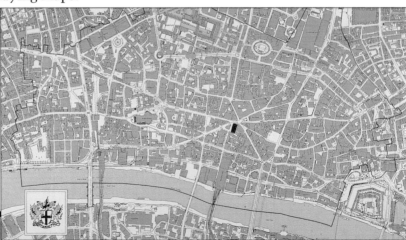

(Right) Ordnance Survey Superplan of the City of London plotted for the Lord Mayor in 1992. Crown copyright.

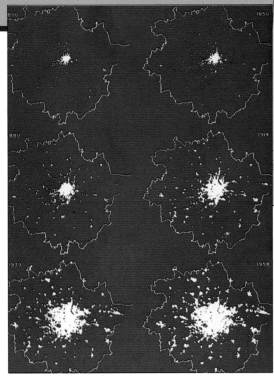

(Left) Six images of the growth of London from the V&A Museum 1964 exhibition catalogue The Growth of London AD 43–1964. (Above) Digital plot of the built up area of London in 1981 from the Office of Population Censuses and Surveys, Department of the Environment. Crown copyright.

Early cartographers often favoured bird's-eye views of cities which give an idea of what the city actually looked like – or what the city fathers wished it to look like. Even today a map can be as much a symbol of pride as a source of information: a role admirably fulfilled by the Superplan of the City embellished with the City's arms and recently presented by Ordnance Survey to the Lord Mayor of London. By the seventeenth century, accurate plans gave a good idea of the sizes and shapes of buildings, landmarks, streets and open spaces. Such plans were the foundation for specialized surveys of disease, poverty, postal services, public transport and, with the arrival of detailed statistics, social conditions from the censuses. Good administration requires good maps, and nowhere more than in the ever changing city.

The lists and directories of the nineteenth century were soon replaced by the street map, and by inventive ways of finding streets and places in the city. The proper regulation of traffic, parking and disaster/emergency management benefit greatly from using up-to-date plans, as during the General Strike of 1926. Public utilities must know where their pipes, sewers, cables and lines are in relation to what is above ground. Modern legislation now requires authorities to monitor and record all streetworks. Today the information needed to collate these maps is compiled most effectively by the creation of databases of geographical information recorded in computer systems. By keeping these up to date and in distinct but relatable 'layers' the authorities might avoid the worst consequences of digging holes in your road. CHRISTOPHER BOARD

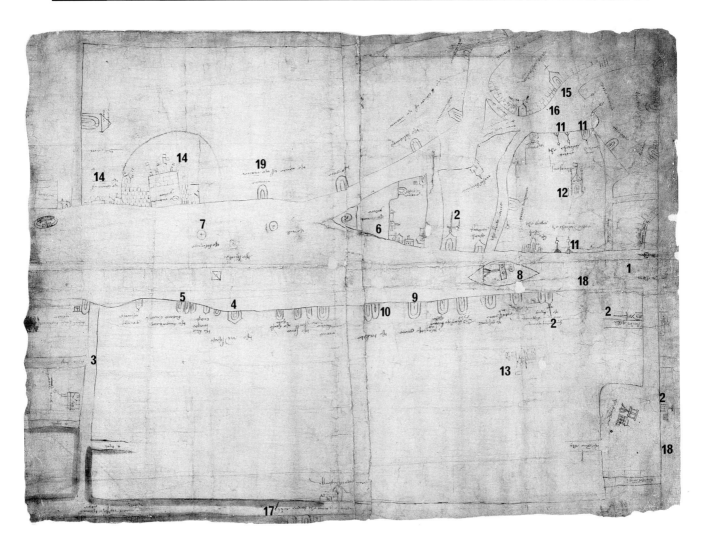

LIBERTIES AND IMMUNITIES

In 1541, in pursuance of the act abolishing all sanctuaries except parish churches, churchyards, cathedrals and hospitals, Henry VIII issued commissions to authorities throughout the land to make maps setting out the bounds and limits of sanctuaries in their towns and cities.

The commission led to the creation of some of the earliest surviving English town plans and possibly accounts for this sketch plan of Southwark (above) which was then a notoriously lawless district. It is oriented with west at the top and shows the area along Borough High Street, immediately south of the Thames and London Bridge (marked by two pillars in the middle of the right edge 1). Although the plan does not specifically

mention places of sanctuary they can still be located since it identifies the churches and hospitals of Southwark and the different jurisdictions, such as manors and liberties, in the area and marks their boundaries. Those of the manor owned by the City are most easily identifiable because of the dagger, one of the symbols for the City, placed over the houses and taverns marking its boundary with the royal manor 2. For the rest of the plan, roads (including the ancestor of the Old Kent Road 3) and local landmarks are shown for orientation. These include the churches, the prisons (Marshalsea 4 and the King's Bench 5), the market installations 6, the bullring 7 and the pillory 8 in the middle of the high road, and the taverns

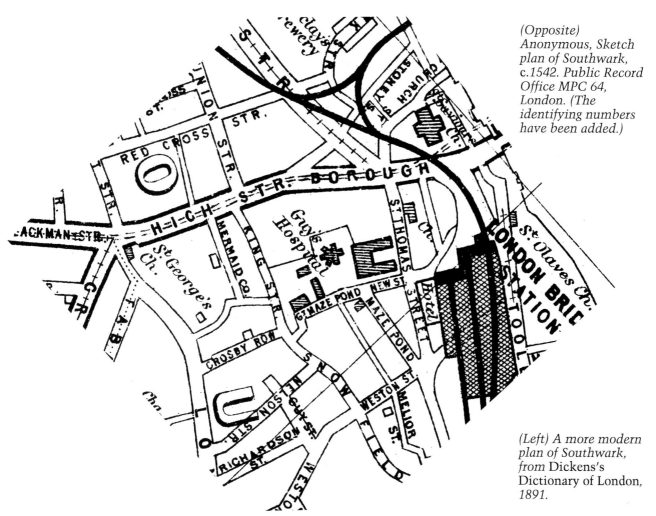

(Opposite)
Anonymous, Sketch
plan of Southwark,
c.1542. Public Record
Office MPC 64,
London. (The
identifying numbers
have been added.)

(Left) A more modern
plan of Southwark,
from Dickens's
Dictionary of London,
1891.

for which Southwark was famous, including the still-surviving George 9 ('the gorge') and the Tabard 10 ('the tabete'), the starting point for Chaucer's pilgrims in *The Canterbury Tales*. Interspersed among them are the entrances to the main precincts 11, such as the priory and church of St Mary Overie's 12, now Southwark Cathedral (shown in elevation middle right), St Thomas's Hospital 13 (elevation shown upside down underneath the pillory – the hospital moved to its present location opposite the Houses of Parliament in 1862), the royal manor house with its park 14 (elevation top left) and also Winchester House 15, the town house of the bishops of Winchester (of which a wall still survives), and its grounds, the walls of which are shown top right 16. Where these do not suffice inscriptions state 'hyer endith the kings lyberte' 17, 'hyer endith the lyberte off the mayre and beghinnith the [liberty of] the king' 18 and indicate the extent of 'the

liberte off the [King's] manor' 19.

This map of Southwark is an ancestor of the countless modern administrative maps, even if these indicate boundaries with lines and colour superimposed over surveyed groundplans rather than with words and thumbnail elevations of buildings. To the modern viewer, however, perhaps its prime importance lies in the conclusions that can be drawn from its often incidental detail about the nature of life south of the River Thames in the 1540s. Here, amidst the tightly packed taverns, markets, prisons, churches and palaces can be imagined publicans, shopkeepers, thieves, drinkers and travellers – some lewd, some licentious, and many out for pleasure. It is not surprising that public theatres soon opened their doors in Southwark which was to become the entertainment centre of Elizabethan London – and the site of Shakespeare's Globe.

PETER BARBER

A CITY FOR MERCHANTS

In 1572, Georg Braun and Frans Hogenberg published the first of what was to become a six-volume series of town plans and views entitled *Civitates Orbis Terrarum* (Cities of all the lands of the world). It was a risky undertaking, and they went out of their way to ensure that the work appealed to potential purchasers, particularly nouveau riche merchants, who were often poorly educated and relatively unsophisticated, by depicting what they wanted to see.

This map-view of London and Westminster is typical. It is a close copy of a much larger plan that had probably been created in the later 1550s

and, though some detail is lost, Hogenberg's fine engraving ensures that much is still to be seen under the magnifying lens. Hogenberg himself added the depiction of the prosperous merchant and his family in the foreground, setting the tone for the whole image. The inscription on the right describes the Steelyard, the centre for the German merchants, in some detail. The crowded river, then the principal highway, suggests the City's wealth. Merchant ships, cranes, cannon in the vicinity of gun foundries, mills, and the bull and bear baiting available on the South Bank hint at Londoners' business and leisure activities. The

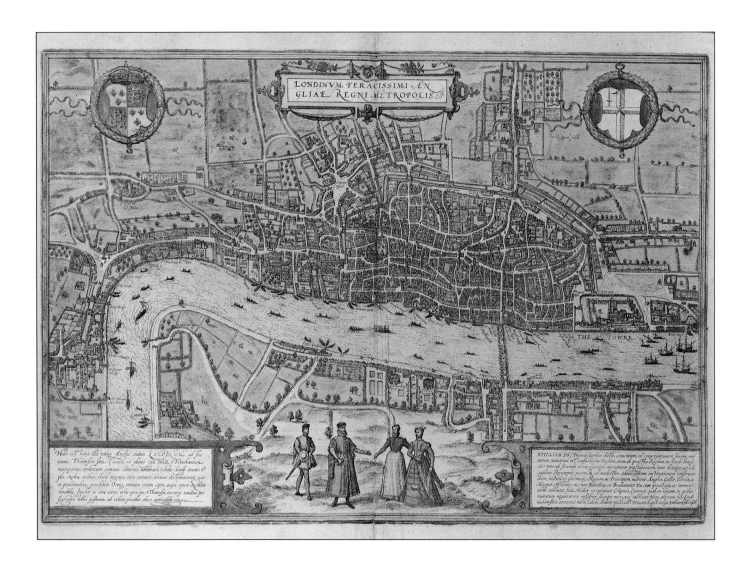

stately quality of life in Westminster is shown, including the great open tennis court and the deer in St James's Park, while the gardens, numerous wells and conduits, the handsome churches, livery halls and town houses of the nobility testify to the high quality of life available to all citizens of London. The Tudor royal arms and the arms of London preside over the City, and the Queen herself can be seen in her royal barge towed by a galley in the middle of the Thames.

While mostly true as far as it went, this is not a complete picture of Elizabethan London. When fixing the tenancies and rents from the livery companies' properties within the City, the merchants who dominated the livery companies made use of larger-scale and more utilitarian plans. This plan of tenements (below) owned by

the Clothworkers' Company near the Fleet River and its accompanying text disclose a warren of passages and courts separating two- and three-storey half-timbered multi-tenanted houses and shops that stood cheek by jowl with large town houses with gardens. Close inspection reveals privies emptying into the Fleet, degrading it from river to 'diche' – and, today, to a culverted sewer running under Farringdon Street.

It could be said that such plans helped to create the wealth that enabled merchants to buy Braun and Hogenberg's volumes. To this day, and throughout the world, the two types of plan continue to be produced and are found, often separated only by a corridor, in the environmental health or planning sections of a town hall and its public relations department.   PETER BARBER

(Opposite) 'Londinum feracissimi Angliae regni metropolis', from Georg Braun and Frans Hogenberg, Civitates Orbis Terrarum, *Cologne, 1572, Vol 1. British Library Maps C.29, e.1 (edition of 1623).*

(Right) Ralph Treswell: Plan of 1–6 Fleet Lane, 16–21 Farringdon St, 1612. Clothworkers' Company Plan Book 47, Guildhall Library. Reproduced in John Schofield The London Surveys of Ralph Treswell, *London Topographical Society, Publication No. 135, London, 1987.*

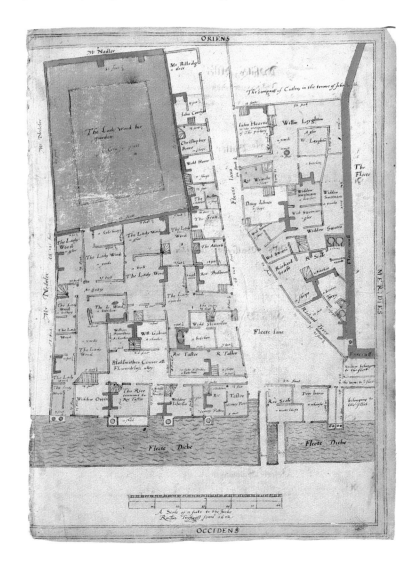

FIRE, FIRE!

One of the greatest recorded urban disasters of all time was the Great Fire of London which, between 2 and 5 (or by the modern Gregorian calendar, 12 and 15) September 1666, destroyed about 13 000 properties and all but the outer fringes of the city recorded by Braun and Hogenberg (see pp.134–5). The event aroused enormous interest throughout Europe and not least in the Dutch Republic, which was then at war with Great Britain. Frederik de Wit, a leading map publisher in Amsterdam, the principal centre for European map-making, also turned his hand to illustrated news sheets (called broadsheets from their format), which combined maps, pictures and text and were the ancestors of modern illustrated newspapers. He recognized a commercial opportunity in the Fire.

De Wit must have put this broadsheet, with its lengthy commentary in Dutch and French, on sale within days of the disaster. He had only had time to set the text and to etch dots, showing what he understood to be the extent of the Fire, on to what was almost certainly an existing plate containing a pre-Fire plan (*plattegrond*) of London and Westminster, with panels listing the parish churches which were illustrated by vignettes on the map. While these broadsheets were satisfying the initial craving for news and information, de Wit continued engraving and, perhaps only a few weeks later, an improved version appeared, this

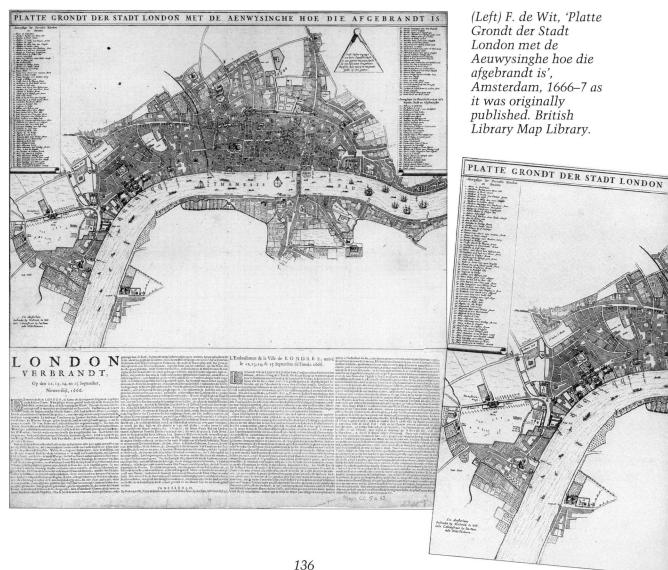

(Left) F. de Wit, 'Platte Grondt der Stadt London met de Aeuwysinghe hoe die afgebrandt is', Amsterdam, 1666–7 as it was originally published. British Library Map Library.

time also containing an imaginative view of the disaster, copied from part of Hollar's panorama of 1647 with the flames added. By the time the plate had been completely engraved, de Wit felt obliged to give the broadsheet an amended title, perhaps in the hope of encouraging sales among those who had already purchased an earlier version. Despite the claim that the map was a 'new model', it was taken from the same plate, slightly expanded at the fringes (far away from the destroyed area), with a few names added. Text and view were unchanged, but to them was now added decoration, in the form of chubby cherubs around the cartouches, or information panels, and scenes from the Fire. These show a lamenting waterman, leaning on an oar and a fishing rod and, behind him, a desperate family with the wife, child in hand, weeping while her husband pays a carter to transport his goods out of danger.

Just as his cartographic images were second-hand, so de Wit may well have copied the individual figures from popular fashion plates. Through them, however, he illustrates contemporary Dutch attitudes to the Fire: genuine horror at the event and pity for the inhabitants who (as the accompanying text makes plain) were exploited by carters, on whom they depended to save their goods from the approaching flames. Yet (as the text also hints) the Fire was a sign of God's wrath: 'the Fire would have been extinguished more quickly had it not come directly from heaven.'

Disasters have always been good business for map-makers. Their maps can satisfy the public's curiosity about the disaster in question, although they usually have to adapt existing plans because there isn't time for a fresh survey to be made. Until the advent of virtually instantaneous news images on the television, the more unscrupulous map-maker was also able to indulge his or her imagination about the disaster at the expense of the gullible and uninformed public. For all their lack of originality, however, maps depicting disasters have an unparalleled immediacy and often, like de Wit's map, provide valuable insights into the popular knowledge and perceptions of the event portrayed. PETER BARBER

(Below) F. de Wit, 'Platte Grondt der Stadt London' – an intermediate version. British Library Crace Collection Portfolio 1.48.

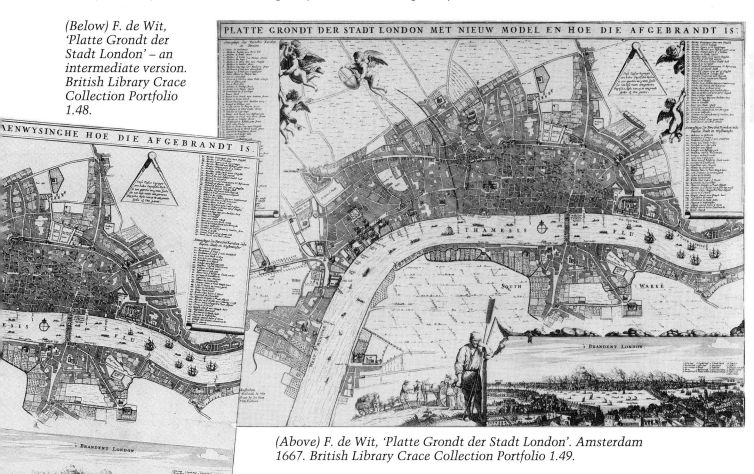

(Above) F. de Wit, 'Platte Grondt der Stadt London'. Amsterdam 1667. British Library Crace Collection Portfolio 1.49.

THE IDEAL CITY

Nothing destroys as effectively as a fire. Between 2 and 5 September 1666, most of the City of London was erased from the face of the earth, leaving only a fraction of the medieval city. The large burnt-out area was a planner's dream. When the King issued a proclamation on 13 September, indicating the radical changes which rebuilding would entail, he already had before him several plans for a new city. Sir Christopher Wren's was the most distinctive and the most radical. It was rational, orderly and classical, showing a complete rejection of the past and a total commitment to Renaissance ideas. It was clearly the product of a mathematical mind, and had the same qualities which later characterized his work as an architect.

Wren was greatly influenced by the sixteenth-century planning of Rome by Sixtus V, in which a rather formless urban landscape had been replaced by a series of focal points – churches, piazzas and obelisks – connected by magnificent avenues. Carriages and processionals demanded long, wide streets; the total idea demanded vistas and distant horizons. Medieval London had focused on St Paul's, but Wren's plan had four focal points. They came from the past, and were the only links with the historic city that he allowed himself. In addition to St Paul's, there was a focus on the Customs House, the Exchange and London Bridge. From each of these radiated wide avenues, the geometric framework of the future city. The Exchange was the most important – a significant switch from the symbolic dominance of the Church in medieval society to that of the secular centre of a capitalist society, and one subservient to the sovereign of a nation state.

If the plan was to succeed a survey had to be completed, in which sites were redistributed, landowners compensated and land bought. Resources were unavailable for such radical changes to the existing city's properties, despite a survey having been completed, and the fact that needs were immediate. Although timber was replaced by brick and many narrow alleyways were eliminated, and although a new city did eventually arise it was not Wren's. Much later l'Enfant's Washington would reflect many of his ideas, but the values of the old City were too deeply etched in London's infra-structure for Wren's plans to succeed.

Almost three centuries later London faced another massive programme of rebuilding. Fire bombs had destroyed about a third of the City, and this seemed to be an opportunity to bring it into the twentieth century. But compared with Wren's ideas the 1944 plans of Holden and Holford were no more than an exercise in tidying and rationalizing the existing road system. The only radical departure was a ring-road designed to keep traffic out of the City. There was no vision of a new future. Small precincts were designed on a more detailed scale; for example, the Paternoster Square scheme opened up vistas of St Paul's. The whole scheme, cautious and pragmatic though it was, was never realized; it was defeated, as was Wren's, by vested interests in the existing pattern of land use. Even if the new roads had been built they could not have coped with the traffic that was only a generation ahead.

EMRYS JONES

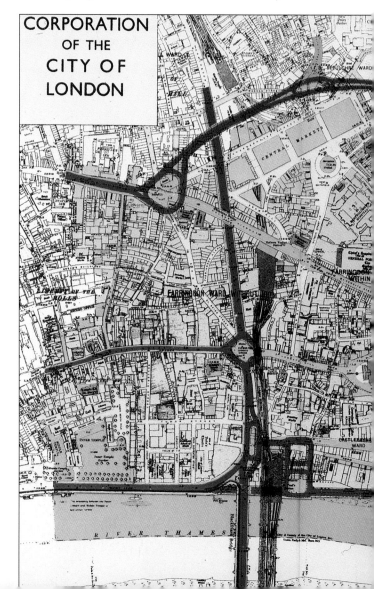

CORPORATION OF THE CITY OF LONDON

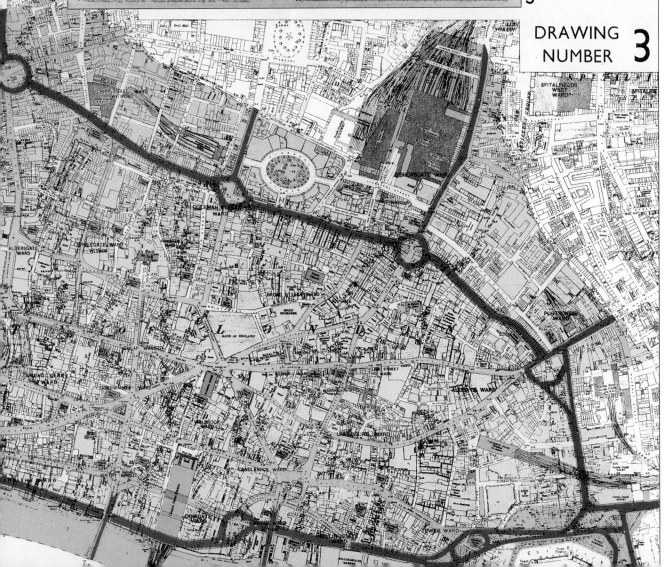

(Left) Sir Christopher Wren's plan for the reconstruction of London following the Great Fire, Guildhall Library.

(Below) Holden and Holford's plan for the reconstruction of London following the Second World War, 1944. Reconstruction in the City of London Report, 1944. Corporation of the City of London. Street improvements. Drawing No. 3.

FINANCE AND FLATTERY

In the early 1720s, John Warburton, Somerset Herald and Fellow of the Royal Society, decided to create a series of 'large, beautiful and most correct' maps of the English counties to replace the existing maps which were generally based on what he scornfully termed 'superficial surveys made near 200 years since' (only a slight exaggeration). Surveyed by Payler Smyth supposedly using triangulation, the maps also provided 'an historical as well as geographical account', by showing the 'Roman military wayes' and the stations among them. The end result, Warburton modestly claimed, would be the 'most usefull and ornamental [wall maps] for libraries, staircases, galleries, etc. that were ever published.'

This map supports some of his claims. It includes such features as the Highgate Ponds, 'Petersham New Park', Belsize and Hampstead Wells, that had only been developed since the 1690s. Hampstead Heath and many roads are shown for the first time. The dotted lines marking roads that passed through commons suggest direct observation, even if the plentiful road forks that end abruptly demonstrate that large areas remained unsurveyed. The most obvious features of the map are, however, the enormous number of

coats of arms – 724 in all – and the associated numbers within the map showing where the holders of these arms lived.

Warburton justified this on educational grounds and as a means for magistrates to detect, from the false arms on their seals, the 'counterfeit passes with which vagrants so frequently impose on the publick.' In fact his motive was to finance his maps by flattering often humbly born subscribers who paid an additional sum to have their arms engraved and their homes indicated in the company of the oldest and best families of the land (who may not have subscribed at all). The method had often been used before, but never with such abandon. Warburton's surveyors took subscriptions on the doorsteps and he caused outrage to his fellow heralds by engraving arms, regardless of whether or not their holders had any legal right to them.

Despite the furore at the time (and, in Warburton's defence, it should be remembered that there were few other means of financing such an expensive private undertaking), social historians have been the long-term gainers. The map is a visual index of snobbery and fashion, showing precisely where the rich and famous chose to say that they lived – the artist Sir Godfrey Kneller

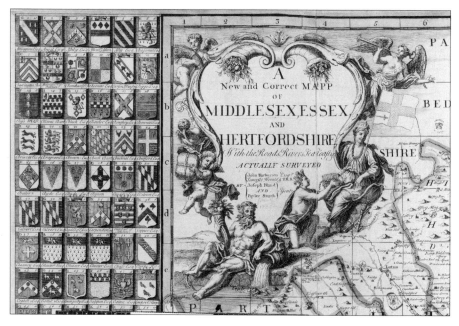

(Left and opposite) Two details from John Warburton, Joseph Bland and Payler Smyth's 'A New and Correct Mapp of Middlesex, Essex and Hertfordshire with the Roads, Rivers, Sea Coasts Actually Surveyed', 1725. Title cartouche and arms in the margin; London and the area to the North and West. British Library Maps 11.d.23.

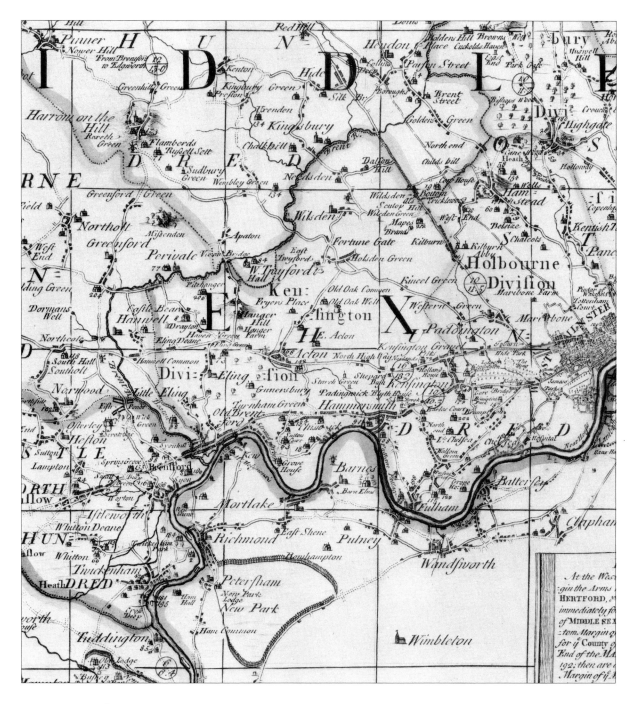

(103) in Whitton and near him the connoisseur Earl of Burlington (16) in Chiswick, with the Duke of Buckingham (162) on the site of Buckingham Palace. It also displays the social aspirations of numerous 'esquires' or mere 'gentlemen' and indicates what they felt was a good address: predominantly in the merchant valhallas of Highgate, Hampstead and Tottenham rather than on the aristocratic banks of the Thames. The mercantile bias is reflected in the cartouche showing an Indian, representing the Americas, presenting its riches to a blushing personification of London with a cherub carrying a bundle of merchandise, Father Thames and another cherub carrying symbols of plenty, and Fame trumpeting the metropolis's renown.

PETER BARBER

Town and Country

Less than two hundred years ago London's built-up area was fairly compact, shaped like an elongated sea-urchin west-east astride the Thames, but with spines extending along the main thoroughfares leading out of the city. These and the river itself attracted the dwellings of the better-off, who could afford to move out of walking distance from their work and were the catalyst converting rural Middlesex and Surrey into 'town'. As the map in the introduction to this chapter shows, London's shape altered considerably as it grew. The London of 1800 depended for

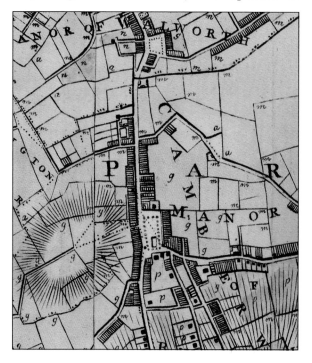

(Opposite) The area between Westminster and Norwood from Thomas Milne's Plan of the Cities of London and Westminster, 1800. Reproduced from Thomas Milne's Land Use Map of London & Environs in 1800, London Topographical Society, Publication Nos. 118 and 119. [British Library, K. Top. 6.95, plate III.]

(Above) Detail from Milne's map showing the land use lettering system.

KEY
a	arable, enclosed (yellow)
caf	common arable fields (brown)
g	enclosed market gardens (light blue)
m	enclosed meadow and pasture (light green)
ma	drained marshalnd (yellow green)
n	nurseries (orange)
o	osier beds or orchards (green)
p	paddocks and little parks (pink)
w	woodland (green, usually overlying dots)
	commons are left uncoloured

transport on the horse, sail and manpower. The main trading artery was still the river, especially for materials of relatively low value for their volume, such as manure and waste from central London which fertilized market gardens.

Thomas Milne's Plan of the Cities of London and Westminster was published in 1800 and is remarkable in a number of respects. Milne was an estate surveyor who took full advantage of the trigonometrical survey being carried out for the Ordnance Survey in compiling this map of land-use in and around London. It is more accurate and detailed than any precursor and is evidently consistent in the way it represents land-use, both urban and rural, of some 260 square miles (673 square km). Prior to this only individual estates had been mapped in such detail and with colouring which became standardized by common practice. Consequently it blazes a trail in mapping landed property, although it seems to have been suppressed as only one complete copy has survived.

Individual fields are marked where they are enclosed, and open or common fields are labelled: both are coloured according to their use. Different periods of building can be distinguished by four types of black pattern, with the linear extensions of the late eighteenth century closely hatched to suggest houses with narrow gardens. Agricultural uses are recorded by letter and colour in this example (see KEY) reproduced from the unique set in the British Library.

From Blackfriars Bridge in the east to Hammersmith in the west and Mitcham in the south, closely built-up ribbons give way to a mixture of market gardens and small parks, homes of an advancing wave of wealthy townsfolk. Away from the main roads south of the river arable and meadow predominate, but gardens north of Mitcham are devoted to lavender culture. The open fields of Battersea and Wandsworth differ because the former, nearer the city, is mixed with market gardening. North of the river, market gardening extends from the edge of Westminster, sometimes mixed with arable in common fields, all the way to Hammersmith. Nurseries are noteworthy around Brompton and osiers are scattered along the river's edge. Distinct villages and hamlets are yet to be joined up beyond Knightsbridge, but all are growing.

CHRISTOPHER BOARD

CHOLERA IN SOHO

As trade routes opened up between London and the East, cholera spread from India. The first epidemic hit London in 1831, with subsequent outbreaks in 1848, 1854 and 1866. The disease was universally dreaded because no known cure existed, and it had a fifty per cent mortality rate.

The use of maps to portray the spread of disease in urban areas had been established in the United States in the 1790s, as reports tracing the course of yellow fever outbreaks came to be accompanied by 'spot-maps' showing the location of infected households. As cholera established itself in Britain, a number of reports were produced which also carried maps showing the distribution of deaths from the disease, notably in Leeds and Oxford.

One of the most influential maps of this kind was that which appeared in Dr John Snow's essay, *On the mode and communication of cholera*, 2nd edition, 1855. Snow was one of the most distinguished medical men of his time – a pioneer of the scientific study of anaesthesia, Queen Victoria's obstetrician and vice-president of the Westminster Medical Society. At the time of the great epidemics of 1848–9 and 1854, most authorities believed that the disease was transmitted by an aerial poison produced by the putrefaction of bodies or vegetables. Snow was convinced that contaminated water was responsible, and in the first edition of his book, published in 1849, he expounded the theory that cholera was caused by 'a poison extracted from a diseased body, and passed on through drinking water which has been polluted by sewage.'

Both epidemics were particularly severe in Broad Street, Soho; in 1854, only twelve of the forty-nine households in the street escaped death. With the help of a map subsequently reproduced in the second edition of the report and illustrated here, Snow was able to demonstrate to the parish authorities that the pump was contaminated, and was a direct cause of the very high cholera rates in the vicinity. In consequence, the handle of the

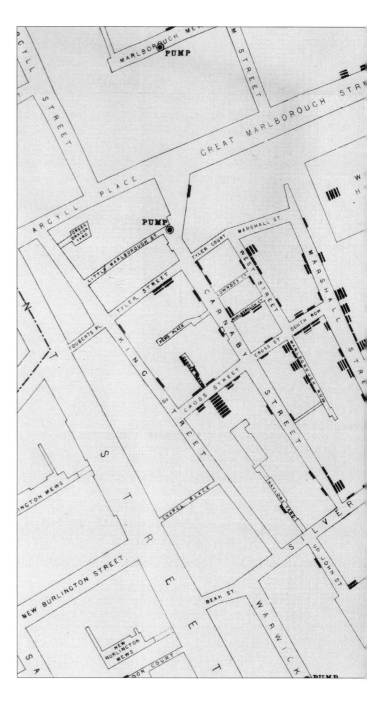

pump was chained. This action obliged the inhabitants to seek other, uncontaminated, water sources and helped to control the epidemic. The street was given its current name of Broadwick Street in 1936. The Newcastle-upon-Tyne public house was renamed the John Snow in 1956 in his honour. Ironically, Snow himself was a teetotaller.

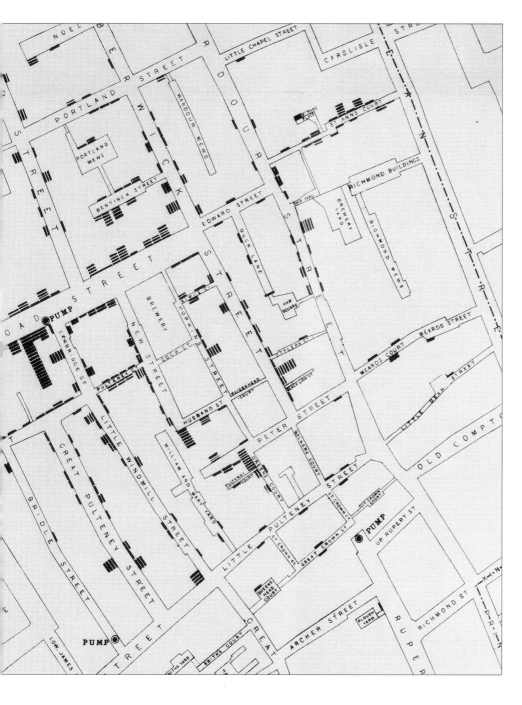

Map showing the distribution of households infected with cholera in Soho. From John Snow's On the Mode and Communication of Cholera, *second edition. Churchill, London, 1852. British Library 7560.e.67.*

Snow's contribution to cartography subsequently developed in two directions. As one of a growing number of sanitary reformers whose cause was made the more urgent by the outbreaks of fatal disease, Snow and his colleagues were significant in persuading the government to establish the local Boards of Health, whose brief was to ensure proper drainage and sewage systems. The Boards in their turn required adequate maps with which to plan urban improvements, and it was from this demand that the Ordnance Survey large-scale plans were born (see pp.156–7). The other mapping tradition was in the field of medical distribution mapping, culminating in the sophisticated, computer-plotted disease atlases of our own time. JAMES ELLIOT

POVERTY AND COMFORT

Charles Booth (1840–1916) was in many respects a highly unlikely social reformer and pioneer in the gathering of social statistics. The son of a Liverpool corn merchant with business interests in the animal skin trade, clothing and shipbuilding, he was nevertheless an enlightened employer who believed in state pensions for the aged and supported the aims of moderate trade unionism. He did, however, take strong issue with the Social Democratic Federation (a forerunner of the Labour Party) which, in 1885, published the results of its own surveys suggesting that twenty-five per cent of the population of London lived in poverty. Considering this figure to be not only factually wrong but an incitement to civil disorder, Booth set out to find the true figure for London poverty. The result was the massive seventeen-volume study, *Life and labour of the people of London*, published between 1889 and 1903.

Booth directed his team of researchers, paid for largely out of his own pocket, with the determination and pragmatism that perhaps only a successful businessman could command. His main sources of information were the notebooks kept by the School Board Visitors, and the 1881 Census. The job of the School Board Visitors was to keep a record, based on continuous home visits, of every family with children of school age in the London School Board area. The amount of detail recorded by Booth's team from interviews with School Board Visitors was astonishing given that they were surveying an area which, in total, had a population of over four million. Every house in every street was noted down and the occupants of each room counted. Particulars on the occupation and income of every working inhabitant, together with the number of children in each family, were recorded. To Booth's surprise (though not to such an extent as to shake his political convictions on how to deal with the problem), the survey showed that over 1.4 million people – nearly one-third (thirty-one per cent) of London's population – were living in poverty.

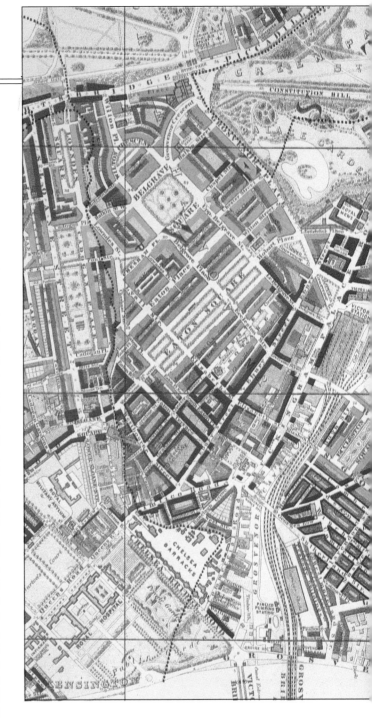

An innovative feature of Booth's work was the maps based on varying kinds and sizes of area in London. At street level Booth classified and coloured streets into one of seven types, 'according to the general condition of the inhabitants', as follows: the 'lowest grade', inhabited by occasional labourers, loafers and semi-criminals – the elements of disorder (black); 'very poor', inhabited by casual labourers and others living from hand to mouth (dark blue); 'standard poverty', inhabited by those whose earnings were small (light blue); 'mixed', with some poverty (purple);

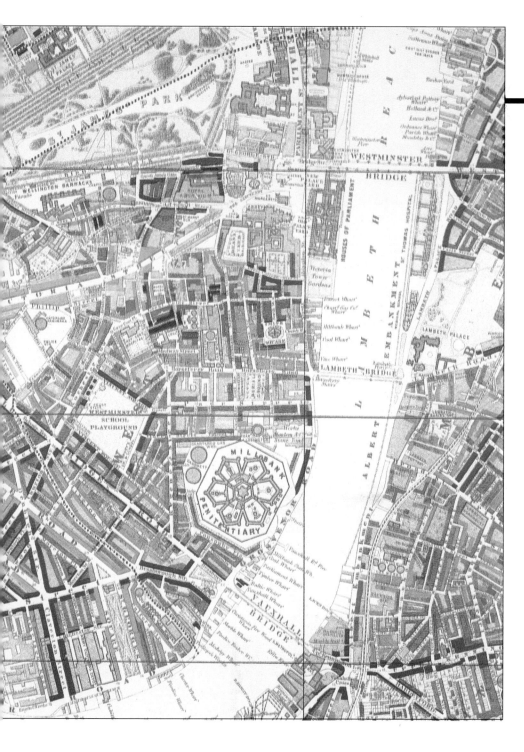

Detail from Charles Booth's 'Descriptive Map of London Poverty 1889'. South-Western sheet. Scale 1:10 560. Reproduced from London Topographical Society, Publication No. 130, 1984.

'working class comfort' mixed with lower middle class, small tradesmen with no servants (pink); 'well-to-do', with middle class families and one or two servants (red); and 'wealthy', inhabited by families with three or more servants and expensive houses (yellow). The map for Westminster and Pimlico is particularly interesting for the way in which it shows the entire range of his classification of streets, from the 'elements of disorder' around Great Peter Street near Westminster Abbey, the numerous mixed streets of poverty and comfort in Pimlico and around Vauxhall Square,

the 'wealthy' main throughfares of Belgrave Road, St George's Road and Victoria Street, and the upper class neighbourhoods of Belgravia and Eaton Square.

Remarkably, the map of poverty by Registration District produced by Booth with its band of poverty along both sides of the Thames to the east of the City and a circle of deprived districts around the City and the West End is not very different to the map of deprivation in Inner London in the 1980s (see pp.148–9).

JOHN SHEPHERD

DEPRIVATION 1981

The Census of Population, which is carried out every decade, is the most important source of information on the number, characteristics and location of the population of Great Britain and Northern Ireland. Its value comes from the fact that it covers every part of the country, is conducted in the course of a single week and hence provides a reliable 'snapshot' of the state of the nation at a point in time. It is based on small geographical areas or enumeration districts which can be built up neatly into local electoral wards, local authority districts, health authority areas, counties, regions and so on, and mapped. Because of these characteristics the census is a key source of information for government departments such as the Department of the Environment (DoE), which is responsible, among other things, for housing, town and country planning and the general economic well-being of towns and cities. In the late 1970s the DoE launched a radically new policy initiative focused on the deprived and declining areas of inner cities. Developed originally under the Inner Urban Areas Act 1978, the philosophy and focus of inner city policy has changed under different governments but, whatever the aims, such policies depend ultimately on targeting extra resources of cash, expertise and facilities to particular areas within cities. This in turn requires the use of census and other data to create suitable indicators of where exactly social and economic deprivation is located. Constructing these indicators is not, however, straightforward, partly because there is no universal agreement on what constitutes urban deprivation.

In a nationwide exercise using information taken mainly from the 1981 census, the DoE used eight different indexes of urban deprivation designed to assess the severity of poverty at the neighbourhood level. Calculations related to the census enumeration district, which was an area incorporating about two hundred households. Eight separate measures of deprivation for each area were combined to create a single index of multiple deprivation, based on unemployment, overcrowding, single-parent households, pensioners living alone, households lacking basic amenities such as a bath or indoor toilet, ethnic origin

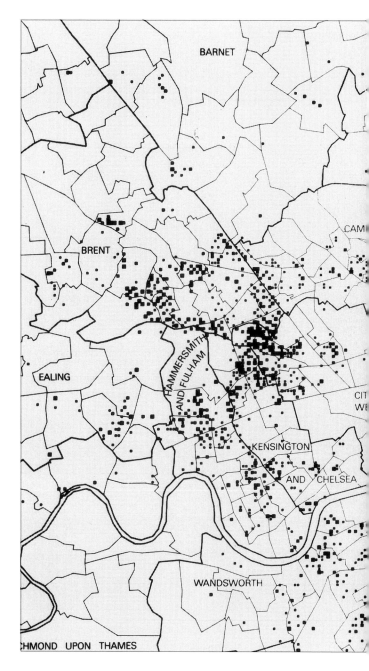

and a standardized mortality ratio. Deprivation 'scores' on this combined measure were grouped into three classes: extremely deprived, severely deprived and deprived, and mapped for major cities and other towns. The map shows the pattern of deprivation in 1981 for the inner and central areas of London. Here each map symbol is located at the centre of an enumeration district, the boundaries of which are not shown.

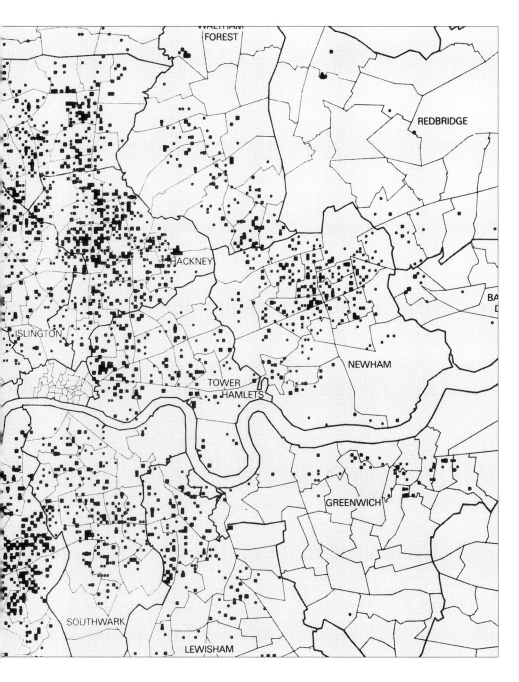

Detail from Greater London Urban Deprivation, Map 0086. Census Unit, Department of the Environment, 1983. Scale 1:50 000. Published by HMSO. Crown copyright.

Compared with Booth's maps of poverty at street level (see pp.146–7), the degree of detail is not so great but the overall pattern is easier to discern: extreme deprivation is concentrated in specific areas (North Kensington, Brixton, Hackney, Spitalfields and the northern parts of the London Borough of Newham); while enumeration districts classified as having severe (larger symbols) and less severe (smaller symbols) deprivation are scattered around these clusters and in a broad circle around the Cities of London and Westminster. Outside these areas isolated enumeration districts stand out as pockets of deprivation. As in Booth's time, the map reveals that the pattern of poverty in London has general and specific attributes, something which continues to challenge politicians and civil servants in their search for a solution. JOHN SHEPHERD

MOVING AROUND UNDERGROUND

When they were established, all London's major railway terminals were outside the core of the metropolis, so the Victorians realized they had to create another transport network to connect the terminal stations and to get travellers from train to work and leisure in the cities of London and Westminster. Built between 1863 and 1884, the first underground railways were steam-operated and shallow, but in the 1890s electric traction became a realistic proposition and so deeper tunnelling in the London clay underlying the capital was feasible. Full electrification soon followed. Some of the new railways, such as the Hampstead and City and South London, reached out into suburbs, while the Central London ran from the Bank of England to Shepherds Bush from 1900 and

was extended in 1908 to serve the Franco-British Exhibition, dubbed the White City, on Wood Lane.

The cat's cradle of nine partially interlocking underground lines presented a cartographic problem which was partly solved by bold colour printing. It appeared on the folding map, 'London's Electric Railways', which was roughly true to scale on a simplified street map. Naturally the postcard craze of the period was exploited to squeeze such a map on to the regulation 5½ × 2½ inch (14 × 8 cm) card. The one illustrated below served as an advertisement for an electrical engineering firm anxious to attract exhibition visitors to their own factory. In order to cope with this shape and size of card the north-south distances

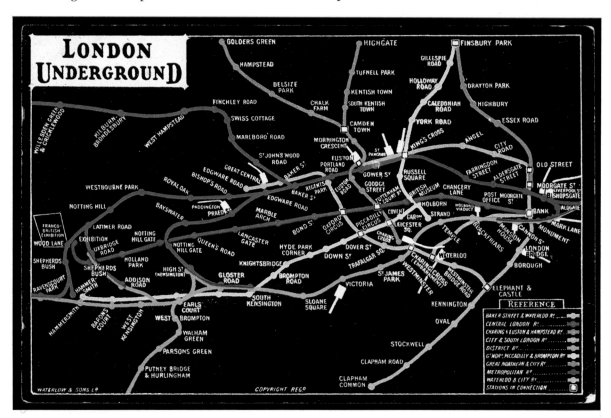

(Above) Postcard of London's Underground Railways, 1908. Waterlow Printers.

(Opposite) Henry Beck's first diagrammatic underground map, 1933. London Transport Museum postcard.

were reduced by up to half and the outlying parts of the system to Golders Green in the north and Clapham Common in the south were shortened.

As the Underground system grew, it became increasingly difficult to map. For the Wembley Exhibitions of 1924 and 1925 a special map portrayed only the central part of the system at a constant scale, with outer lines, including the one to Wembley, shown in a diagrammatic manner. When Henry Beck, a temporary draughtsman laid off by the Underground railway, redesigned the map between 1931 and 1933 he enshrined the earlier principle of exaggerating and elongating the central part of the system, but established the straight line diagram for which he is rightly famous. The Thames became a caricature and the Central Line became the new axis, running with only a couple of kinks from Ealing to Liverpool Street as if it were west to east. Later maps straightened this axis completely. Modifications have had to be made as each extension opened and each new line crossed the whole system, but Beck's concept has survived and has become the model for many other urban transport maps across the world.

Not only has this fundamentally different approach to design made the map more legible, it has made it more memorable. By employing horizontals, verticals and diagonals and pulling apart the lines and stations in the centre of London he made more room for station names. So successful has the design become that it is used as a symbol for London on T-shirts and other tourist souvenirs. It has also been used in advertisements to symbolize communication or interconnection. Indeed it has virtually replaced the true-to-scale maps, which can be found in most Underground stations, as the correct map because the latter look unfamiliar and therefore suspect, even wrong.

CHRISTOPHER BOARD

POSTAL LONDON

Letters cannot be transported, nor delivered, nor (in the past) charges evaluated without distances being known, together with the exact location of the addressee. For these reasons accurate maps are essential.

Vast quantities of mail are posted and delivered in London every day, and they must be transported and sorted en route. As a result, a number of large sorting offices have been built in the capital, most of which are connected by the Post Office's own automatic underground railway, completed in 1927. This enables the swift interchange of letters from one part of central London to another, and to some of the main railway stations for transporting to other parts of the country and abroad. The sorting offices are now mechanized and an ever greater percentage of mail is sorted automatically.

For delivery purposes London was divided into various sections (SE, NW, etc.) in 1856–7. This system formed the basis of the modern postcode, which can encompass anything from a whole street to one part of one building, if the company is a large user. Postcodes were first allocated in the 1960s.

The Royal Mail has always used maps to assist in transport and delivery and, indeed, was instrumental in commissioning some of the first accurate surveys of England and Wales and the standard-ization of measurements between places. However, before the sweeping reforms of the late 1830s, the Post Office was a slow, cumbersome business with a multi-layered administration which was reflected in the methods of posting, distribution and delivery. This can be seen in this section of Bowles's two-sheet plan of the Cities of London and Westminster with the Borough of Southwark, published in 1814. It was a commercially published map used by the Post Office to delineate delivery walks of what would now be described as postmen, but were then termed letter carriers. These carriers not only delivered the mail but also collected it, as the postage was normally paid by the addressee.

London has had its own collecting and delivery service since 1680. The London District Post originally cost a penny for one item. Later the area was divided; by the period of this map outlying districts within a radius of 12 miles (19 km) were charged threepence and central areas in a radius of 3 miles (5 km) twopence. However, this was for local mail. If a letter was to be sent to the country it had to be transferred to the General or Inland Office and charged differently. There was also a third system, termed the Foreign Office, which handled letters either going to, or coming from, abroad. The Foreign branch was the most limited in area of delivery, from Westminster to the Tower, and it was abolished in 1831. These three systems overlapped, each with their own receiving houses and letter carriers for delivery.

The areas of the walks on the Bowles map were hand-coloured and named – Sadler's Walk, Cadis's Walk, etc. Listed are the number of letter carriers for each walk – five Foreign carriers and ten Inland carriers for Sadler's Walk, with the local District Post excluded. Today, there are updated versions of the same thing, precisely marking each postman's walk, and these are changed occasionally after re-measurement or because of new buildings and resulting changes in occupation.

DOUGLAS MUIR

Bowles, Two-sheet plan of the Cities of London and Westminster with the Borough of Southwark, 1814. Post Office Archives.

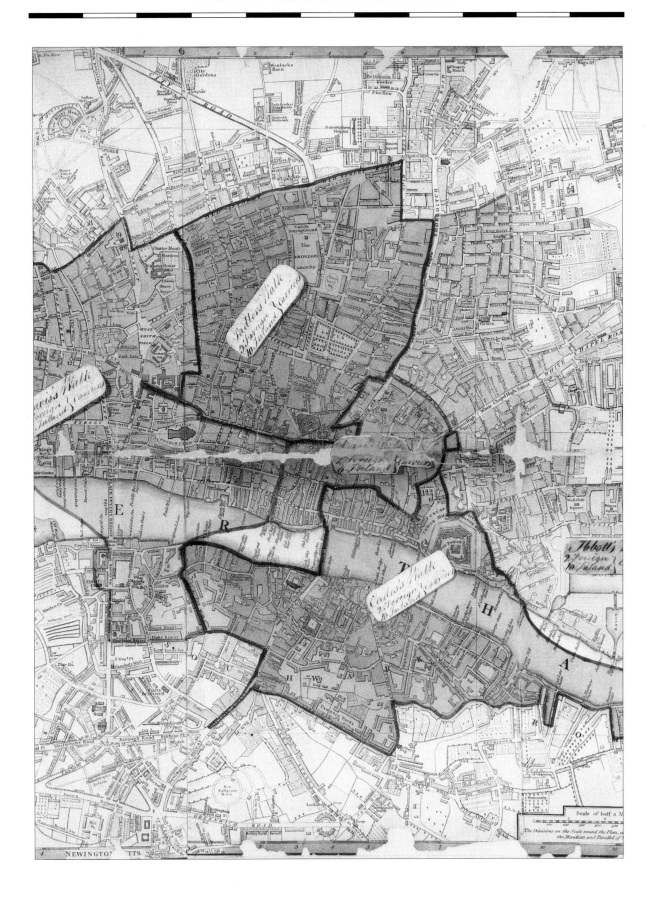

IN FALSE COLOUR

We are now familiar with images of clouds sensed from satellites on daily television weather forecasts. For some time now it has also been possible to use sensors in satellites to record the electro-magnetic energy, essentially from the sun, that is reflected off and absorbed by the varied surface of the earth. Several sensors using different but narrow wave-bands can record the energy transmitted by such objects as water, concrete, bare earth, grass and metallic objects. Using different parts of the spectrum enables the sensor to discriminate better between the elements which make up a landscape. However, 'resolution' (the physical size of the smallest feature that can be recognized) is an important constraint on what can be detected and therefore displayed on a graphic image of the ground. In general, the higher the resolution, the smaller the size of unit on the ground that can be detected. The Landsat 5 satellite view of London illustrated here has a spatial resolution of 90 × 90 feet (30 × 30 metres). But the French SPOT-1 system launched in 1986 has a spatial resolution down to 32 feet (10 metres) and is employed for the National Remote Sensing Centre's poster 'London from Space.' This means that while Landsat 5 can show us woods, Spot can show small clumps of trees, if not large individual ones. The time interval between successive passes over the same place is 18 days for Landsat but 26 days for Spot.

The image of London shown here looks unusual to the human eye because it uses colour film which does not register the blue wavelength in the visible spectrum but uses two red and one infra-red wavelength. These three bands, further modified or enhanced by computer processing, enable the viewer to distinguish many aspects of London's landscape quite clearly. As users of such images we have to sacrifice some realism in favour of the greater amount of information on types of land cover that is produced.

Not only can the strong linear features, such as the M25 and other motorways, be easily seen but so can other main roads and railways. The Thames is magenta, as are some other wet features carrying sediment (gravel pits and sewage farms west of Heathrow Airport), but cleaner

reservoirs in the same area show up as smooth purple masses surrounded by yellow concrete banks. Many golf courses with their distinctive green fairways can be seen, but in them and elsewhere around built-up London, woodland is generally lumpy purple; the same colour, with even greater lumpiness, characterises the outer suburbs such as leafy Beckenham and Bromley.

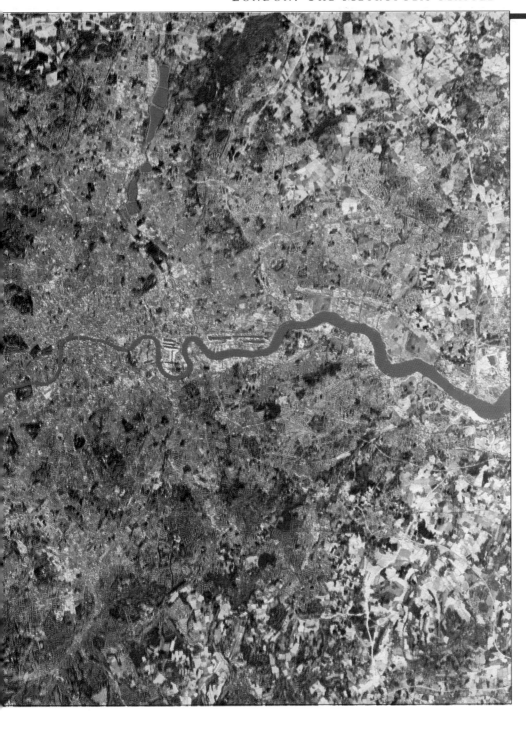

Detail from Satellite View of London *taken by Landsat on 21 October 1984. London Topographical Society, Publication No.134 (1986).*

Outer suburbia is also betrayed by a texture based on the wider spacing of its roads and avenues. As the eye moves towards the centre of London, the dappled purple and magenta of the inner suburbs give way to yellow and magenta as the spottedly rebuilt mixture of large blocks and remaining terraced houses mingle with industrial sites and offices. Neither the West End nor the City stands out, but the royal parks and squares of Bloomsbury allow one to make out where the city cores are. Even some of the Thames bridges can be discerned crossing the magenta ribbon (here reminiscent of the logo used for *EastEnders*). The colour may be false but the shapes and textures offered in satellite views are fascinating puzzles.

CHRISTOPHER BOARD

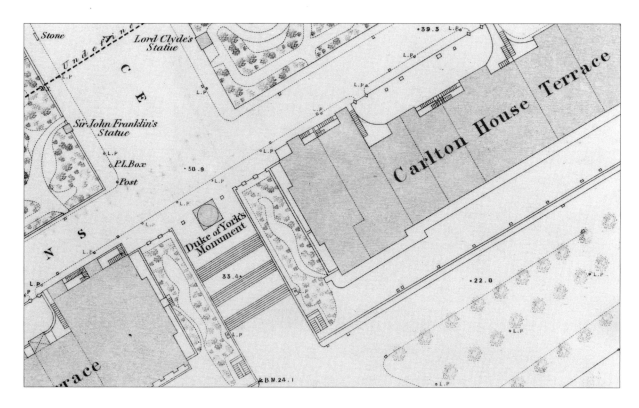

CAPITAL CLOSE UPS

The need for detail about what lies above and below the pavements of London and other cities is not new, and there has always been a direct correlation between the degree of accuracy required and the density of development and of property values. Enormous scales of up to 10 feet to the mile were used in a programme of urban map-making which started in the 1840s and continued for the next half-century.

Unlike other cities which were largely surveyed at the 10-feet scale, London's maps were produced at 5 feet to the mile (1:1056) and, when the survey of the provincial areas came to an end towards the close of the nineteenth century, London's large-scale maps continued to be produced.

In due course, over eight hundred sheets covered London at the 5-feet scale, and this set of maps, later revised, became the standard London series of the Victorian era for planning and administration. These maps, with their wealth of detail and finely executed engraving, are regarded as being among the most beautiful of the early Ordnance Survey products, and are primary sources

for historians and even modern planners, who still find the maps invaluable.

Today's large-scale mapping of the capital (and everywhere else in the country) is based upon new mapping introduced by Ordnance Survey after the Second World War – at 50 inches to the mile (1:1250) for urban areas, and at smaller scales for less developed countryside. Being in computer form, a whole series of freedoms are offered to the map customer; no longer are we restricted to fixed sheetlines, to scale of presentation, or even to a standard specification of content. In essence the computer will hold a seamless map of the nation from which any part may be extracted at will.

This modern map is known as Superplan. It is the harbinger of a new look and style for Ordnance Survey mapping of urban areas, designed for immediate use, constantly updated, and giving customers what they want in an increasingly customer-orientated age. And while the customers may admire the beauty and fastidiousness with which Victorian England was mapped by Ordnance Survey, it is the unfussy, accurate and

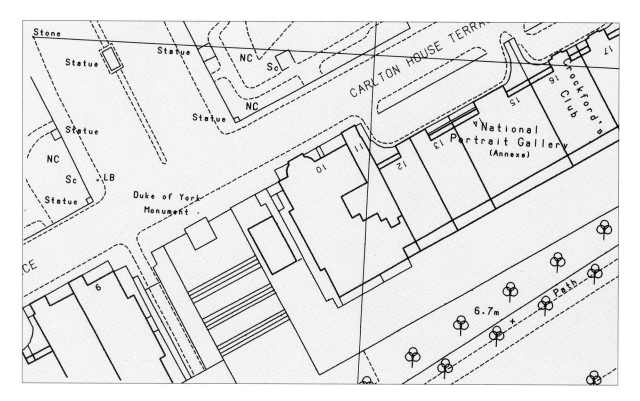

available map, with this week's revision, which they now want and can get.

The extracts shown above illustrate the differences and similarities between the large-scale mapping of the capital in Victorian times and the Superplan series of the 1990s. The 1:1056 map of London on the opposite page shows an immense amount of interior detail in buildings and gardens, and the characteristic copperplate lettering of the early conventional maps. Minute street furniture, such as lamp-posts, letter boxes and drain covers, is shown but, despite the very large scale, no house numbers have been added to the buildings. Furthermore, the image is split between two sheets.

In the Superplan extract revised the day before this copy was made, minor detail such as garden paths and flower beds have been generalized and simplified, and vegetation has been reduced to brief descriptions such as NC (for non-coniferous trees). Non-essential street furniture has been removed and only party divisions are shown within buildings. The National Grid reference system has been added, as well as house numbers, and the stipple infill once shown in buildings has been replaced by enhanced building outlines, generated by the computer. Unlike the

(Opposite) Detail showing Carlton House Terrace and the Duke of York's Steps from Ordnance Survey, Five Foot Plans. London Sheet VII.72, and Sheet VII.73, both surveyed in 1871 and published in 1874.

(Above) The same area shown in Ordnance Survey, Superplan, 1992. Crown copyright.

early maps of London, Superplan can be altered on the spot to suit the customer's needs and – as here – it can be centred on the area required. This copy was produced in ten minutes from the time the National Grid reference was handed to the print operator.

And this is only today's offering. Tomorrow we will be able to recognize not only the lines on the map as fences, rivers, pavements and so on, but the areas they contain – properties, open spaces, planning zones, and the like. Tomorrow's customers will be able to specify colour to highlight their particular interests, and to link specific items on the map to a variety of other related information, even if, like developers' plans, it is still on the drawing board.   JOHN LEONARD

ON THE ROCKS

Sometimes accurate maps can make all the difference between life and death. The distinction between knowing your whereabouts and being lost is often uncertain; and the greater the uncertainty, the greater the risk. When geographical knowledge was very limited, it was quite common for frightening, half-remembered or even imagined monsters to be added to maps to warn future travellers of the risks involved. But it is equally likely that maps have been improved by travellers returning with new and more accurate information. In recent years increased environmental awareness has resulted in accurate charting of natural hazards like ice, fog, storms, tides and earthquakes. Such 'risk' maps are continually updated and reassessed as new information comes to light. While we cannot claim that tides, for example, are no longer dangerous, they are certainly less dangerous than they were.

Risk assessment is a human judgement. As a result there will be many different interpretations of what consititutes a risk, let alone how severe it is. So maps based on risk assessment clearly depend completely on the interpretations and motives of their makers. For example, the risk of being burgled varies from dwelling to dwelling, street to street and area to area. Individuals will perceive this information in different ways. The police, insurance companies and estate agents – all interested parties – will divide the areas up and base their activities accordingly. Insurance companies have often produced risk maps assessing the danger of subsidence, fire, explosion, flood or earthquake.

Different kinds of risk call for different types of maps, even if they are produced for the same people. Road maps, for instance, are made to assist road users, but a map assessing the quality of the road surface will differ immensely from a map of major road congestion. Travellers often require special risk maps because of the variety of information required. Travel at sea brings many risks: wrecks, rocks and sandbanks, currents, traffic, old ammunition dumps, weapons-testing areas, all essential knowledge for the navigator. Air space has to be mapped carefully, and because of the distances travelled co-ordination of

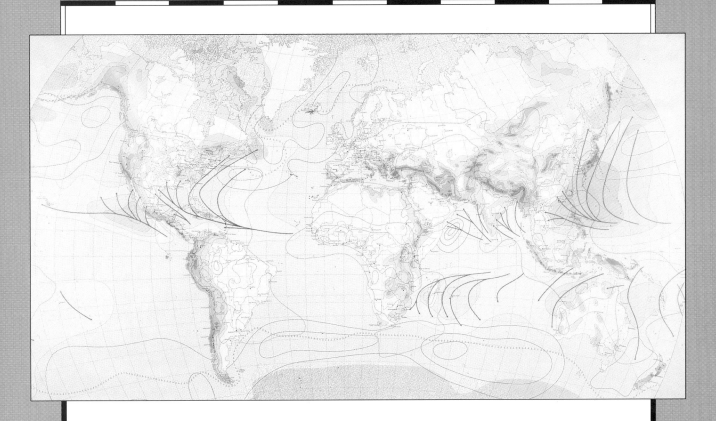

Münchener Rückversicherungs-Gesellschaft. 'World Map of Natural Hazards' (Munich: JRD Karlografische Verlagsgesellschaft Mb, second edition 1988). Amongst other things the map shows the risk from earthquakes, tsunamis (tidal waves) and volcanic activity (yellow and orange – the darker, the more at risk); hazard from windstorms (pink, with pink arrows to show direction), risk of sea-ice, icebergs and sea fog (blue speckles).

information at an international level is essential, presenting huge logistical problems.

Risk maps therefore are compiled from a variety of sources: some from past observations, others from interpretation and inference. As for all maps, the past is a guide to the future. The clear intention of those who compile risk maps is to warn, protect and motivate people to cope with the uncertainties and partial knowledge of what lies ahead in time and space. CHRISTOPHER BOARD

AT THE EDGE OF THE WORLD

The world of the medieval European was centred on his or her own region and on the Mediterranean, the heart of the classical world, the main stage for the Bible and the destination for pilgrimages and crusades. Beyond that 'civilized' core there were varying degrees of danger, even if it was generally agreed that Paradise was to be found at the easternmost end of Asia.

Where, in the eleventh century, a map-maker could get away with a vague reference to an abundance of lions in north-eastern Asia and a picture of one (see p.29), two hundred years later he was expected to depict the semi-human occu-

pants of these remote areas whom Christians had the duty to convert. The cartographers relied on the writings of ancient authors, notably Pliny the Elder, medieval travellers and classical legends as translated, copied, inserted into encyclopaedic works and illustrated in texts over the centuries. Despite the inevitable misunderstandings, magnificent maps such as the Hereford *Mappamundi* of about 1280 and the smaller Psalter World Map (see p.23) were created.

It was generally accepted that the most awesome creatures lived in the deserts of Ethiopia on the southern fringes of the known world (i.e. the

(Left) Anonymous, fragment of world map, c.1290 showing monsters in Africa. Duchy of Cornwall.

(Opposite) Pir ben Haci Mehmed ('Piri Reis'), fragment of world map, 1513 showing monsters in South America. Topkapi Serail Museum, Istanbul. R 1633 (muk).

right side). They are artistically depicted on this fragment of a world map of about 1290 from the binding of a manorial court book (opposite). A few of these creatures were notably benevolent, like the loyal and patient elephant, the handsome, gentle and sweet-breathed panther ('pantera') and the gold-digging ants ('formice'). Others were mildly amusing or could anyway be disregarded, such as the timid parandrus (top left) that blended into its surroundings like a chameleon when frightened, or the archabatite who, in this version, wandered around naked and on all fours. Some were impressive, like the troglodites, cave-dwellers who ran so fast that they could catch wild beasts. Others, though, were distinctly bad news. Hyenas were cunning and murderous, catofeplases killed humans merely by looking at

them (but luckily their heads were so heavy that they usually looked at the ground) while, as the illustrations show, the cannibalistic andropophagi and the dog-headed cynomolgi liked nothing better than a juicy human thigh . . .

These monsters took a long time a-dying. Many disappeared from Africa after 1492, only to reappear on sixteenth-century maps showing the new frontier in South America. Here they were joined by cannibals and new monsters, such as the Patagonian (literally 'big feet') giants. Giants also appeared in the mists of the Scottish Highlands in the maps of Mecator. As scares of landings of Martians in this century demonstrate, related beliefs endure to this day, although cartographers have retired from the fray.

PETER BARBER

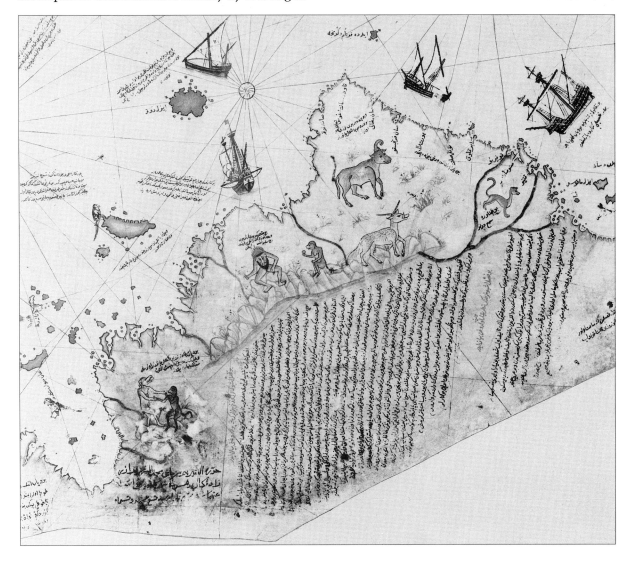

TRADITIONAL WARNINGS AND COASTAL DANGERS

The Catalan Atlas of 1375 is arguably the most beautiful of all surviving medieval maps, which is fitting as it was part of the collection of Charles V of France. The central third of the atlas is illustrated here, but not shown are the introductory panels with text and diagrams, or the eastward extension which turns it from a chart of the Mediterranean into a map of the world. Once the lavish ornamentation is stripped away, the displayed portion is no more or less than a standard portolan chart.

Derived from the Italian word *portolano* (meaning written sailing directions), such charts originated in the thirteenth century. Another French king, Louis IX, is considered to have made the first recognized reference to such a portolan chart when sailing off the coast of Sardinia in 1270. Completing the French connection, the earliest surviving chart, the Carte Pisane (named after the place of discovery) is, like the Catalan Atlas, preserved in the Bibliothèque Nationale in Paris.

The practical advantages of the portolan charts were readily apparent for those navigating in the Mediterranean and Black Seas. Indeed, by the mid-fourteenth century Aragonese ships were required by law to carry them. The scale of these charts was not large, as it was held back by the twin restrictions of the size of a calf's skin and the need to extend (at least) from Ireland to the Black Sea. So although some rocks and shoals could be shown (by crosses and dots), the detailed knowledge of the hazards of a particular harbour approach would be committed to the Captain's memory. Instead, the chart offered distance, using a scale of old marine miles, and directions through the complex web of rhumb lines (the lines connecting compass points) constructed around an unstated centre circle. Perhaps the charts' most important function was to act as an aid for remembering sequences of place names,

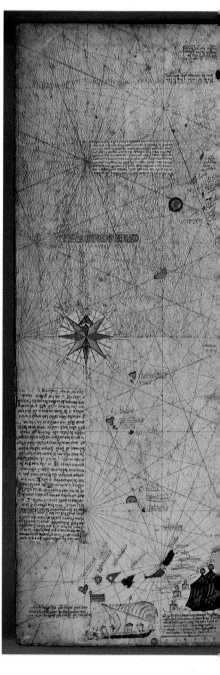

Panels 5–8 (of 12) from the Catalan Atlas, *c.1375. Bibliothèque Nationale, Paris. MS Esp. 30.*

listing about a thousand of them around the Mediterranean and Black Sea coasts. Even apparently decorative features, such as flags flying from town symbols, helped a Christian sailor to avoid straying into a Muslim-held port.

The portolan charts appeared almost fully formed. It remains a mystery where precisely they came from. Their highly recognizable outlines are a striking contrast to the landsmen's

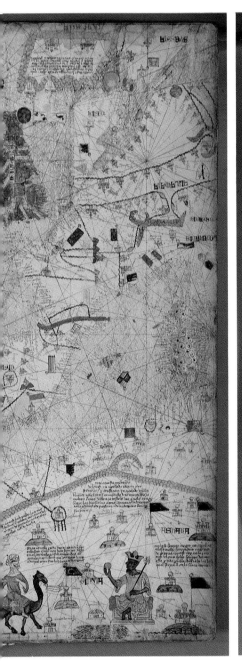

maps of the time. Over the centuries after 1300, charts and atlases were produced from a variety of different Mediterranean ports. Unlike repeatedly copied texts, the charts' outlines were reproduced faithfully and the place names refreshed with new information until a marked deterioration in both aspects becomes visible in the sixteenth century. For no other types of map is it true that a production of 1650 is routinely inferior to one of 1350.

The Catalan Atlas was never intended to be used at sea but the way its sheets were attached to panels foreshadows the typical productions of some of the last practitioners, a group of seventeenth-century English chartmakers working beside the Thames. Typically, they fixed their charts to hinged boards, ideal for stowing away on board ships.

TONY CAMPBELL

FOR THOSE IN PERIL ON THE SEA

If an early topographical map was wrong the traveller might get lost; the inaccuracies of sea charts frequently cost lives. The chart that, in its original form, was itself a contributory cause of one of the greatest natural disasters to a British fleet recorded that sad event in its second edition. The maritime survey that Captain Greenville Collins published in 1693 as *Great Britain's Coasting Pilot* included the first chart of the Isles of Scilly with any pretensions to accuracy. Where previous efforts, dating back a century before to the work of the Dutch pilot, Lucas Janszoon Waghenaer (see pp.166–7), showed a highly schematic arrangement of the islands, Collins' outlines match with the modern chart well.

The problem was not in the inner relationships of the islands and rocks that make up the Scillies but rather in the geographic positioning of the group as a whole, specifically their latitude. Confusion about their correct position led to the marginal latitude indications being removed altogether from the detailed chart of the Scillies group at a very early stage. But on the smaller-scale sheet that set the Scillies into their Cornish context Collins placed the most southerly hazard, the Western Rocks, nine minutes of latitude (or nine nautical miles) too far to the north, and it was those same Western Rocks that would claim the *Association*, flagship of Sir Cloudesley Shovell, plus two other ships (a total of two thousand men)

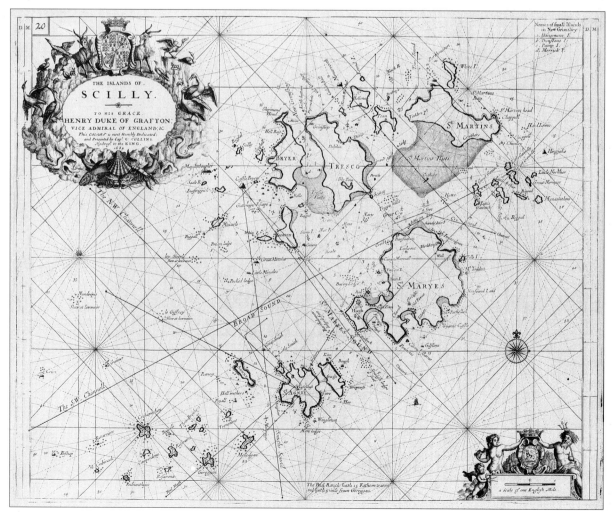

on an October night in 1707. When the second edition of Collins' atlas was issued in 1722 the fateful Gilstone Rock, on which the ships were wrecked, was inserted, with the sombre note beside it 'Sr Clously lost'.

The effect of pushing northwards the latitude of the Scillies and, to a lesser extent that of the Lizard (which together guarded the western approaches for British vessels returning to home waters), gave a false sense of confidence. In an era of imprecise navigational instruments and unsophisticated techniques, it was preferable to exaggerate marine hazards rather than underplay them. The thick scattering of wrecks around the Cornish and Scillonian coasts is a grim testimony to the dangers of those waters.

Latitude could be obtained relatively easily from the sun or stars (provided, of course, they were visible). A ship's master would have reasonable confidence in his north-south position, and trust in the stated latitudes on his chart. Longitude, on the other hand, was a function of elapsed time from the point of departure and clocks were incapable of measuring that with any accuracy. Common practice, therefore, was to arrive at the correct north-south position and then 'sail down a latitude'. The trick was to time landfall for daylight hours, as Admiral Shovell failed to do. The west coast of Australia took its toll too, not because of inadequate charts but from an underestimate of the long Indian Ocean passage. Only with John Harrison's chronometers of the late eighteenth century – impervious to heat, moisture and the ship's roll – was the longitude problem finally solved. Even in August 1992 inadequate charts were blamed when the *QE II* ran aground off Cape Cod!

TONY CAMPBELL

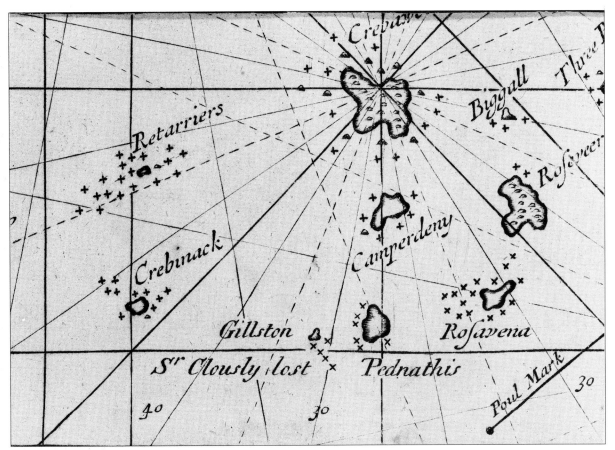

(Opposite) Chart 20 (the Isles of Scilly), Captain Greenville Collins, Great Britain's Coasting Pilot, *London 1693. British Library 7 TAB 108.*

(Above) Detail from a later, coloured edition of the same map. British Library.

SAFETY FOR ALL

From the end of the thirteenth century or even earlier, Mediterranean sailors were using charts for navigation. These so-called portolan charts were skilfully drawn with inks of different colours on prepared sheep or goatskins by cartographers mainly living in Genoa, Venice and (perhaps a little later) Majorca and Barcelona. During the course of the fifteenth century these cartographic skills reached Portugal and by the early years of the sixteenth century the Portuguese cartographers Pedro Reinel and his son Jorge were drawing Atlantic charts.

At that time the sailors of north-west Europe were largely ignorant of the use of charts; for generations the courses and time taken to reach one point of land from another with favourable winds were passed down from father to son – a form of navigation known as 'capeing'. So when the northern seaman saw the portolan charts aboard visiting Mediterranean vessels they ridiculed the idea of using goatskins for navigation.

However, an intelligent and experienced sea pilot named Lucas Janszoon Waghenaer, who saw the potential in developing the portolan chart, lived in the leading North Netherlands seaport of Enkhuizen. The Dutch already had experience in printing, book-binding and engraving and Waghenaer realized that if seacharts could be engraved on copper he could then sell to seamen as many copies as he wished to strike from the plates. He set about collecting hydrographic information from his many sea-going compatriots and engaging draughtsmen and engravers. In the course of 1584–5 Waghenaer published his great pilot book, *Spieghel der Zeevaerdt*, containing printed sailing directions and forty or so charts covering the coasts and principal ports of western Europe from Norway to Spain. Being a skilful pilot himself, Waghenaer fashioned his charts to meet the needs of the navigator. To the symbols 'x' for a submerged and dangerous rock and '±' for a safe anchorage, already in use on portolan charts, he added further images to represent buoys, beacons, church spires, windmills, conspicuous trees and so on. He included on the charts views of the coastline as seen from seaward, enabling the navigator to recognize land-

falls. Perhaps most importantly, he introduced on to his charts figures showing depth soundings at the time of half tide in anchorages and over harbour bars. The four charts of the entire coast of Brittany are not only practical seamen's charts, but are very beautiful.

Spieghel der Zeevaerdt was an immediate success. The title page, which displayed the use of the currently available navigational aids, became

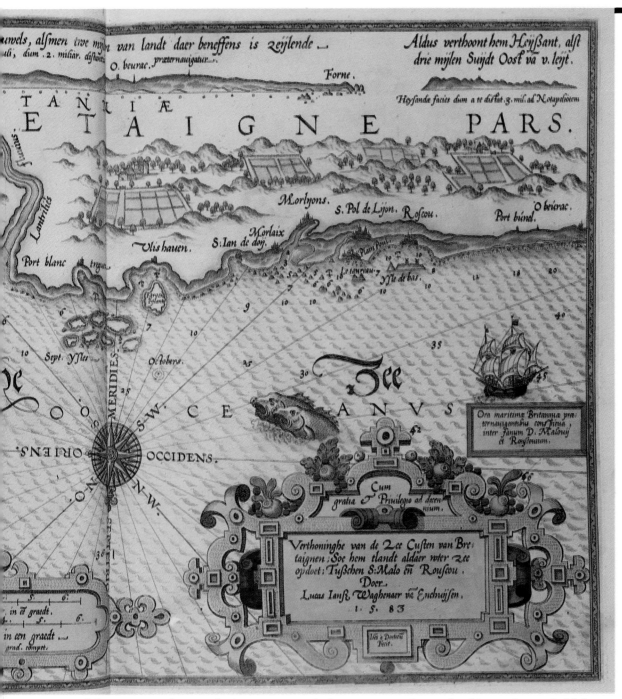

widely recognized. Translations were made into several European languages including Latin (1586), then the common language of educated Europeans and, in 1588 – with half an eye on use in the war with Spain – English. So popular did the book become that for the next century all illustrated pilot books were commonly called 'waggoners' in tribute to Waghenaer.

REAR ADMIRAL STEVE RITCHIE

'Zee Custen beghinnende van S. Malo tot voor de haven van Ronscou', in Lucas Janszoon Waghenaer Spieghel der Zeevaerdt. *Leyden: Christoffel Plantin, 1585. British Library C.8.b.1, Chart 6.*

FINDING A SAFE HAVEN WHEN AT SEA

For most people, provided they holiday outside the Mediterranean, the significance of tides relates primarily to the amount of beach left available and the timing of sandcastle construction.

For sailors, on the other hand, tides remain a constant concern when navigating in coastal waters. Tides have always been most crucial when entering or leaving port, whether it be a

Guillaume Brouscon, untitled pilot's manual. Brittany, c.1540–50. British Library Add. MS 22721. Ireland and England Sheet.

sailing ship approaching an undredged entrance centuries ago or a supertanker needing the extra draught of high tide to avoid running aground. The fortnightly springs offer additional water at high tide, but also extra rock hazards at low water.

Today's skipper is provided with tide tables – no more difficult than checking the time of the last bus home – but earlier sailors had to work out 'the times of tides' for themselves. By the eighth century the Venerable Bede had commented on the relationship between the moon and the tides, giving a monthly cycle in which each tide was deemed to be 45 minutes later than the last. Armed with this knowledge, it was possible to codify the tidal information for an individual port. This was necessary because the moon's effect was unequally delayed by local circumstances, for example the narrowing effect of the funnel shape of the English Channel. However, the time of high water on the day of a full (or new) moon was predictable and the so-called 'establishment of the port' was devised to convey this. First found in the *Catalan Atlas* of 1375 (see pp.162–3) this provided selective ports with a coded reference in the form of a compass direction. This was logical, given the maritime practice of estimating daytime hours from the sun's position. Hence East meant 6 a.m., South noon, West 6 p.m., and so on.

The graphic process was taken a stage further in the pocket-sized handwritten atlases produced by the Breton, Guillaume Brouscon, in the mid-sixteenth century. Just as many modern road signs avoid the problem of language, or indeed of literacy, so Brouscon imaginatively combined charts with tidal information. Using compass roses as clocks, he ran a line from each significant port to the compass direction denoting the hour of high tides on a day of new or full moon. A later refinement by the Elizabethan Thomas Hood would place a letter, representing the compass point, by the port concerned. A still more direct approach, and one that survived into this century, was Edmund Halley's use of a Roman numeral to state the time of high water (VI.5 being 6.30 a.m. or p. m., for example).

Knowing the 'establishment' would not of itself give all the answers. Though an early sailor usually kept track of the moon, Brouscon and others provided a further table, with Golden Numbers and other delights, from which the date of that month's full moon could be calculated. A little elementary mathematics would add or subtract the necessary three-quarters of an hour for each elapsed or anticipated day. Compressed in this way into a handful of small pages, Brouscon's pilot's manual gave sufficient explanation, tables and charts for most navigational needs.

TONY CAMPBELL

DECEPTION IN THE DESERT

As long as there is an easy way up, there can be few features on a map more welcome to navigators than an escarpment running east-west when travelling south. It provides a positive position line. The northern escarpment of the Hamada el Homra in the Tripolitanian desert is one such example. The Italian-based 1:400 000 map showed features in great detail down as far as latitude N 31° 40', but thereafter indicated and, in some cases named, only the main dry water courses and heights or cliffs shown by brown hatch marks. There was no mention of the extent to which they could be relied upon. The task of a small expedition of two vehicles was to find the vehicle pass

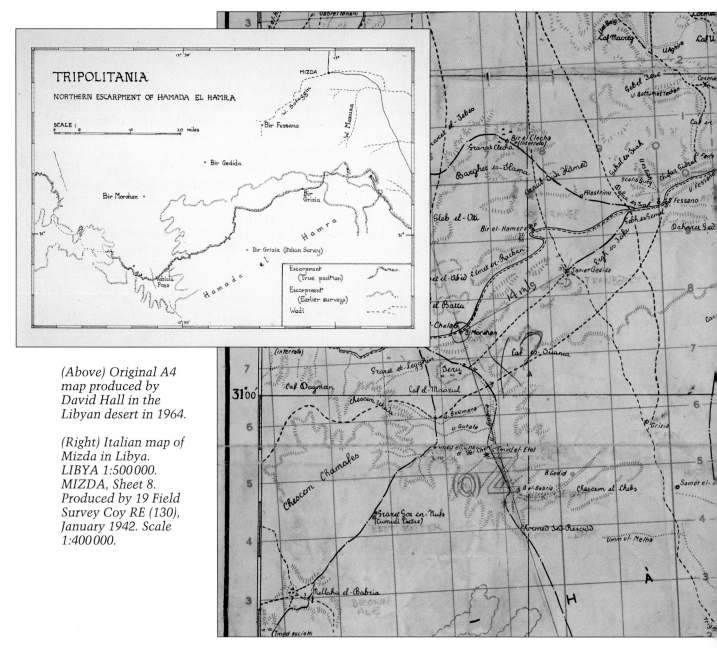

(Above) Original A4 map produced by David Hall in the Libyan desert in 1964.

(Right) Italian map of Mizda in Libya. LIBYA 1:500 000. MIZDA, Sheet 8. Produced by 19 Field Survey Coy RE (130), January 1942. Scale 1:400 000.

up the escarpment on to the Hamada el Homra and explore the flat and featureless plateau to the south.

Trusting our map and instruments we set a course of 158 degrees on the sun compass from the known point of the well of Bir Morahan, and the map made it clear that the cliffs of the escarpment should appear close and to the east of our route after about 3 miles (6 km). It seemed strange that there was no sign of that escarpment from Bir Morahan. We had driven the right distance, but

there was no sign of any cliffs anywhere apart from a slight blue haze of a possible escarpment at least 9 miles (15 km) further south. The well's position was now far behind us and there appeared little or no relationship between the map and the ground. This was not a matter of being 'lost' because, had the map been a skeleton plotting chart showing only lines of latitude and longitude, with Bir Morahan marked, we would have known our geographical position. Time prevented a search, and so striking on a new course in an easterly direction the expedition eventually found the escarpment which was indeed an extension of the blue haze.

Bewildered by the map, I returned with a guide, Ahamid bin Dau, and two camels and, having bought sufficient simple supplies to complete a compass traverse of part of the escarpment, we headed first for the same well of Bir Morahan, intent on identifying the error on the map. Aerial photographs provided some helpful detail, and apart from nearly losing our camels one night, we ended the journey ten days later with the material for a revised map of part of the escarpment, adding to it two years later after a further camel survey. The resulting simple map showed up the 15-mile (25-km) error of the Italian map, and it was used with delight by travellers in subsequent years.

When faced with similar broad-brush hatching which marked a possible southern part to an escarpment and stony upland off the north-east of the Tibesti, we used the map with caution, but discovered and surveyed some 70 miles (112 km) of the south and eastern part of what we named the Hamada el Akdamin ('Stony Desert of the Ancient Ones') because of the profusion of neolithic remains. Some desert maps show on them the enticing words 'Relief data incomplete', with nothing to assist the navigator. On the other hand the detailed maps of the Wahiba Sands in Oman show line upon line of long dunes with valleys between them, so the navigator can rarely have much idea which valley is which. Detail of such features as lone trees is essential, just as in south-east Libya the lone archenu tree marked on the map, a short distance away from the massif of Archenu, identifies the position without doubt. The marking of selected small features can therefore be a vital ingredient to good desert maps.

DAVID HALL

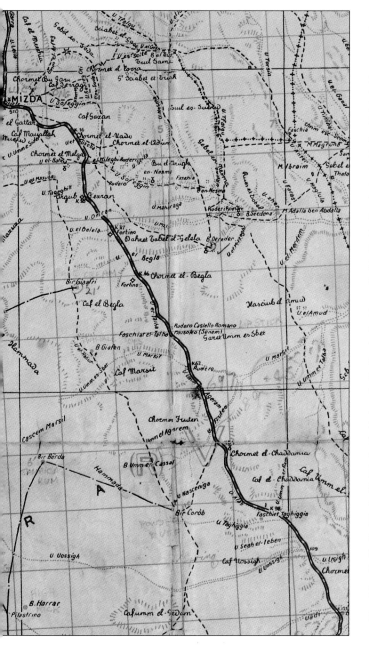

MAPPING EARTHSHOCKS: PAST AND FUTURE

The unexpectedness of earthquakes, and their extreme violence, leave people feeling utterly helpless. There are rarely forecasts or warnings, while the brief duration of shocks means that little can be done to reduce harm during an event. Little wonder that earthquakes were the subject of numerous mythical explanations and, to many, they remain archetypal 'acts of God'.

Mapping patterns of seismic threat to establish which areas are relatively safe and which are most prone to intense shaking is one way of coping with this menace. Once these patterns have been established, planning measures and building codes can be sensibly applied to limit future losses. Mapping earthquake hazards requires both observation and understanding. The non-mythical study of earthquakes extends back centuries, but the invention of sensitive recording instruments (seismographs) and the development of a global network of earthquake observatories has led to the increasingly accurate recording of seismic events. Thousands of shocks are now recorded each year and a clear global pattern has emerged, with well-defined belts of intense activity (seismic zones) separating areas of less frequent disturbance and regions with little earthquake activity (aseismic areas).

The actual occurrence of shocks, however, is an inadequate guide to seismic risk as many are so small as to have no impact. The potential for damage depends on the size of the shock as measured by magnitude scales (e.g. the Richter scale) and many local factors. It is the impact of the earthquake, therefore, as measured by the twelve-point Modified Mercalli intensity scale, that is important. The maximum intensity is usually recorded at the epicentre, immediately above the focus, and the strength declines outwards through zones of roughly equal impact (defined by isoseimal lines). The recorded impact of the famous 1906 San Francisco Earthquake is shown

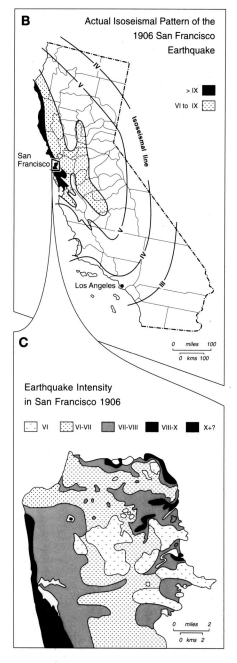

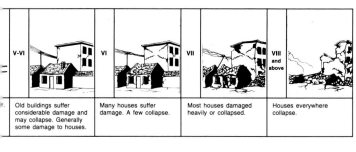

V-VI	VI	VII	VIII and above
Old buildings suffer considerable damage and may collapse. Generally some damage to houses.	Many houses suffer damage. A few collapse.	Most houses damaged heavily or collapsed.	Houses everywhere collapse.

D

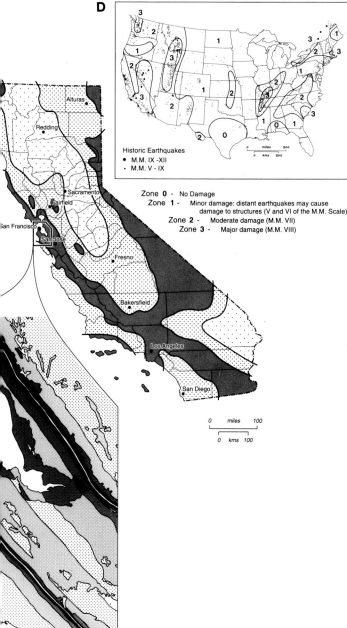

Historic Earthquakes
● M.M. IX -XII
· M.M. V - IX

Zone 0 - No Damage
Zone 1 - Minor damage: distant earthquakes may cause damage to structures (V and VI of the M.M. Scale)
Zone 2 - Moderate damage (M.M. VII)
Zone 3 - Major damage (M.M. VIII)

here and reveals the characteristically irregular pattern due to topographic and geological factors. The enlargement for central San Francisco shows much greater complexity, reflecting the variability of ground conditions and construction.

Earthquake prediction, or the identification of likely levels of threat, relies heavily on the notion that the past is the guide to the future. In this way, detailed mapping of earthquake impacts over time reveals patterns of frequency and intensity (hazard zones) of very long duration from a human perspective. This cataloguing process has been completed for most earthquake-prone countries. For example, the seismic geography of the United States, mapped by the US Office of Emergency Preparedness in 1972, reflects the distribution of historic, significant earthquakes up to 1970. The four hazard zones reflect a range in threat from 'negligible' (Zone 0) to 'potentially severe' (Zone 3), and show plainly where the greatest precautions should be taken and those areas where none are required. The enlarged version for California, produced by the California Division of Mines and Geology in 1972, provides better details. Neither of these maps indicates the likely frequency of earthquakes but this can be worked out by subdividing the hazard zones to show the probability of damaging shocks.

Yet even the map of California seems extremely generalized when compared with the mosaic of impacts of the 1906 earthquake. However, by dividing the gross hazard zones on the basis of ground conditions, a famous 1:125 000 scale map ('Maximum Earthquake Intensity Predicted in the Southern San Francisco Bay Region, California, for Large Earthquakes on the San Andreas and Hayward Faults') was created. The intricate patchwork is a clear guide as to where the effects of an earthquake will be greatest, providing an excellent framework for planners, architects, engineers, insurance companies and developers to reduce risk.   DAVID K. C. JONES

Collage, based on 'Global Challenge and Change. Geography for the 1990s'.

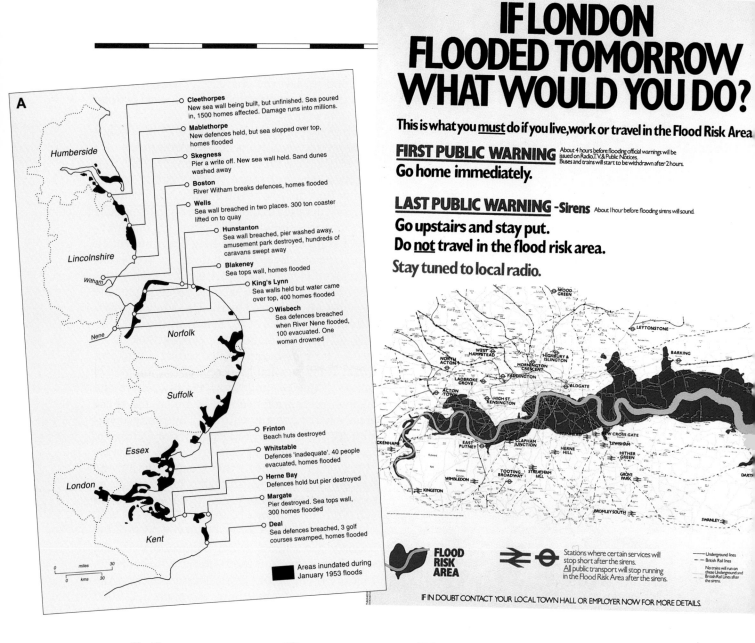

A

Cleethorpes
New sea wall being built, but unfinished. Sea poured in, 1500 homes affected. Damage runs into millions.

Mablethorpe
New defences held, but sea slopped over top, homes flooded

Skegness
Pier a write off. New sea wall held. Sand dunes washed away

Boston
River Witham breaks defences, homes flooded

Wells
Sea wall breached in two places. 300 ton coaster lifted on to quay

Hunstanton
Sea wall breached, pier washed away, amusement park destroyed, hundreds of caravans swept away

Blakeney
Sea tops wall, homes flooded

King's Lynn
Sea walls held but water came over top, 400 homes flooded

Wisbech
Sea defences breached when River Nene flooded, 100 evacuated. One woman drowned

Frinton
Beach huts destroyed

Whitstable
Defences 'inadequate'. 40 people evacuated, homes flooded

Herne Bay
Defences hold but pier destroyed

Margate
Pier destroyed. Sea tops wall, 300 homes flooded

Deal
Sea defences breached, 3 golf courses swamped, homes flooded

Humberside
Lincolnshire
Witham
Nene
Norfolk
Suffolk
Essex
London
Kent

miles 0 30
kms 0 30

■ Areas inundated during January 1953 floods

IF LONDON FLOODED TOMORROW WHAT WOULD YOU DO?

This is what you **must** do if you live, work or travel in the Flood Risk Area

FIRST PUBLIC WARNING About 4 hours before flooding official warnings will be issued on Radio, T.V. & Public Notices. Buses and trains will start to be withdrawn after 2 hours.
Go home immediately.

LAST PUBLIC WARNING - Sirens About 1 hour before flooding sirens will sound.
Go upstairs and stay put.
Do **not** travel in the flood risk area.
Stay tuned to local radio.

FLOOD RISK AREA

Stations where certain services will stop short after the sirens.
All public transport will stop running in the Flood Risk Area after the sirens.

—— Underground lines
- - - British Rail lines

No trains will run on these Underground and British Rail Lines after the sirens.

IF IN DOUBT CONTACT YOUR LOCAL TOWN HALL OR EMPLOYER NOW FOR MORE DETAILS.

MAPPING COASTAL FLOOD HAZARD

Human populations have always tended to concentrate near rivers or along coastlines and so have had to cope with the perennial problem of flooding. Maps play important roles in this, both in providing clear descriptions of the extent of such disasters and in reducing the areas at risk in the future.

At least seven disastrous floods have affected the east coast of Britain since 1236. On the night of 31 January/1 February 1953 numerous breaches were made in the sea defences over a 300-mile (500-km) length from Yorkshire to Kent. Some

330 square miles (850 square km) of land was submerged by seawater, 24 000 houses swamped, factories and power stations on Lower Thameside brought to a standstill and 307 people drowned. The effects in Holland were even worse, as its dyke system was overwhelmed.

However, the extent of flooding in 1953 as portrayed on the map (above left) clearly indicated the need for a coherent response. A year later the Waverley Committee of enquiry identified the cause of the flooding as both short-term (a deep atmospheric depression) and long-term (sea-

(Far left) Flood Defences of the East Coast from Spurn Head to Deal. Map based on the Report of the Departmental Committee on Coastal Flooding May 1954. Cmd 9165. Crown copyright reserved, CBH 24640.

(Left) Poster, 'If London flooded tomorrow what would you do?' Published by the Greater London Council (after 1964).

(Right) Map based on figure 63 in The Potential effects of climate change in the United Kingdom. Department of the Environment, 1991.

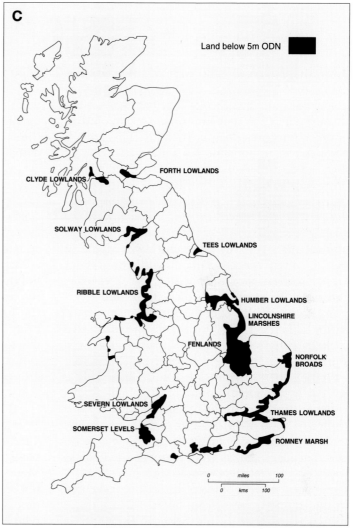

level rise). Consequently, major defence works were undertaken to raise walls and embankments over the entire length of affected coastline and construct lifting barriers across such rivers as the Hull, Lea and Thames.

The construction of the Thames Barrier suffered inevitable delays due to technical problems and labour disputes. Originally due to be completed in 1981, it eventually became operational in 1984 after the expenditure of over £500 million. For three decades extensive tracts of London had remained vulnerable to flooding. The temporary raising of walls through the capital had provided some security but emergency action plans had to be drawn up. Those at risk had to be told the extent of the area under threat, the warning procedure, what they should do if they were flooded and how transport would be disrupted. The 1977

poster reproduced on the page opposite is one of several issued by the Greater London Council to inform the public and is an excellent example of the way maps can be used to indicate hazard zones.

Unfortunately, the threat of coastal flooding remains despite improved defences. Accelerated sea-level rise, apparently due to global warming, could place further areas under threat in the next century, as indicated on the map above. Some 200 000 people live in areas currently threatened by coastal flooding and the costs of a major London flood are estimated at £10 billion. As our hold on certain lowlands becomes less secure, flood maps will not be confined to portraying zones at risk but will increasingly define boundaries for development as the lowest-lying ground is abandoned to return to wetland.   DAVID K. C. JONES

DANGER AHEAD

Before the days of radio warnings of road accidents ahead, motorists were forced to rely on guidebooks and handbooks. The best-known are those produced by motoring organizations and oil or tyre companies, such as Michelin. This French company is responsible for a long tradition of maps and guides of many parts of the world, providing motorists with information to enable them to avoid the worst or most dangerous roads. When few roads were in good condition traffic was light, so the emphasis in road maps then was on road quality. In the 1920s and 1930s Michelin marketed two special maps showing the state of French roads in the spring of each year. Five main categories of roads were recognized and overprinted in dark blue over the official road classification. The best, modern roads, surfaced with asphalt, concrete, or small paving stones were shown by short dashes, as between Lyon and Villefranche. Roads in good condition with a relatively permanent surface of chippings or *pavé* are overprinted with longer dashes and are typically the main arteries along the Rhône valley. Ordinary roads carry no overprint and were usually macadamized, as were many of the C class roads and some *routes nationales* in very hilly regions south west of Lyon. Bad roads, indicated by short cross bars, can be found on main routeways such as the one between Lyon and Le Puy via St Etienne. Finally, the very bad roads are shown by a series of small crosses, often on short sections over particularly difficult terrain, such as the well-known Col de la République southeast of St Etienne.

Even the ordinary series of Michelin road maps at 1:200 000 in the 1920s gave the positions of hump-back bridges on roads and fords, as well as three grades of gradient and information about whether roads were in regular upkeep or worn out. For some years after the Second World War the same series of maps showed places still badly damaged and bridges that were impassable.

With increasing prosperity in France, road surfaces improved so much in the 1950s and 1960s that their quality was no longer mapped. As traffic volumes increased in the 1970s and 1980s, autoroutes and other new kinds of roads were added, but the emphasis shifted to the dangers created by volume of traffic, especially in the holiday season. The bottlenecks and queues leading up to them still dominate traffic bulletins at the beginning and end of August and for some years the organization Sécurité Routière has produced road maps to help the holiday motorist to avoid these. These Bison Futé guides also mark alternative routes (*itinéraires bis*) which are usually signposted on the ground.

Now that much more freight is being carried by road, it has become vital to prevent lorries of different tonnages using relatively minor yet important roads in France during the spring thaw. Maps, regarded as working documents and carrying legends in French, English and German, are prepared each winter for the guidance of drivers who have to comply with regulations depending on the weather at the time. Threats to impound lorries, heavy fines and even imprisonment for repeating the offence encourage drivers to take this workaday map seriously. Maps produced for holiday-makers each summer are, by contrast, brighter and bolder to persuade drivers to heed the sound advice of the road safety organizations.

CHRISTOPHER BOARD

Carte Michelin. État des Routes Printemps, 1929 France Sud. Sheet 99 E.R. Scale 1:1 000 000.

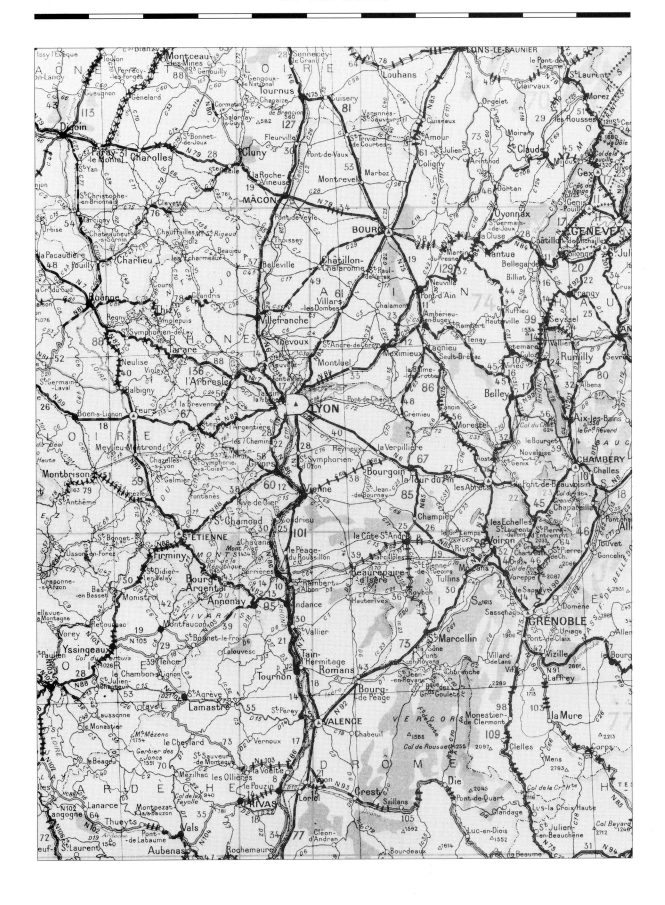

SAFETY IN THE AIR

The safe conduct of commercial aviation is a three-dimensional headache in space and time, involving large numbers of aircraft that can't slow down and stop at a red light if all is not well. Indeed, most aircraft would stall at any speed below about 90–110 mph (150–180 kph), so the whole air traffic control (ATC) system must ensure a continuous passage for each aircraft and adequate vertical and horizontal separation from its fellows. Not surprisingly, the result for the layman may appear to be a weird maze of jargon and abbreviations, and aircraft sporting names like Alpha Romeo or Yankee Juliet (the international phonetic alphabet for call signs AR and YJ).

The main map gives a bird's-eye view of the UK system which is controlled in England and Wales by the London Air Traffic Control Centre (LATCC) and in Scotland by the Scottish Centre (SCATCC). The main elements within these areas are the airways and the Terminal Control Areas (TMAs) which control entry to the airports. Within the TMAs there is a division between Approach Control and Airport Control which, as their names suggest, marshall aircraft into 'holding areas' until they can be fed in an orderly procession into the airport's landing system.

The inset map takes the lid off ATC and shows details of the airways and TMAs. In addition it shows the tools of the trade that enable the system to work. Knowledge of the whereabouts of aircraft in the control areas is obtained by radars that not only give the position of the aircraft but also, by triggering a response from the aircraft, can obtain its identification, speed, height and other useful information enabling a three-dimensional pinpoint on the aircraft. Voice communication is made through VHF radio, while navigation along airways, in holding areas and on airport approaches is accomplished by referring to VHF Omni-directional Beacons (VORs), usually with distance measuring equipment (DME). The VOR can be visualized as sending out signals along each one-degree radial of a full 360-degree circle, so that aircraft can home in on the beacon from any direction, 'turn corners' at the intersection of any two VOR beams and follow a holding pattern before entering an airport landing stream.

Airport radars control both air and ground movements, while aircraft landing at the airport use the Instrument Landing System (ILS) to find their way down to the runway, even in almost zero weather conditions. Not shown, of course, are the navigational computer maps available to the aircraft crew giving all the essential details of their course and position.

Internationally, each national ATC system should mesh with its neighbours. However, facilities vary widely around the world and even in Europe we find thirty-one systems controlled by fifty-one control centres which in no way constitute a co-ordinated system. Eurocontrol has sixteen members at present, but hopefully recent attempts by the EC to establish central control management will result in a more representative international body and rid us of disputes and tiresome delays, and make for increased safety.

In the near future VORs may be replaced by Ground Position systems based on satellite information accurate to a few metres, enough to benefit the car driver, let alone the aircraft captain. The ILS landing aid is due for replacement, probably by a Micro Landing System (MLS), giving a wider approach beam which will allow multiple approach paths to the airport. Air transport has improved its safety record over the years, but increasing traffic is bringing increasing concern for the future and makes technical and organizational advances vital. Maps are not only essential operational tools, they can also highlight danger points in a system, such as where increasing traffic could produce dangerous crossing points on the airway system and make the need for relief routes advisable.

KENNETH SEALY

Map derived from Perspective Chart of Controlled Airspace in the United Kingdom, *published by the Civil Aviation Authority, 1976. It was produced for display and instruction and is not for operational use. The 3-D representation of the air corridors helps to clarify a highly complex situation for people not familiar with it.*

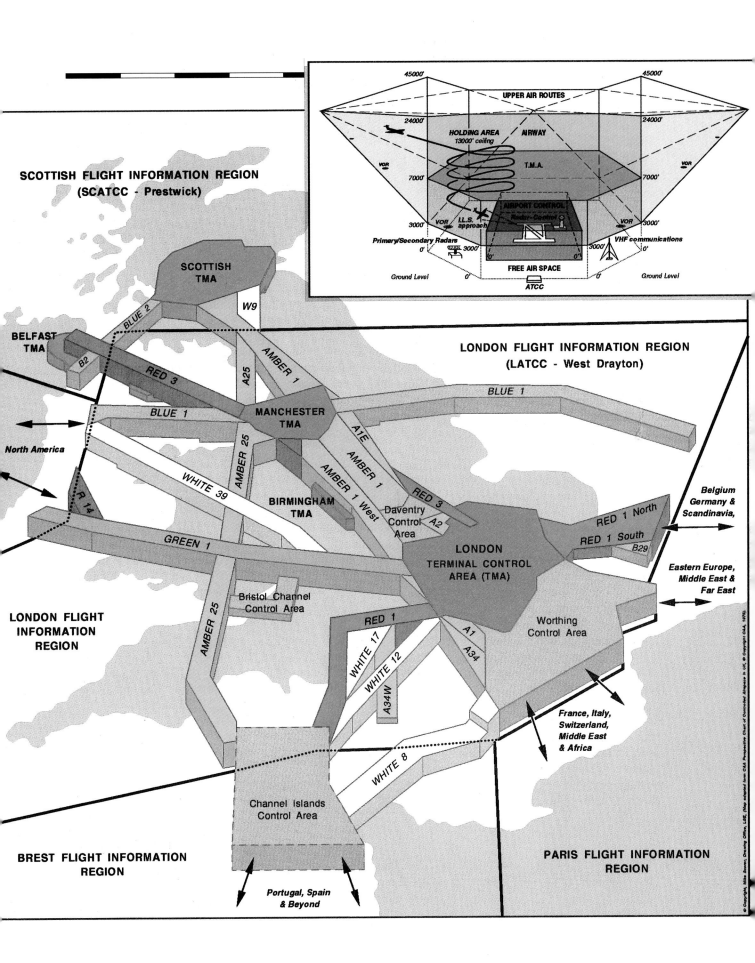

SCOTTISH FLIGHT INFORMATION REGION
(SCATCC - Prestwick)

UPPER AIR ROUTES

45000'   45000'

24000'   24000'

HOLDING AREA
13000' ceiling   AIRWAY

VOR   T.M.A.   VOR

7000'   7000'

AIRPORT CONTROL
Radar Control

VOR   I.L.S.   VOR
3000' approach   3000'

Primary/Secondary Radars   VHF communications

0'   3000'   3000'   0'

FREE AIR SPACE

Ground Level   0'   0'   Ground Level

ATCC

SCOTTISH
TMA

W9

BLUE 2

BELFAST
TMA

B2

RED 3

A25

AMBER 1

LONDON FLIGHT INFORMATION REGION
(LATCC - West Drayton)

BLUE 1

BLUE 1

MANCHESTER
TMA

A1E

AMBER 25

North America

WHITE 39

AMBER 1

AMBER 1 West

BIRMINGHAM
TMA

RED 3

Belgium
Germany &
Scandinavia,

R 14

GREEN 1

Daventry
Control
Area

A2

RED 1 North

RED 1 South

B29

Eastern Europe,
Middle East &
Far East

LONDON FLIGHT
INFORMATION
REGION

AMBER 25

Bristol Channel
Control Area

LONDON
TERMINAL CONTROL
AREA (TMA)

RED 1

A1

A34

Worthing
Control Area

WHITE 17

WHITE 12

A34W

France, Italy,
Switzerland,
Middle East
& Africa

WHITE 8

Channel Islands
Control Area

BREST FLIGHT INFORMATION
REGION

Portugal, Spain
& Beyond

PARIS FLIGHT INFORMATION
REGION

© Copyright, Mike Swann, Drawing Office, L&T, (Map adapted from CAA Perspective Chart of Controlled Airspace in UK, © Copyright CAA, 1975).

179

MAKING 'FALSE CLAIMS'?

Both the map showing robbery in Belgium and the one of 'London Badlands' are statistical and cartographic manipulations presented expertly, but they lead the unwary reader to jump to conclusions, inferring that the risk of burglary or violent theft is greater in one area than another. For example, would the residents of central Belgium feel more afraid of suffering an aggravated theft and react accordingly? How would those living in 'high-burglary' SW9 (Stockwell) react to seeing that they were the district most at risk in London? Would they be more inclined to invest in insurance or house fortifications?

The Belgian map shows the incidence of violent robbery, which appears to occur in areas which have a high density of population. This map seems to support the popular misconception that increasing urban density is associated with increasing crime and that this holds true for central Belgium. However, such a pattern is influenced by the way this crime is defined. The number of aggravated robberies is shown per 10 000 houses, and statistics do not indicate the risk to individuals, although some might infer that this is greater in districts which have high percentages. We can see that between Mons and Namur, small areas of apparently little risk adjoin high risk communes. However, the reader cannot judge what effect different rates of reporting and recording crimes may have on the figures.

This Belgian map clearly shows boundaries of areas where such a crime is prevalent, but is entirely dependent on the way in which commune boundaries are defined. It is also assumed that crime rates are uniform within each commune, which is highly questionable. The number of robberies per 10 000 dwellings is plotted irrespective of the number of people in each dwelling, so risk is expressed in terms of robberies per dwelling rather than per individual. For example,

the true risk of crime affecting an individual in the coastal area of Brugge may be greater than that in central Brussels.

The 'London Badlands' map shows the percentage of claims made against burglary insurance with one company, grouped by London postal districts. As with the Belgian map, this one is equally open to misinterpretation. For example, the gentrified area of renovated Stockwell (SW9) purports to show the highest burglary rate, whereas evidence suggests that better-off individuals may be keener to report burglaries than those less wealthy groups, who may be more typical of nearby postal districts, such as SW2 (Brixton) or SE24 (Herne Hill).

Stockwell's 11.9 per cent incidence of burglary may not reflect where the burglars are assumed to strike most, and not everyone in Stockwell faces the same risk of burglary as the map suggests. The risk is much greater in unprotected corner houses than it is in a fully alarmed mid-terrace property. Furthermore, the varying social and economic composition of the population of postal districts may lead to high rates of reported burglary in Hampstead being cancelled out by low rates elsewhere in NW3. As long as premiums are calculated for postal districts (postcode areas), the actual risk of burglary in any one street or house cannot be appreciated.

No map can ever be completely reliable or accurate to the finest level of detail, but it is nevertheless an interpretation of the real world. If London's Badlands were to have used only four groups of percentages, like the Belgian map, instead of ten, it would have looked very different. If we are tempted to blame the cartographer as the message bearer we should remember that map-readers bear some responsibility for interpreting the message correctly.

LINDSAY CONSTABLE

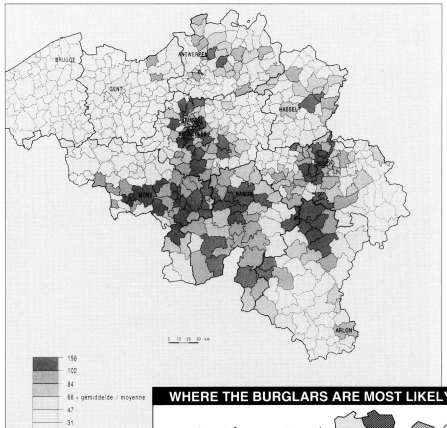

(Left) Vol Qualifié. Robbery or aggravated theft per 10 000 dwellings in Belgium 1984–88. © 1990. Martine Pattyn, General Staff of the Gendarmerie, Rue Fritz Toussaint 47, 1050 Bruxelles, Belgium.

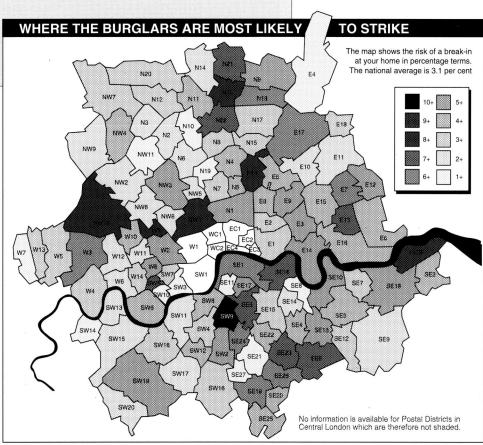

(Right) 'London Badlands: where the burglars are most likely to strike'. The percentage risk of break-in for London postal districts as determined by Prudential Insurance burglary claims. **Evening Standard** *7 July 1992.*

INSURING AGAINST MAN-MADE DISASTERS

Human beings are often careless, but they have learned that it is prudent to insure against this tendency. Accidents, however they are caused and whoever is to blame, will happen. Maps compiled for insurance purposes have a long history and some of the early examples are very attractive. Eighteenth-century London saw the introduction of insurance maps showing building materials and spaces between houses. In Britain, Chas E. Goad has dominated the production of

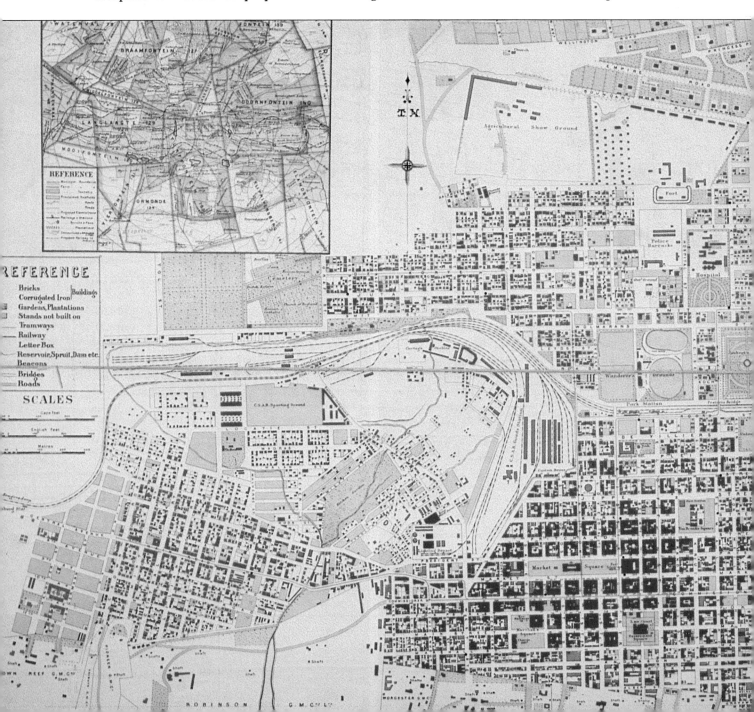

fire insurance plans since 1885. These plans provide an unrivalled source of information for geographers and genealogists because they show the use of buildings, house numbers and street names. Earlier plans were hand-coloured to emphasize different building materials (an indication of flammability) and special attention was given to mills containing inflammable material, doors, windows and floorplans as well as the location of firefighting equipment such as hydrants. In the United States, the Sanborn Fire Insurance Company maps are reputed to cover virtually every house in the country.

Of course man-made disasters happen throughout the world, but they are better known when they occur in famous cities like London (see pp.136–7). However, the impact of a disaster on a new city in a remote part of Africa can be more shattering for its people and government. It is highly likely that the Great Dynamite Explosion, which killed 80, injured 700 and made 1500 homeless in Johannesburg on 16 February 1896, stimulated detailed mapping of the city. Several railway trucks of dynamite had been left baking in the summer sun at sidings near the city centre, when their 55-ton load was set off by shunting. The explosion was heard 100 miles (160 km) away and half the windows in every house in Johannesburg were broken. A contemporary panorama of the destruction shows wood and corrugated iron houses, common in a city then less than ten years old, completely demolished. They were more vulnerable than the brick constructions, which lost only windows.

The map shown here was undoubtedly drawn up for insurance purposes. Its large scale allows it to distinguish brick from wood and iron buildings and to give an accurate assessment of how much land in the city was actually built on. It also adds details such as pillar boxes and horse-drawn tramways. It is thus an unrivalled source of detailed information, originally sent to the Colonial Office in London. It may well have been based on Goad's contemporary plans of the city.

Goad's plans are now widely used as a source of information on shopping centres. Such inventories will provide future historians with specific information about town centres, where the locations and ownership of businesses have continually changed. Lest it be thought that cartographers bother only about fires in cities, in countries which suffer prolonged dry periods and thus forest fires, maps like those of Catalonia are now being produced to chart the vulnerability to fires of the forests in that region of Spain.

CHRISTOPHER BOARD

Donaldson and Hill, 'New Map of the City of Johannesburg and suburbs', compiled by D. Seccadanari, Engineer and Cartographer, revised up to June 1904. Public Record Office, Kew. CO700 Transvaal.

PICTURE CREDITS

BIBLIOGRAPHY

GENERAL

BAGROW, LEO — *History of Cartography.* Second edition. Precedent Publishing Inc., Chicago, 1985.

BROWN, LLOYD A. — *The Story of Maps.* Dover Publications, New York, 1979.

CAMPBELL, TONY — *Early Maps.* Abbeville, New York, 1981.

CRONE, GERALD R. — *Maps and their Makers.* Fifth edition. Dawson, Folkestone, 1978.

DICKINSON, G.C. — *Maps and Air Photography: Images of the Earth.* Second edition. Edward Arnold, London, 1986.

HARLEY, J.B. AND WOODWARD D. — *The History of Cartography.* Chicago University Press, Chicago. To be published.

HARVEY, P.D.A. — *The History of Topographical Maps: Symbols, Pictures and Surveys.* Thames and Hudson, London, 1980.

HODGKISS, ALAN G. — *Understanding Maps. A Systematic History of their Use and Development.* Dawson, Folkestone, 1981.

HODGKISS, A.G. AND TATHAM, A.F. — *Keyguide to Information Sources in Cartography.* Mansell, London, 1986.

MONOMIER, MARK — *How to Lie with Maps.* Chicago University Press, Chicago, 1991.

ROSSOLIN, FLORENCE (Ed.) — *Cartes et Figures de la Terre.* Centre Pompidou, Paris, 1980.

THROWER, N.J.W. — *Maps and Man: An Examination of Cartography in Relation to Culture and Civilization.* Prentice Hall, Englewood Cliffs, New Jersey, 1973.

WALLIS, HELEN AND ROBINSON, ARTHUR (Eds.) — *Cartographical Innovations. An International Handbook of Mapping Terms to 1900.* Map Collector Publications, 1987.

Those who are interested in looking at a wider range of graphic representations would do well to look at the following:

TUFTE, E.R. — *The Visual Display of Quantitive Information.* Graphics Press, Cheshire, Connecticut, 1983.

TUFTE, E.R. — *Envisioning Information.* Graphics Press, Cheshire, Connecticut, 1990.

PARTICULAR ASPECTS

ANDREWS, J. — *A Paper Landscape. The Ordnance Survey in Nineteenth-Century Ireland.* Clarendon Press, Oxford.

BARKER, FELIX AND JACKSON, PETER — *The History of London in Maps.* Barrie & Jenkins, London, 1990.

BENDALL, A.S. — *Maps, Land and Society. A History with a Carto-bibliography of Cambridgeshire Estate Maps c.1600–1836.* University of Cambridge Press, Cambridge, 1992.

BROWNE, JOHN PADDY — *Map Cover Art.* Ordnance Survey, Southampton, 1992.

BUISSERET, DAVID (Ed.) — *Monarchs, Ministers and Maps. The Emergence of Cartography as a Tool of Government in Early Modern Europe.* University of Chicago Press, Chicago, 1992.

CAMPBELL, TONY (Ed.) — *What Use is a Map?* British Library, London, 1989.

ELLIOT, JAMES — *The City in Maps. Urban mapping to 1900.* British Library, London, 1987.

GEORGE, WILMA — *Animals and Maps.* Secker and Warburg, London, 1969.

GLANVILLE, PHILIPPA — *London in Maps.* The Connoisseur, London, 1972.

HARLEY, J.B. — *Maps and the Columbian Encounter.* University of Wisconsin, Milwaukee, 1990.

HARVEY, P.D.A. — *Medieval Maps.* British Library, London, 1991.

HARVEY, P.D.A. — *Maps in Tudor England.* British Library, London, 1993.

HILL, GILLIAN — *Cartographic Curiosities.* British Library, London, 1978.

HODSON, Y. — *An Inch to the Mile – The Ordnance Survey One-Inch Map 1805–1974.* Charles Close Society, London.

HOLMES, NIGEL — *Pictorial Maps.* The Herbert Press, London, 1992.

HOWSE, DEREK AND SANDERSON, MICHAEL — *The Sea Chart.* David & Charles, Newton Abbot, 1973.

KAIN, ROGER AND BAIGENT, ELIZABETH — *Cadastral Mapping in the Service of the State: A History of Property Mapping.* University of Chicago Press, Chicago, 1992.

MASON, A. STUART — *Essex on the Map. The Eighteenth Century Land Surveyors of Essex.* Essex Record Office, Chelmsford, 1990.

MOLLAT, MICHEL DE LA RONCIÈRE ETC. *Sea Charts of the Early Explorers, 13th to 17th Century.* Thames & Hudson, 1984.

O'DONOGHUE, YOLANDE *William Roy 1726–1790. Pioneer of the Ordnance Survey.* British Museum Publications, London, 1977.

RAVENHILL, WILLIAM *John Norden's Manuscript Maps of Cornwall and Its Nine Hundreds.* University of Exeter, Exeter, 1972.

ROBINSON, ARTHUR H. *Early Thematic Mapping in the History of Cartography.* University of Chicago Press, Chicago, 1982.

SKELTON, RALEIGH A. *Explorers' Maps: Chapters in the Cartographic Record of Geographical Discovery.* Spring Books, London, 1970.

SMITH, DAVID *Victorian Maps of the British Isles.* Batsford, London, 1985.

SMITH, DAVID *Maps and Plans for the Local Historian and Collector.* Batsford, London, 1988.

WILKES, MARGARET *The Scot and His Maps.* Scottish Library Association, Motherwell, 1991.

WOODWARD, DAVID *Art & Cartography. Six Historical Essays.* University of Chicago Press, Chicago, 1987.

JOURNALS

The Cartographic Journal, published twice yearly by the British Cartographic Society. (See *Societies* for address.)

The Geographical Journal, published three times a year by the Royal Geographical Society. (See *Societies* for address.)

Imago Mundi, published annually, c/o The Map Library, The British Library, Great Russell Street, London WC1B 3DG.

The Map Collector, published quarterly, c/o 48 High Street, Tring, Hertfordshire HP23 5BH.

SOCIETIES

The British Cartographic Society, founded in 1963, to promote the subject of cartography, to advance cartographic education and to encourage research. Contact: Honorary Secretary, Charles Beattie, 13 Sheldrake Gardens, Hordle, Lymington, Hampshire SO41 0JF.
The Charles Close Society for the Study of Ordnance Survey Maps, founded in 1980, the only society known to be devoted exclusively to the products of a single mapping organisation. It publishes a journal three times a year, guides, booklets and monographs. Contact: David Archer, The Pentre, Kerry, Newtown, Powys SY16 4PD.
The International Map Collectors' Society. It publishes a quarterly journal. Contact: Caroline Batchelor, 'Pikes', The Ridgeway, Oxshott, Leatherhead, Surrey KT22 0LG.
The London Topographical Society. It publishes a map of a view facsimile annually and/or an issue of *The London Topographical Record.* Contact: Bishopsgate Institute Library, 230 Bishopsgate, London EC2M 4QH.
The Royal Geographical Society, founded in 1830, has a major map collection. Its journal carries reviews of atlases and maps, and its articles are often illustrated by maps of some historical significance. Contact: The Secretary, 1 Kensington Gore, London SW7 2AR.

*A*CKNOWLEDGEMENTS

Peter Barber would like to thank the following: his family for their forbearance, his colleagues in the British Library for their assistance, particularly Geoff Armitage, David Beech, Michael Boggan, Tony Campbell, Jane Carr, Peter Carey, Karen Cook, John Davies, Michael Hoey, Graham Marsh, Andrew Ogilvie, Henry Okeyemi, Anne Taylor and Helen Wallis. From outside the library he would like to thank Philip Attwood, Andrew Burnett, Margaret Condon, Andrew David, Francis Herbert, Paul Goldman, Yolande Hodson, Peter Jackson and the council of the London Topographical Society, and Luke Syson.

Christopher Board would like to thank the following for their help in the publication of this book: Roma Beaumont, Carl Fulton, Christine Gazely, Jane Pugh, Mike Scorer and Amy Swanson.

Both authors feel that special thanks are due to Julian Flanders, Deirdre O'Day, Julian Stenhouse and Suzanne Webber of the BBC for making the writing of this book a pleasurable experience, and to all the contributing authors for their tolerance and understanding on receiving requests for contributions at short notice and in the holiday period.

INDEX

George I, King of Greece 85
Germany:
    colonial map 84–5
    Czech maps 83
    military reconnaissance 104–5
    propaganda maps 81
    trench maps 122–3
Ghana 87
Gillray, James 71, 75
globes 74–5, *see also* projections
Goad, Chas E. 183
Gordon, Lord George 118
Gordon riots 118–19
'Gough Map' 48–9
Great Dynamite Explosion (1896)
    183
Great Fire of London 136–8
Great Toyshop, Ludgate Street 76
Greater London Council 175
Greater London Urban Depriva-
    tion 149
Greece:
    ancient 6
    coin map 81
    colonial map 84–5
Gregory XIII, Pope 72
Grey Leagues 108
Guinea 20–1
Gulf War 101, 125
Gulliver's Travels 20, 26, 36–7
Gutierrez, Diego 160

H

Habsburg empire 80–1, 112
Hack, William 10–11
Halley, Edmund 18, 169
Hamada el Homra 170–1
Hamont, Jean-Baptiste, Sieur
    Desroches 128
Hancko, F. 115
Handel, George Friederic 126
Harrison, John 165
Haverhill, Suffolk 98–9
Helions Bumpstead, Essex 98–9
Henri IV, King of France 24
Henry VIII, King 110, 132
Hereford *Mappamundi* 22, 160
Hogenberg, Frans 134–5
Holden and Holford's London plan

(1944) 138–9
Holland, Samuel 126
Hollar, Wenceslas 39, 137
Holy Land, route map 44, 45
Hondius, Jodocus 24–5, 36
Hood, Thomas 169
Hooghe, Romeyn de 39, 128
Horthy, Admiral Nikolaus 80
Humboldt, Alexander von 18
Hungary, maps of 50, 80–1
Huningue fortifications 91

I

importance and size 16–17
Inkermann, battle of 116
Inner Urban Areas Act (1978) 148
insurance companies 180–3
invasion defence maps 110–11
Italy, maps 72–3, 84, *see also*
    Rome
itinerary *see* route

J

Jacobites 76, 78, 126
Jamaica, map (1682) 11
James I, King 89, 96, 97
James II, King 82
Japan 36, 42–3
Jefferys, Thomas 121
Jerusalem 22, 29
Johannesburg 183
Justus Perthes of Gotha 54

K

Kampuchea 91
Kashmir Valley 16–17
Kenwood House 118
Kircher, Athanasius 18
Kneller, Sir Godfrey 140
Kupe 58

L

Lafreri, Antonio 121

Land Utilization Survey 107
landed property 143
landmarks 39, 45, 54, 57, 58, 171
Langley, Buckinghamshire 106
latitude 12, 165, 171
Laxton, Nottinghamshire 98–9
Lazarus 50
Leeds 56
Leeds and Liverpool Canal map
    52–3
L'Enfant, Pierre Charles 138
Leopold II, King of Belgium 84
Lepanto, battle of (1571) 121
Lewis, G. Malcolm 41
Liber Floridus de St Omer 74
Libyan desert 170
Lille, siege of (1708) 123
Lincoln 32–3
Line of Tordesillas 87
London:
    armorial 140–1
    Badlands map 180–1
    city views 130–1
    deprivation 148–9
    flood risk 174–5
    Great Fire 136–8
    insurance maps 180, 182
    merchants' map 134–5
    Milne's Plan (1800) 142–3
    postal districts 152–3
    poverty 146–7
    reconstruction 138–9
    riot-control map 118–19
    satellite view 154–5
    Soho cholera (1852) 144–5
    Southwark (1542) 132–3
    street maps 56
    Superplan 94, 131, 156–7
    taxi drivers 42–3
    Underground map 39,
        150–1
London District Post 152
London School of Economics
    (LSE) 46–7
Long Melford Hall, Suffolk 94–5
longitude 165, 171
Looff, Johannes 10
Louis IX, King 162
Louis XIII, King 128
Louis XIV, King 75, 76, 90–1, 108,
    128